SO FAR
FROM HOME

CEDAR MILL COMM LIBRARY
12505 NW CORNELL RD
PORTLAND, OR 97229
(503-644-0043)

WITHDRAWN
CEDAR MILL LIBRARY

D0980714

Julia Gilliss and her daughter,
Julia Melville Gilliss
(Based on original in Gilliss Collection)

SO FAR
FROM HOME

An Army Bride on the Western Frontier,
1865-1869

JULIA GILLISS

Edited
(from a transcription by Charles J. Gilliss)
with Introduction & Annotation by
PRISCILLA KNUTH

OREGON HISTORICAL SOCIETY
PRESS

FRONTIS: This illustration shows Julia Stellwagen Gilliss, the writer of these vivid and immediate letters to her family "back home" in Washington, D.C., and her first child. It is based upon a photograph made on August 1, 1867, probably in Portland, Oregon. Baby Julia, "the fattest little butterball," and her mother were "comfortably fixed" at Fort Vancouver, Washington Territory, while Capt. James Gilliss traveled up the Columbia River into the interior to report to Gen. George Crook in the Boise district to find out his new station. Julia wrote that the baby's picture was "not half as pretty as she is, and she has squinted her eyes just like I do." (Illustration by Karen Beyers, based upon a photograph in the Gilliss Family Collection.)

LIBRARY OF CONGRESS CATALOGING-IN-PUBLICATION DATA
Gilliss, Julia, 1843-1926
So far from home : an Army bride on the Western Frontier, 1865-69 / Julia Gilliss ; transcription by Charles J. Gilliss ; edited with introduction and annotation by Priscilla Knuth.
    p. cm.
Includes bibliographical references.
ISBN 0-87595-135-X (alk. paper)
1. Gilliss, Julia, 1843- —Diaries. 2. Officers' wives—Northwest, Pacific—Diaries. 3. Frontier and pioneer life—Northwest, Pacific. 4. Northwest, Pacific—History. 5. United States. Army—Military life—History—19th century. 6. Frontier and pioneer life—Oregon. 7. Oregon—History. I. Gilliss, Charles J. II. Knuth, Priscilla. III. Title.
F852.G49 1991
979.5'041'092—dc20   91-37429   CIP

The paper used in this publication meets the minimum requirements of American National Standard for Information Sciences—Permanence of Paper for Printed Library Materials, ANSI Z39.48-1984.

Copyright © 1993, Oregon Historical Society, 1200 S.W. Park Avenue, Portland, Oregon 97205
All rights reserved. No part of this publication may be reproduced or transmitted in any form or by any means, electronic or mechanical, including photocopying, recording or any information storage or retrieval system, without permission in writing from the publisher.

Designed and produced by the Oregon Historical Society Press

Dedicated by
CHARLES J. GILLISS & WILLIAM WEIR GILLISS, JR.,
to their family.

CONTENTS

"... when I write it almost seems as if I was among you talking. I see you all so plainly."

MARCH 2, 1866

INTRODUCTION

THESE LETTERS from an army officer's bride to her family in Washington, D.C., (a city newly complicated by rapid growth of the United States government) were written just after the Civil War, and describe the beginning of a very different life for her in the distant Pacific Northwest. In that time, she had an opportunity to begin married life in a rather wonderful way. She was responsive to people and the earth as she saw them as well as educated, and her record communicates much about her times and experiences; she had a talent for description. The letters are worth recognizing for the reminders and realizations they offer of family life at Western military posts, nearby towns (if any), and the kinds of certainties and uncertainties involved in such a "movable feast."

Julia Stellwagen Gilliss was twenty-two, just beginning a venture with unexpected Far Western dimensions when she began writing these letters home to her family in 1865—to maintain some "connections" in her changed life and to share new wonders; she was close to her family. Born in 1843 and the first child of Charles Kraft and Eliza Tucker Stellwagen, Julia married James Gilliss, twenty-five, eldest son of James Melville and Rebecca Roberts Gilliss, on October 12, 1865, in Washington. Three weeks later they began their first long journey together—to the Pacific Northwest by

Julia, Annie and Edward Gilliss
(ca. 1863–64)
(Based on original in the Gilliss Collection)

sea—destined, they thought, for Fort Walla Walla in Washington Territory.

From her responses, Julia must have had some taste for adventure. Evidently she had an unusually good education, one that derived not only from school but from her parents' backgrounds. Her father came from an early Pennsylvania German heritage centering around Philadelphia, where he was born. About 1849, after his store there was robbed, he lost his silverware and clock and watch repair business and moved with his family to Washington, D.C. With the aid of his father-in-law, he became a draftsman for the Navy; he was also a photographer and a painter. Julia's mother was the granddaughter of Sir William and Lady Alice Booth of Jenifer Castle in Devonshire, England, and her father, James Tucker, brought his family to the United States in 1819.[1]

When Julia married James Gilliss, he was a captain in the U.S. Army. His father, a naval officer, established the Naval Observatory in Washington in the 1840s, and was its superintendent during the 1860s. Father and son had been to Washington Territory in 1860 "to assist in taking observations of the total eclipse."[2] At the beginning of the Civil War, son James obtained a commission in the Army as a second lieutenant of the Fifth Artillery. He was brevetted "for gallant and meritorious services at the Battle of Malvern Hill" with the Artillery in 1862, and again for the Battle of Spottsylvania Courthouse in 1864, the year he was promoted to captain and quartermaster. At the Battle of Cedar Creek in October, James was captured by Southern troops wearing Union blue uniforms, and sent to Libby Prison at Richmond. Exchanged about five months later, he reached home the day before his father died—suddenly—in February 1865. From February until October, Captain Gilliss served in the office of Gen. Daniel H. Rucker, chief quartermaster at Washington, D.C. He must have courted Julia during this time.

Army transfer orders arrived about the time of James' and Julia's wedding in Epiphany (Episcopal) Church; the young couple started for the Pacific Coast and distant Washington Territory that fall of 1865, at a time when the regulars were replacing the volunteers in the West. The immediate post-Civil War Army had more officers than it knew how to utilize, and frontier posts offered obvious possibilities as the Army regrouped.

For the Gillisses, as it did for many couples, the voyage provided an extended honeymoon. Julia mentions that there were "brides enough on board to have made the fortunes of any one minister."[3] Though she proved to be a poor sailor, the journey—by sea from New York to the Isthmus of Panama, then by rail across that region, and by sea again to San Francisco and on to the Columbia River— was all new experience. There was much to tell her parents, her younger sister Annie (born 1847), and still younger brother Edward (born 1854). James, too, had a brother and sisters: Rebecca, Fannie, and Jack (John?) are mentioned in Julia's letters.

Her letters are not parochial or uninformed. Julia provides a variety of material, not only on army life in the Pacific Northwest but on social customs (and prejudices) of the time and on necessities and niceties of frontier living in the post-Civil War 1860s. She is among those who have added dimensions and depth to the perception of family life on the Army's western frontier—its intricacies, limitations, and some of its differences from the more rigidly organized East.[4]

As a bride and then a young mother far from the "civilization" of her home in Washington, D.C., Julia enjoyed much of her adventurous and make-do life with a loving husband. And she responded to the country and its scenic beauties with descriptions occasionally as "rapturous" as Albert Bierstadt's paintings (she mentions him several times). In a way, Julia's letters reflect a general view of the West and echo the response of her father's friend, the painter Emanuel Leutze, known especially in the United States for two large paintings, "Westward the Course of Empire Takes Its Way," and "Washington Crossing the Delaware"—surely symbols, even monuments, in schoolrooms and books for decades after.[5]

In the Pacific Northwest Julia saw and experienced some extremes, from comfortable hotel and disputed army post "architecture" to canvas roof and dirt floor. The military posts where she lived in the later 1860s were in different stages of their usages and functions: Fort Dalles, up the Columbia River and just east of the Cascade Range, in the 1850s a primary departure point for military expeditions and exploration of the interior, had lost importance as the backwash of miners and settlers passed it going east to newer goldfields; Fort Stevens, a part of new coastal defenses at the mouth of the Columbia River, was expanding; Fort Vancouver, on the north bank of the Columbia near Portland, once the location of a regional fur-trading center for the British Hudson's Bay Company, was by Julia's time a depot army post in a civilized area near a regional hub; but Camp Warner, in southeastern Oregon, was new and incomplete, far from anywhere.

Like new Camp Harney, to which Julia gave short shrift, Camp Warner at its second site (viewed and approved by brevet Maj. Gen. George Crook), was in what was still "Indian Country." Within the period of the Gillisses' stay at Warner, 1867 through 1868, the post mushroomed. While Crook "pacified" the Indians in and around the interior gold-mining country, Warner had a very active function; there Julia realized some critical aspects of Indian-white conflicts. The Camp Warner of Crook's activities continued to be useful through the Modoc War in the Tule Lake-Klamath country, but was abandoned in 1874. By that time, of the army posts Julia had seen at close view (including fleas, flies, dust and mud, as well as bands, billiards, and sutlers' stores), only Fort Stevens, as part of a river-mouth coastal defense system, and Fort Vancouver, as a regional depot, were active.

There is fun in Julia's comments on croquet with Mrs. General Crook at Camp Warner, on other things army wives might do for entertainment, and on a Christmas party when materials for celebration were anything at hand plus imagination. There were difficult times, too. Money was short, for army pay in greenbacks was heavily discounted. Appreciated luxuries were sometimes as simple as a box of apples rescued from the sea. The Gillisses were remarkably healthy for the times and places, and Julia's pregnancy went well, though later their child nearly died. The descriptions of home remedies, attention to diet, and visits to post doctors Julia wrote are informative, and so are the health hazards—in Washington, D.C., and in the Pacific Northwest. Sometimes Julia's comments sound almost current.

Julia had absorbed the views of many in her social world regarding "different" peoples—of faiths and of color, including the "uncivilized" Indians. Yet it appears from comments and advice to her parents that her social flexibility was greater than theirs; her new experience was broader.

Compared to "wagon train" pioneer wives, Julia had some differences and advantages beyond an exceptional education and pleasant personality. Unlike them, she did not expect to stay and put down roots in a family home in the Pacific Northwest. (Surely, even the "moving" people, the men who took themselves and their wives and families from the East in steps often marked by where the children were born, must have crossed the continent in some expectation of staying in Oregon.) Beyond her new family life, just beginning with husband James, the Army provided a ready-made social structure and a "place." (The fact that James was not an "Academy" man probably had effect, if any, less in social and more in political aspects of army functioning—like James' delayed transfer?) One might note that Julia's social experiences in the West, on shipboard and around Fort Vancouver and Portland, were often with regional "first families" or the equivalent; she had come from a socially polished world in Washington, D.C. Further, the fact that James was a quartermaster made him, and his wife, of interest to civilians concerned with necessary business between themselves and the Army.

By the later 1860s, the army supply structure on the regional frontier was relatively organized or was being reorganized with growing interior settlement. Even if there were still gaps and inconveniences, the Army's difficulties with supply over great distances may have been less harassing for Julia than keeping the family fed was for a good many pioneer wives in the more "civilized" Willamette Valley; settlement there was rather recent. The Gillisses were not well off, but James did have an assured income, even if its value was discounted and its arrival may have been late; and there were food supplies of some kind, if not always what they wished.

The Army provided a living place as well. For the Gillisses for much of their stay in the region these were generally good living spaces—which Julia was fortunate enough not to share with another army officer's family (a point she appreciated).

There must have been worries and difficulties Julia did not mention or make much of—perhaps so her family in the East would not worry, or perhaps her husband said little about some that would have concerned him. The quartermaster's office at distant frontier posts—dispensing money and contracts—might so easily develop disapproved (at headquarters) entanglements. Many did. James' primary function was to supply the sinews of war as best he might, rather than strike the blows or determine policy, but sinews still required strict attention and some special flexibilities.

Julia appreciated the niceties of feminine dress and fashion (though not *all* fashions), but she was practical about what was appropriate to life when one lived "amid sand heaps and pine trees," and social affairs (except in San Francisco and Portland) were limited to events officers' wives could organize at an "outback" post. She had no use for an opera cloak at The Dalles; a "linsey woolsey" dress and gingham sunbonnet, she suggested, were better. She tried to dress the baby, too, in what she felt was appropriate to her surroundings and activities. At The Dalles, Julia reported, she was "the first wearer of rats and waterfalls." And she provides a wonderful recipe for freshening her "curls."

A good part of the concerns of the new bride were domestic, of course. Julia mentions her efforts and successes with food, noting on February 4, 1866, that she had "not spoilt anything yet so that it was uneatable." Like most housewives, she sent home a few recipes and suggested remedies. Army housekeeping had its own advantages and disadvantages; disadvantages compared to the East probably, but not compared to most of the West or the Middle West.

In her new homes, at least at Fort Dalles and Fort Stevens, Julia had some scope in "decorating." She enjoyed making them as pretty and comfortable as she could, perhaps much as James may have enjoyed putting in gardens. In many ways she was fortunate to begin "homemaking" at Fort Dalles, where she had almost too much of a

General George Crook
(ca. 1866–67)
(Based on original in Gilliss Collection)

house—actually a "suburban villa"—to work with. That house Col. (and Inspector) J.K.F. Mansfield in 1858 described as "quite showy and handsome and fanciful in external appearance . . . [resembling] the fancy residence in the country near our large cities," even if it was cheaply built.[6] It was a good deal different than the Gillisses' first home at Crook's Camp Warner, where the heat from the stovepipe melted the snow and dirt on the canvas roof and brought it down in streams on the "floor." Julia's verbal pictures of quarters at Fort Dalles, Fort Stevens, and Camp Warner are even more vivid than her sketches.

Army wives were "perceptive observers," as Sandra L. Myres notes.[7] True enough, Julia did have at least one servant during most of her stay in the Pacific Northwest to afford her more time. She was fortunate in Mrs. Kelly and Mary Ann, and even in the faithful Swiss of her last letters—more so than Emily Fitzgerald, who about ten years later wrote plainly and differently of her experiences as an army doctor's wife in Idaho and Alaska.[8]

In spite of real enjoyment and the adventure of new country and life, Julia missed her family: father, mother, sister Annie, brother Eddie, and baby Kitty (Elise). It was a *long* time for her—and many hoped-for but not received transfer orders later—before her breathless note from Camp Bidwell late in 1868 announced the arrival of the order for James to report to Washington, D.C. And then a final delay, due to military ego and protocol, for another two months!

There must have been a joyous family reunion. The family history reports that after the Gillisses returned to Washington, James was stationed in Sioux City, Iowa, then at Chicago until November 1875. (They lost their home during the famous Chicago fire of 1870.) From 1875 to 1880 Captain Gilliss was at the Cheyenne Army Depot in Wyoming, and the three years following at Fort Monroe, Virginia. He was promoted to major and quartermaster in 1881. The family grew, too, in the years after Oregon, and four more children were born: Charles J. late in 1872, Florence S. early in 1875, William W. in April 1880, and Helen in November 1881.

When the family moved again it was to Fort Leavenworth, Kansas, where Major Gilliss was Chief Quartermaster of Division (1883-

Margaret Dailey (Mrs. George) Crook
(ca. 1866–67)
(Based on original given Julia Gilliss by Mrs. Crook)

87); after that he was in the Quartermaster General's office in Washington, D.C. (1887-93). The next move was to St. Louis, Missouri, where in 1894 he was promoted to lieutenant colonel and Deputy Quartermaster General. Later he was at Governor's Island, New York, and Washington, D.C., and became colonel and Assistant Quartermaster General in 1897.

Just after the Spanish-American War in late 1898, Colonel Gilliss was back at Governor's Island when, as Julia had worried much earlier, he died suddenly on November 13—after a good day, like his father. As Colonel Gilliss had planned, his "papers were in perfect order."

Julia died in Washington, D.C., on December 16, 1926, and was buried beside her husband in Arlington National Cemetery. In the tradition of Isabella Bird, Julia's legacy for us is in her letters—a record that provides realization of places and times beyond the usual comments on politics, power, and dollars and cents. We are grateful for her pictures of family life and the Pacific Northwest as she experienced them.

EDITORIAL STATEMENT

THE LETTERS of Julia Stellwagen Gilliss were transcribed by her son, Charles J. Gilliss. Some of the originals were missing, and he added a few interesting parts from his mother's little book, "Army Life in the Sixties," the single copy of which she completed in 1899 and had bound to give her brother, Edward J. Stellwagen. At the time Charles Gilliss worked with the material in 1943, he had both the book and his mother's letters. It is fortunate that he preserved the record through transcription. Now, as Julia's grandson W. Weir Gilliss, Jr., reported, neither book nor original letters exist.

Most of the letters have been used in this publication, and omitted parts, indicated by ellipses (. . .), are repetitions or family detail. Several little sketches and paintings Julia made of Fort Dalles and Camp Warner have survived, and thanks to W. Weir Gilliss, Jr., who provided both the copy of Charles J. Gilliss' transcription of the letters and the original sketches, they are preserved in the Oregon Historical Society's Regional Research Library.

There were a few places where names were not clear or may have been misread in transcription. In editing, all names have been checked with available sources, and explanations and corrections made in text or notes. Editorial insertions are in brackets. Part of the material Charles Gilliss used from "Army Life in the Sixties" has been taken from the appendix he added and placed under appro-

priate dates, which he indicated. He made a few parenthetical insertions, and Julia did, too (in most cases, it is clear who made the
insertions). Occasionally Julia underscored a word for emphasis;
these appear in italics.

The usage of the time then as now was to abbreviate recognized
military titles. Except for one or two complete spellings as examples,
this policy has been followed here. At the time, James was AQM, Assistant Quartermaster. Other military abbreviations are AAQM, Acting Assistant Quartermaster; QMD, Quartermaster Department;
ACS, Assistant Commissary; CO, Commanding Officer.

Julia's affectionate nicknames for her sister, Annie, are matched
by the variety of her own signatures—Junie, Julie, et cetera—no
doubt names favored by family or husband. James consistently
refers to her as Junie in the several notes and letters he wrote to the
Stellwagens at the time the Gillisses' first child was born in the
spring of 1867.

As Julia mentions, some of her letters were written as a journal on
shipboard or over several days; sometimes she has finished in a
hurry to catch the next outgoing mail. All the letters presented here
were to her parents or sister or brother, and sometimes in her
"continued" conversation, she does not repeat the identifying
salutation.

Where it added to clarity, some dated spellings or misspelled
words have been corrected (Julia spells very well, better than a good
many prominent regional pioneers). A number of expressions used
as two words in the 1860s have been joined, and some punctuation
added, along with additional paragraphing. Months and a few other
abbreviations are generally spelled out, most contractions done in
today's style, and ship names italicized.

Beyond such minor mechanics, the material and the expression of
ideas and feelings, the flavor, are Julia's own.

ACKNOWLEDGMENTS

WE ARE GRATEFUL to W. Weir Gilliss, Jr., for the material he preserved and sent to the Oregon Historical Society, and for family history he provided; and to Nancy Joan Gilliss for further help with family material. Thanks also go to Mrs. Elizabeth Reichow, who carefully retyped from the photocopy, and to Donald P. Abbott for proofing help.

Members of the Oregon Historical Society Press staff, under the direction of Bruce Taylor Hamilton, have labored with affection on this collection of letters. Lori McEldowney worked as the staff editor, Susan Applegate kept production matters in line during her tenure at the Press, the late George Thomson Resch designed the interior of this book, and Karen Bassett-Rosane who helped this project through its final stages. The illustrations are by Karen Beyers, a Portland artist who took Julia's words to heart.

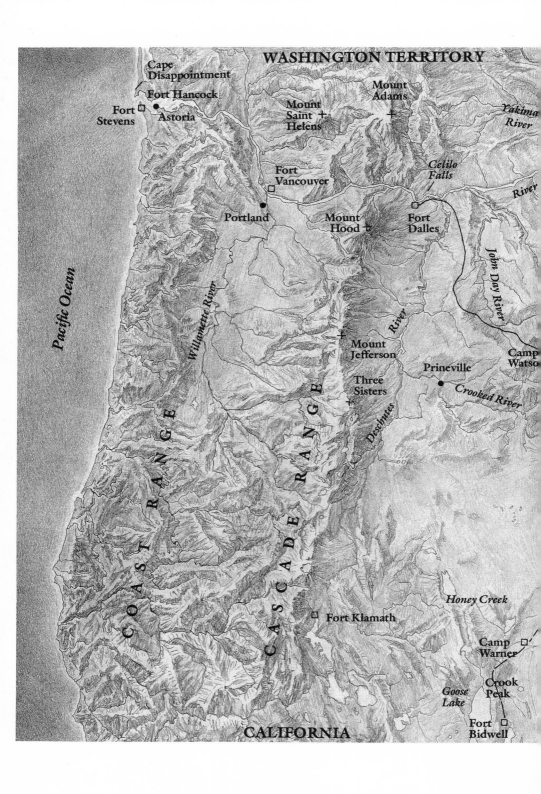

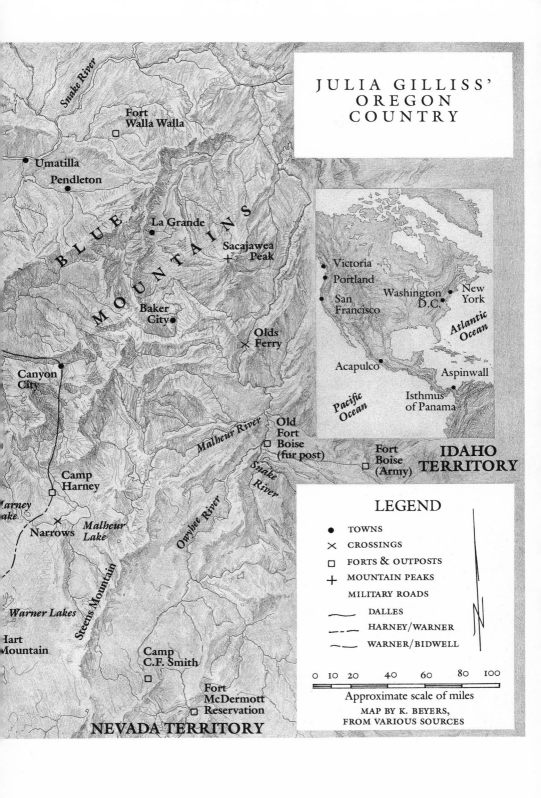

JULIA GILLISS'
OREGON
COUNTRY

Snake River
Fort
Walla Walla
Umatilla
Pendleton
La Grande
Sacajawea
Peak
Baker
City
Olds
Ferry
Canyon
City
Malheur River
Old
Fort
Boise
(fur post)
Fort
Boise
(Army)
IDAHO
TERRITORY
Camp
Harney
Snake
River
Harney
ake
Narrows
Malheur
Lake
Owyhee River
Warner Lakes
Steens Mountain
Hart
Mountain
Camp
C.F. Smith
Fort
McDermott
Reservation
NEVADA TERRITORY

Victoria
Portland
San
Francisco
Washington
D.C.
New
York
Atlantic
Ocean
Acapulco
Aspinwall
Pacific
Ocean
Isthmus
of Panama

LEGEND

● TOWNS
✕ CROSSINGS
□ FORTS & OUTPOSTS
+ MOUNTAIN PEAKS
MILITARY ROADS

——— DALLES
–·–·– HARNEY/WARNER
–··–··– WARNER/BIDWELL

0 10 20   40   60   80   100

Approximate scale of miles
MAP BY K. BEYERS,
FROM VARIOUS SOURCES

BLUE MOUNTAINS

SO FAR
FROM HOME

LEAVING HOME

Voyage from New York
to the Pacific Northwest

OCTOBER-NOVEMBER 1865

ASTOR HOUSE, N.Y.,
October 31st, 1865.

Dearest Mama & Papa   We had a very pleasant trip on in spite of travelling at night. The train was composed of new cars, more beautifully fitted up than any I ever saw before. The one we occupied had mirrors all along the sides and high backed velvet chairs with a spring that placed them at any angle you wished. It was not crowded and the passengers seemed unusually select. There was a special car on the train of rosewood with crimson brocatelle hanging made like a room, without those permanent seats; it was brilliantly lighted but I do not know who occupied it.

We arrived in New York a little after four this morning and I don't believe the people here ever go to bed. Stores were open and the bustle and lights in the streets were as much as we have at home in midday. We have a delightful room at the Astor, furnished prettily enough for a parlor, with a great large window looking down on ever restless Broadway. There I am sitting now and the perpetual motion of the crowded thoroughfare below me seems wonderful—that each individual and vehicle should get disentangled from the mass and go on his way with life and limb perfect. It has been raining all the morning, but the clouds seem breaking now.

We have just finished breakfast in the cosiest most home-like of ladies ordinaries . . . . Jim has gone to his Uncle Tom's . . . or I know he would write with me.[1] He thinks you had better keep our marriage certificate for us, as it would most likely get lost if we had it . . . . Give my warmest love and kisses to Annie [sister], Eddie [brother] and baby Elise and tell them they must write to me whenever they can. I want a letter from you by every steamer and you shall have one in return. Address care of Capt. James Gilliss, A[ssistant] Q[uarter] M[aster], Fort Walla Walla, Washington Territory. Do not feel sad at missing us . . . . God bless you all   *Julie*

Our steamer sails tomorrow. She is the *Henry Chauncey* and this is to be her first trip to Aspinwall [Colon, Panama].[2] We have secured an entire stateroom by paying for three tickets, and the extra berth, which is really a nice lounge, will add greatly to our comfort. We went out this morning to buy a few last steamer necessities, and to take a look at the never failing beauty of New York Harbor. After the last three days of storm, the brilliancy of today is marked, and the strong breeze blowing up the bay is deliciously crisp and fresh. The water is all sparkles and white caps, gulls are circling overhead and the fussy, bustling little ferries are plying busily in all directions.

Bedloe's and Ellis and Governors Islands look like gems of green in the October sunlight. The first named, tiny as it is, has on it a large and well equipped hospital, where all through the war, the sick and wounded have been well cared for.[3]

This note is only a good-bye to you; I will try to keep a diary for you while steaming southward, but do not know how kindly I shall take to salt water. Goodbye.

P[ACIFIC] M[AIL] S.S. HENRY CHAUNCEY,
November 6th, 1865. Off Cuba.

Dear Parents   I had intended keeping a diary from the time we sailed, but I find it very difficult to make the ink flow properly and a stronger reason is that I would have to write after the date of each day, seasick, feel mean, and that would have been the sum and substance for the last five days. We left New York on the first with the most beautiful clear sky and brilliant sun. At noon precisely the salute was fired, the vessel loosed her moorings and the *Henry Chauncey* with its living freight of fourteen hundred souls ploughed her way out of beautiful New York harbor . . . leaving the long lines of Highlands melting away in mistiness on our right we struck into the open sea . . . . Friday night we passed around [Cape] Hatteras, but even the watchful eye of the Captain could detect no difference in the smooth surface, and it was not until we struck into the short chopping sea of the Gulf Stream that we felt more motion than you ordinarily have in a steamboat on a river. We soon passed out of that and we are still gliding on in and out among the West India Islands as if old Ocean was taking a lengthy nap. 'Tis true an almost tropical sun on the water makes as little clothing as possible necessary. I have been so disgusted with the sea during the first few days experience that I felt as if I never wanted to see another drop of salt water, but the feeling is disappearing and I find much that is interesting.

Bishop [William I.] Kip, wife, son and son's wife are on board and are the only friends I have made. I am delighted with them all.[4] The son has only been married a short time and his bride is about my own age, just leaving her home and parents for the first time and "a fellow feeling makes us wondrous kind." Though for that matter there are brides enough on board to have made the fortunes of any one minister. Almost all the young people are married couples of from eight months down to a week. And old Mrs. Kip told me that every time she has made the trip and that has been five or six times, there was a great majority of brides all bound for California . . . .

Yesterday, being Sunday, we had church in the long cabin. The Bishop preached, but I was too sick to leave my berth. In the evening I felt much better, and the Kip family took me by force up on deck. In a very short time I was so much improved that we sat there till nine o'clock singing all the hymns in the prayer book that we could find tunes for. There are two other ministers on board and a very pleasant party of persons and a great many good voices and the music of so many combined was very, very sweet, in the moonlight on the sea.

We have the most elegantly fitted up vessel on this side of the Isthmus. It is large and commodious and is a floating palace hotel. It is her first trip and she is so fast that the Captain says he will have to slacken our pace or we will get into Aspinwall a day too soon and that is not allowed. I think the smooth passage that we have had is almost unprecedented. And even down here in this region of perpetual rain we still have bright skies and fair winds to waft us onward. We are so close to Cuba that we can see a house on the beach. It is a barren looking island, not a tree or shrub being visible from the beach. I would not live in these warm, damp countries if I could possibly help it. Everything is so damp and sticky. Even pins rust fast in your clothes in the course of a day. Imagine the whole shipload of passengers busy taking quinine for the next two days as a preventative against the fever on the Isthmus. It is always customary.

"Tuesday 7th." Still bright and clear. Last night we saw a bright flashing light on our larboard side which we concluded to be the lighthouse on St. Domingo. We see a great many flying fish and yesterday a large orange-colored bird hovered around the vessel for an hour or two, as if weary of flying and longing to rest its wings. Among the pleasant people is Professor [J.D.] Whitney and his wife. He is, I think, State Geologist of California, and has a class of young men with him.[5] They add greatly to my pleasure by showing me the marine treasures they are constantly fishing up, using queer buckets and dips. Last night we played "cribbage" on deck until too dark to see, when we had some delightful music, both vocal and instrumental (piano) in the cabin from various lady passengers. The Bishop's son and daughter have challenged Jim and self to a game of cribbage this evening. We have chess, backgammon, cards and plenty of amusement, but it is like hotel life, there is no *home* in it. Jim watches over me with the most loving care, and I do not care much for any other society. I do not think I can be too thankful for my good husband.

On Thursday morning we shall reach Aspinwall. How I wish you could have some of the limes, oranges, lemons and bananas that we shall get there. Please write to us every steamer and just direct [to] Capt. Jas. Gilliss, A.Q.M., Fort Walla Walla, Washington Terr., Per Steamer, via San Francisco and just put on ordinary 3 ct stamp.   *Julie S.G.*

> P.M.S.S. GOLDEN CITY,[6]
> November 13th, 1865.

     Dearest Mama & Papa   After sending off my last letter we arrived at "Aspinwall."

Such a queer picture: the wharf all black and dirty; the semi-nude natives paddling around in little boats and running around the beach; beyond, the quaint, red roofed houses of the station rising among the groves of cocoa nuts and bananas. We went ashore and walked among the shops and fruit stalls. The natives are as dark as negros and keep up a constant chattering of Spanish. They seem remarkable for their love of dress and the extremely fine quality of the fabrics used for them. The women wear turbans and very broad brimmed hats and carry flat baskets on their heads filled with oranges, lemons, limes, cocoa nuts, bananas, sponge cake and nut candy, which they make delicious. Jim bought one of their queer, fine, wicker baskets and filled it with fruit for me, but we are cautioned against eating bananas. It is considered very dangerous to eat them here where they grow. They do not taste any better than when they reach us, and being in this tropical sun, they are said to ferment as soon as eaten.

Our ride across to Panama was delightful. There were three trains sent over, and the first one had one car reserved especially for the Captain's friends and a favored few. Jim and myself were among the invited and there were only a few of us, [so] the car was pleasantly filled without being crowded. A party of gentlemen made up a lunch basket to bring with us . . . . then we started and for hours in rapid succession before [us was] the most magnificent panorama I ever saw. A cloudless sky and a burning sun beating over us would have been almost insupportable, but for a delightful breeze which the old travelers with us said was almost unheard of before. The deep intense green of the foliage lights up beautifully in the sunshine. Peak after peak of high land rises in quick succession from the beach, clothed to their very summits with the tangled luxuriance of the tropics.

On we went like a great snorting snake, writhing along past groves of the graceful feathery palm and huge leaved banana; through thick mangroves with their polished glittering leaves; the waving cocoa nut with its immense clusters of fruit, ready to drop to the ground. Brilliant colored flowers spring here and there; the white plumage of the crane is seen in almost every pool of water, and the deep dark recesses of the tangled undergrowth are fit hiding places for the wild beasts that lurk within the shadows. The picture is gorgeous, brilliant, magnificent, but you feel that it is hollow, dark and deadly, that the poisonous marsh ... underlies all; this beauty is only the pitfall that we may always find beneath the glitter and display of the tropic climate.

We pause over the iron bridge of the Chagres and the view is beautiful looking up the stream under the arch of the bridge, till it winds like a silver thread around the base of the green velvety peaks of the high land.[7] The huts of the natives are very picturesque but that is all. They are a rude framework thatched with a kind of reed that grows in the marshes. The natives seem to be piled in without regard to numbers; the children are clothed in only the garments furnished by nature and bear a striking resemblance to the monkeys of their own forests. The station houses which are at intervals of several miles along the road are very pretty. They are large and airy, painted white with windows on all sides and large verandahs all around. They are always situated in the midst of groves of orange, limes or any of the trees of the Isthmus. They all have the most magnificent flower gardens.

After several miles the scenery becomes monotonous. The eye wearies of the never failing stretches of the same foliage and flowers, the very air with its deep heavy perfume becomes oppressive and every breath becomes painful. We only saw one ... india rubber tree; the bark is perfectly red and the leaves merely a scrubby bunch at the top.

On reaching Panama, which we did almost five o'clock in the evening, we found steamboats there to convey us to the Steamer which lay off the island of Taboga. But Panama! . . . Oh for an inspired pencil to transmit to canvas the scene that met my eye as I stood on the deck of the Steamer that evening. Right before us rose a high peak covered with verdure, sloping down to the very waters. Just at its base nestled the old town, quaint and moss grown with the sunlight darting through the openings and windows of the ruined buildings. Towers and spires pointing their taper fingers up to Heaven, stood out in bold relief against the evening sky. Some of the crumbling ruins have palm trees waving from the tops, and vines clambering in and out the crevices. The long line of old convents have lost their upper structures and the ground floor of most of the buildings are occupied by stores. But from the distance the view is enchanting.

Stretching away to the northward is a curving line of coast with its hard shining beach . . . . Add little red vessels asleep on the bosom of the bay . . . . But above all, like the most gorgeous curtains, rested clouds and coloring that well could rival Italian for famed skies. Never have I beheld such magnificence, never conceived such depth and richness of color. Breathless and almost spell-bound one watched the ever varying glories of that sunset until the deep crimson, orange, purple and frost-white faded into the dim blue, and "Night drew a sable mantle o'er the earth and pinned it with a star."

Our universal feeling of admiration and regret followed the last lingering ray and we longing watched the receding shores, as we steamed out of the beautiful bay of Panama and committed ourselves once more to the perils of the mighty deep. And yet I have never felt utterly lonely when the land had vanished and waters rolled on every side. It always seems as if you could look beyond the waves if your sight was only a little stronger.

We have had land in sight for two or three days and a range of the most beautiful mountains follows us along as we skirt the shores of "Tehuantepec."[8] Tonight we expect to reach "Acapulco" where we must endeavor to get our letters ashore. Tell Eddie we saw a large school of porpoises yesterday leaping and playing in the water. The weather is intensely warm but we are quite well and send many a thought to our loved ones at home, gathered cosily around a fire, while we have to indulge in a steam bath day and night, willi nilli .... With our warmest love and heartfelt longing to see you all.   *Julie*

OCCIDENTAL HOTEL, SAN FRANCISCO, CAL.,
November 25, 1865.

My dearest parents   After all our tossing about on the weary ocean, we have finally, thankful for the protection which has guided us, arrived at this city of hills. Yesterday morning about ten o'clock, the *Golden City* with her tired passengers, steamed majestically through the Golden Gate into the magnificent bay of San Francisco. We were very glad once more to press our feet on mother Earth, but still a little regret would creep in that all the friends who have been tossed about together through the last twenty-three days are scattered apart to the four winds of Heaven to meet again— when? We had a very pleasant party on board and so many still remain in San Francisco, that I do not feel like a stranger in a strange land. Yet a single glance around tells me I am far from home. This city is a great deal larger than I expected. Built all over the sides and crest of several large hills, some of the streets seem almost perpendicular, and to stand either at the summit or the base transition either way seems nearly impossible. Yet streetcars crawl through most of them and vehicles dash up and down in a manner frightful to witness.

We had a charming voyage up the Pacific, not quite so crowded, as the large opera troupe left us to go to Peru, but this deprived us of most of our fine singing. We went into the land-locked bay at Acapulco, hoping to have a day on shore, but we were not allowed to land. Cholera being feared, all incoming vessels were quarantined, with a ferocious looking ship flying French colors to enforce obedience.[9] We could only look from a distance on the queer adobe buildings with their tropical surroundings, and then turn our eyes to the wonders of the bay. We rode at anchor for a few hours, so completely shut in by green hills, that the eye could not detect a break which promised an opening to the outer sea, but we had come in, so the pathway opened before us when we started on the right track. We went close in shore at many places on the Mexican coast but were always forbidden to land, and also were kept at a distance from the canoes of the fruit dealers, which we were very anxious to patronize, but were obliged to do without until we reached San Francisco.

The stores here are beautiful and the goods truly magnificent. New York loses her supremacy and is forced to stand on the same level as her younger western sister. All the merchandise here seems to be of the finest conceivable material. I do not believe there are any goods that are imitations or of inferior quality in the city. Wanting more pins very badly I walked up and down through several streets before I could find a store that looked as if such trifling articles were kept within. Another thing that strikes a stranger is the profusion and magnificence of the fruit and vegetables. Nowhere under the sun have I seen such heaps and piles of every kind of fruit that grows, and in such perfection as here . . . .

The houses are mostly of frame, *very ornamental* but low on account of earthquakes, these all surrounded by gardens and covered with flowers. I have seen hedges of scarlet geranium all in full flower *five* and *six feet high. Now* in *November* they have strawberries here and all our most delicate hothouse plants growing in wild profusion in the open air. And yet this delicious balmy atmosphere is considered very unhealthy. Everyone gets the rheumatism, and the ladies here at the hotel say that a cold degenerates into consumption more quickly here than elsewhere. And the constant rumbling of earthquakes keeps the inhabitants in a nervous shake. It is rather a poor joke when you go out for a quiet walk to have the ground heave and swell like the ocean waves beneath your feet, and to have the fronts of houses fall out on your head without a moment's warning.

They are now building the new houses with iron rods encircling each room. There was a slight shock here just a few hours before we arrived. One great precaution is that although most of the streets are paved with cobblestones there are no pavements.[10] All the sidewalks are wood, and completely undermined with rats. And yet along these broken, wooden walks sweep the most superbly dressed ladies in the world, for I believe there is nothing under the sun that you cannot get here if you have the *money*. But there's the rub. Everybody seems to be wealthy and I expect they are, for a moderately well off person would soon become impoverished. Prices are exorbitant. Everything must be paid in gold, and even then costs twice as much as it does at home in greenbacks.

Chinese abound. Some have adopted the American style of dress, but very many retain their own costumes. Their houses all bear the same unfailing sign, "Fine washing and fluting done here," and really I don't suppose in any three or four other cities put together can you find so many *washermen* and washerwomen. And yet you have to pay as much here for a single piece, as you do at home for half a dozen. They all wash by the piece and have their regular prices for every article of apparel. We are having our wash done in the laundry of the hotel, but the rates are the same. I like this hotel very much but the dining hall especially is, in my estimation, perfection. And such a table; I believe the most rigid advocate for dyspepsia diet, would become a gourmand here . . . . Jim has just gone to attend the funeral of Colonel De Russy, . . . who has been for some time the commander of the Presidio.[11] Just as our vessel entered the harbor yesterday, the steamer for Walla Walla passed *out*. So we shall have to stay here for a week. I should be very glad, if it were not so expensive. I have just been out walking through the market. It would set a Washington housekeeper crazy to see it.

Sunday Morning. We are going to Grace Cathedral today to hear Bishop Kip. I wish you could know them. They are one of those kind of families that you cannot help loving every member of it, and feeling drawn toward them in spite of yourself . . . .

If you wrote me anything of importance by the last steamer please rewrite it, for I think possible that I may lose the letter if it was directed to Walla Walla. The Captain Johnson who James was ordered to relieve was relieved some months ago by some other officer, so that they have no use for James there, and I suppose General [Henry W.] Halleck will send him somewhere else, possibly Fort Vancouver.[12] But there seems to be as many officers out here as are wanted.

Be sure when you write to tell me every little scrap of home news about you all, for it will be eagerly looked for by your loving   *Daughter Julie*

OCCIDENTAL HOTEL, SAN FRANCISCO, CAL.,
Sunday, November 26th, 1865.

Dear Annie and Eddie   I cannot help writing for it seems as if every word was a tiny thread connecting me with you all at home. I try to imagine just what you are doing and saying and wonder if you miss me. I have just returned from church and the lingering words of our beautiful service carried me back to dear old Epiphany and made me feel that our church is a home for me all the world over.[13] We had a very fine sermon from the Bishop. His church is very much like St. Marys Cathedral, Burlington, but much handsomer. Young Mr. Kip and his wife walked home with us . . . .

I have just been to lunch. We had pyramids of oranges that looked like pumpkins and grapes like those found by the spies, for Jim and I had a *half* a bunch divided between us and it stuffed us so we could not eat the other half. I have frequently seen at dessert, *one bunch* that *filled* a tall fruit stand. But tell Papa I'm sorry I can't find Savoy cabbages. No one is acquainted with them. Everything here is prodigious.

Eddie dear, I'm sorry I have no stamps for you yet, but I hope to find some . . . . I would love dearly to have you all out here to see the sights, but in spite of them the more I see of other lands the more I love my own . . . . One thing I do not like about San Francisco is that all the places of amusement and the stores are kept open on Sunday just the same as through the week, and I think it is a worse place for boys than New York.

OCCIDENTAL HOTEL, SAN FRANCISCO, CAL.,
November 29th, 1865.

Dear Mama & Papa   As the steamer makes her return trip tomorrow, I do not want her to reach home without a message from me . . . . I am enjoying myself very much here, am constantly beset with visitors and have made some very dear friends. We are both quite well and consequently can run about everywhere. Night before last we went to the Academy of Music . . . . Yesterday we rode out to the "Mission Dolores," the first settlement of this great mushroom city. The buildings there are quaint old Spanish houses and sheds very much dilapidated, and moss-grown; they have green tiled rooves and look like the houses down in the old Mexican towns. The chapel has been rebuilt and is a gloomy forbidding old stone edifice. Attached to it is a Cemetery (now owned by the Roman Catholics) which is in a terrible state of ruin. We came home in a car propelled by a dummy engine, as a heavy fog bank obscured the sun, and settled down thickly over the city. Today we are going on another jaunt, making the most of our time here, for we sail for Fort Vancouver [Washington Territory] on the next steamer. Jim's orders to that effect are out . . . .

Is it not singular that the winter here is the lovely season. *Now* the air is balmy and the climate perfect, but in summer the morning is murky and the afternoon gusty and cold. This (at present) is the rainy season but it has not rained since I have been here. We were at Bishop Kip's at luncheon two days ago, and are to dine there this week. He showed me his gallery of paintings some of which are very fine. He has Le Brun's "Washing of the Blackamoor," which was stolen during the troubles in France and brought over to New Orleans where it was bought by the Bishop's father.[14] He has a portrait of his wife when she was Miss Lawrence, by Inman, that is the loveliest piece of flesh and blood I ever saw.[15] They have a great deal of style and I imagine are quite wealthy. In fact they are the summit and head of California society, but as with all truly refined people there is not a particle of affectation or pomposity about them.

I have just heard the vessel sails for Oregon Tuesday and I expect before you receive this we will be enjoying Vancouver. Little did I think when at school I used to make out with a pencil on a map this western country, that I ever should become a traveler and trace with footprints on the land itself, the same places. But I enjoy it all. Even at this short period the pleasures of our voyage are dwelt upon and talked over while all that was disagreeable and worrying is almost forgotten, and I would be willing to undertake it again tomorrow if I knew that every revolution of the wheel would take me that much nearer home. But still I am happy, very happy in my husband's love and care, and should think that Earth held nothing else to ask for, if I only had you all around me . . . . I can *wish* you all a "Merry Christmas and Happy New Year," though the distance makes it impossible to send any more substancial token, so I will have to wait 'till our return and bring Christmas with me. It is exceedingly fashionable for things, especially letters, to be lost in their transit from West to East and vice versa. I enclose a sample of our California newspapers; I think it is decidedly original. The Cholera has appeared here, but the papers this morning say it is only cholera morbus, but as all three cases terminated fatally I am inclined to think it is genuine.[16] They are trying to hush it up I suppose.

I have stopped writing for an hour; this time it was the Bishop and Willie Kip called on us . . . . I am really ashamed to send home such short letters as I do, but I try to compensate by writing often; as I would like to hear from home whenever it is possible, so I think you would like to hear from me. There, I must stop again. Lunch is ready and I am always ready to eat.

Well lunch is over and since then I've been out riding to Lone Mountain, and clear across the opposite side of the city to Telegraph Hill. I am very tired climbing such a steep ascent, for you can only ride to the base. We got home at six o'clock just in time for dinner. Tomorrow we are going to the Cliff House on the seashore where there are innumerable pelicans, sea lions, seals, seaweed etc.

As I told you, our first order to Walla Walla was changed, as a Volunteer Lieut. has been put in charge of the Quartermaster's work there, and the post is no longer sufficiently important to send a regular officer there. Col. E.B. Babbitt of the Q[uarter] M[aster's] D[epartment], our chief in this city, has asked General Halleck to order my husband to report for duty to Colonel Lovell at Fort Vancouver.[17] Where he will assign us I do not know, will tell you as soon as our orders are issued. I hope we will have a post station, for money does not seem to last very well out here. Everything is paid for in gold, except the services of Uncle Sam's officers, so we have to use our greenbacks on a coin basis, and yesterday we only received sixty-eight cents on the dollar. We will manage somehow! If we cannot buy all that we want, we must want less. We have engaged our passage on the *Sierra Nevada* and I must say she looks old enough to fall to pieces on the voyage, so I am glad that it will only last a few days.[18] Will write you next from Oregon if our trip is prosperous . . . .

ON NORTHWEST SOIL

Setting Foot in Portland

DECEMBER 1865-JANUARY 1866

ARRIGONI'S HOTEL,[1] PORTLAND, OREGON,
December 10th, 1865.

My dearest Parents   Here we have alighted once
more in our wild erratic flight, but no nearer a definite knowledge of
our destination. I really think if Mr. War Department, was compelled to say for what especial purpose Jim was ordered out here, he
would be considerably nonplussed. There are so many officers,
quartermasters especially, out here that they do not know what in
the world to do with another. They did not want him in San Francisco so Genl. Halleck ordered him to report at Fort Vancouver for
assignment to duty. Col. Babbitt thought possibly they might station him at Portland. Well, after another delectable sea voyage, behold us dumped down in Portland.

Such a voyage! Rain, wind, a rolling, pitching old tub of a vessel,
always on one end or the other. Waves always sweeping the decks,
staterooms and cabins full of spray, damp berths, moist everything.
What the table could have offered, I have no idea. I don't think anyone tried it. Our fellow passengers in misery, were only a Chinese
Mandarin and his wife, and a half a dozen men and women who saw
each other when they went aboard and when they came ashore; no
oftener. Ugh! I'm glad that trip is over; and I surely thought that

17

the voyage and ourselves were finished together when we entered the Columbia river and rolled over the Bar.

Jim went to Vancouver yesterday and reported; they don't want him there, there is little or no employment for a quartermaster in Portland, and they think maybe a quartermaster is wanted at Fort Boise, Idaho Territory. So our next move may be in that direction. If they keep on at this rate we shall be edged over to the East, if they keep us going long enough. Portland is apparently quite a large city for this country and there is a great deal of business carried on but it rains all the time. It has rained for five weeks and looks as if it would continue for five months; they say it generally does rain all winter, that their clear weather does not begin until April but the summers are lovely. It rained during our trip up the Columbia river and I had not recovered from sea sickness so that I could not see the scenery for which it is remarkable. I am a miserable sailor; I do not think I can ever become accustomed to the motion for I am just as sick the last day out as the first, and only get well when I get on shore.

This is a funny hotel, very comfortable, but so different from anything I ever saw. Very nice easy chairs, but with the most remarkable crochet "tidies" pinned on the backs and arms, to the great discomfort of the occupant. The lamps are clean and give good light, but are glass with pieces of red flannel in the oil. Is it for ornament, I wonder? The table is good, everything very neat and clean, and when one can sleep and eat well, nothing else matters, when you are on the wing as we are.

This country is interesting, abounding in game (and the most delicious milk). I don't know what is their gauge for an individual appetite, but they furnish one person with enough for a regiment. Tell Annie that would just suit her, but for me *who never had an appetite* 'tis rather appalling. I have not been out yet, so I have only been able to form an opinion of the town through the squares of my window veiled with showers; but the steamer sails for San Francisco so soon that I want to have my letter ready to send. You can write to me at *any time* as the overland mail comes every day, only you must not write (per steamer) on your letters. I am so impatient to hear from home that I can hardly contain myself. Just think, not one word have I heard since we left New York, and I have written five. I know you have written, but your letters have not caught us yet . . . . With a great deal of love to you both from your affectionate and happy daughter,   *Julie S.G.*

ARRIGONI'S HOTEL, PORTLAND, OREGON,
December 16th, 1865.

Dear Annie   Although I am very busy packing up again I thought I would take a few moments to write to you. Jim has at last received his *third* order, which sends him to "Fort Dalles," about a hundred and twenty-five miles above here, on the Columbia river.[2] The post is highly spoken of, and has the best quarters for officers on this coast. The city of [The] Dalles lies right at the Fort. I was all impatience to go as soon as Jim's orders were received, but the river was filled with floating ice and the boats stopped running. We have had a thaw now and we will leave here Monday morning. The boat runs daily, but only leaves Portland at five o'clock in the morning, which is an unconscious hour, as it is not *daylight here till seven* and dark in the afternoon at five, and the sun does not get directly overhead at noon. It is so dark, I must stop till I have a light.

I went out and took a walk with Jim today and was astonished at the number and variety of the stores. They have some better stores here than we have in Washington, but mud! Oh! Oh! if you would take a trip out west, you never would grumble about mud again. Especially here in Oregon; it is commonly called Web Foot country, for they say everyone who comes here have webs grow between their toes like ducks. It does rain incessant, but has not been as cold as we have it at home. There are some very nice people here and quite pretty houses; several churches. We have a church at the Dalles . . . . Tell Uncle William his brother is living in Oregon City, and his eldest daughter is married to the Captain of a steamboat. . . .[3]

I suppose you are all busy dressing the church; I hope you won't forget to dress our parlor with church scraps. If they could only get hold of the acres and miles of evergreens out here they would be delighted. They look beautiful cased in ice. There is so much water here that when cold there is nice ice. Jim is going to get me a pair of skates and take me skating. I see the peak of Mt. Hood every day, out of the window, covered with snow and looking much nearer than it really is. We shall have a better view of it from the Dalles . . . .

I try to bear very patiently the thought that Jim is really not needed out here, there is scarcely anything for him to do, but it is very hard to think he could have been so much more useful nearer home if they had only chosen to keep him there. I wish his good friends in Washington would work to have him recalled. These forts are nearly useless, the Indians are scattered far away, the posts themselves right in the heart of civilization, and one by one they are being abandoned. I suppose in a year Fort Dalles will share the common fate and then we shall be started off to another one.   *Julie*

PORTLAND, OREGON,
December 24th, 1865.

Dearest Mama & Papa   We are still in the above named place but hope to leave in a few days. Last Monday we made the attempt, that is we went on board the steamboat and steamed out to the confluence of the Willamette with the Columbia. We laid there for two or three hours, our progress impeded by the masses of floating ice; at last we were obliged to abandon the attempt and turned our faces Portland-ward. But we were compensated for our disappointment by the magnificence of the view which burst upon us as the vessel headed around. The sun was just rising, and the groves of evergreens with snow nestling among their branches were gilded with the sunshine which glanced on their icy casings. Down to the very water's edge they grew and climbed to the tops of the hills beyond, while far above towered the snowy peaks of Hood, St. Helens, Adams, Raynier [Rainier] and Jefferson. Cold, glittering and glacial looked their shaded sides, while where the sun rays played they were bathed in a deep rosy hue. Standing aloof in their superior majesty, yet seeming guardians of the slumbering little green hills at their feet. Down in mid-distance where the river danced and flashed in the sunlight like a thing of life, the mists rolled back on either side like a curtain, and a deep, rich purple haze flooded the landscape, through which the ice-bound trees sparkled like jewels. The keen, morning air was cut by the circling wing of the seagull and wild ducks skimmed along the surface of the water. Mt. Hood was up, and by the blue smoke from her crater upward curling, seemed (like the little cottages around) to be preparing for her morning meal.[4] *We* breakfasted on board and in a couple of hours ran back into Portland where we have been ever since, bound in with ice and snow. I have had several sleigh rides, but we are very anxious to get settled at Fort Dalles, and the rains today give promise of it. This roaming unsettled life is very tiresome, and hotel life very superficial.

At Cascades, Wash[ington] Ter[ritory], December 27. Well here we are, progressing by *slow* and easy stages toward our destination. We left Portland day before yesterday morn before daybreak and slowly cut our way through the floating masses of ice for 65 miles to this point, where the boat has to stop on account of the rapids and falls in the river. This is the first "portage," and here we take the steam cars for five miles around the falls, and take another boat at the upper terminus. When the boat stopped we went ashore in the rain and found only the locomotive awaiting us. The company thinking that the boat would not be up, had left all the passenger cars at the other end of the line. So the only alternative was to ride on an iron horseback, so the passengers seven in number packed themselves in the tender while I as the only lady of the party was honored with a *seat* in the engine proper. There I sat as cosy as possible, kept very warm by the fire under the boiler, while poor Jim and the rest of the gentlemen had decidedly cold standing accommodations. We went on charmingly until we were within a mile of our stopping place when the track was discovered to be completely covered with snow, rocks and loose dirt which had slid down the mountain side. There was nothing to be done but stop 'till the track could be cleared, and spades and shovels were in requisition.

After a delay of two or three hours, the work was found to be so much greater than was anticipated that all hope of getting through it before night, was abandoned, and we had to foot it the rest of the way. What fun! you would have laughed to see us. The snow was melting, and slippery as could be; on we slipped, stumbling, laughing; occasionally the treacherous snow would let us through to a much greater depth than we anticipated. We had quite a steep hill to descend, and we rolled carpet bags, portmanteaux and baskets ahead of us while we rolled after them catching at every twig that protruded through the snow, to stay our rapid motion. But all things must have an end, and in a very short time we arrived at the village in a glow from our efforts and laughter. 'Tis the tiniest little mite of a place you can imagine, boasting only one store and no hotel. But we are very delightfully situated at a Mr. [John] Andrews who very kindly allowed us to board with them. They have a very pretty place, nicely furnished and just as pleasant and homelike as possible. I have taken a great fancy to Mrs. Andrews. She is the perfect embodyment of kindness and hospitality. She says she is rather the recipient of favor in having us for company, for though plenty of her friends very gladly will spend the summer with her, they prefer the cities in winter. It is not very cold here for 'tis so sheltered by the mountains, but the river is still frozen between here and the Dalles, a distance of about fifty miles so that the boats cannot come down yet.

High above the village stand two blockhouses in which lived . . . those only who were saved in the terrible Cascades Massacre. Every other person was murdered, and now the village has only two occupied houses. All the others are boarded up, tenantless shells, a pathetic monument to the extinction of entire families. The Indians that are here now are of the Flathead tribe, and look very picturesque when they stand out on the rocks, watching for salmon which they spear with great dexterity, but on closer acquaintance they are dirty and unpleasant. I shall see very little of them, however, as we hope the boat will arrive tomorrow to take us up the river.[5]

The country is magnificent. In fact I don't believe the scenery through which we passed on our way up here can be excelled by any in the world. High on either side rise the mighty summits of the Cascade range while through the cleft between, roars and tumbles the water of the Columbia with its great masses of floating ice gliding rapidly with the current. Far, far back as the eye can see till lost in the clouds, stretch the "everlasting hills," their sides sloping down to the very water's edge. Numerous waterfalls leap and dash down, caused by the melting of the snow, while here and there a permanent cascade of greater magnitude greets the eye. We saw one, the "Horse Tail Fall," which dashes down a perpendicular height of eleven hundred feet. Soon we came to the famous "Cape Horn," a magnificent rocky point about 400 feet high. The rock is worn by mountain streams into a succession of connected boulders covered with a luxuriant green moss, which occasionally shows the perpendicular strata and volcanic character of the stone. In each of these crevices a torrent has rushed down, and been held spell-bound by the Frost King, and while the moss around is green and fresh, the poor imprisoned waters await the sunbeams' power to loose the spell that binds them. From every rock and jutting point the giant icicles hang like huge stalactites, and gleam cold and frozen amid the surrounding darkness. Terrible gales sometimes rage around this point and more than one vessel has gone down a prey to the fury of the wind and waves. Above, the waters of this lordly stream are confined in the narrow limits of a hundred feet, and as if chafing at its confinement, breaks into a hundred falls which come madly leaping, rushing, roaring in wild impetuosity over its rocks and islands. Soon we came to Castle [Beacon] Rock, a solitary stone rising for fourteen hundred feet above the ground. My paper warns me to stop which I will do after sending our love and a kiss to all our loved ones from Jim and   *Julie* . . . .

CASCADES, WASHINGTON TERRITORY,
Monday, January 8th, 1866.

My dear Parents   On board steamer *Idaho* . . . I was just on the point of writing to tell you that James had gone to walk to the boat [from The Dalles] which is lying a few miles up the river being prevented by ice from advancing to the wharf.[6] He left before breakfast this morning, as soon as he heard that the boat was down, as he has received several letters in regard to his business at Fort Dalles, which is becoming important.

Well! about ten o'clock who should come in but Capt. [John] McNulty, captain of this very boat.[7] He had come down on horseback and all the passengers, including a good many ladies and children, were walking or coming on an ox sled. The snow is very deep, and from the appearance of the weather the Captain said he thought

possibly it might be weeks before the boat could come down any further. With a mental determination not to be separated from my husband so long, I asked why I couldn't go up, as others were coming
down. He said so I could, but without any trunks. So I packed a carpet bag with immediate necessities and the Capt. brought me his
horse with a Mexican saddle.[8] The bag was strapped on one side of
the saddle and I with my beaver coat over my riding dress, & a thick
worsted hood on my head, making a striking picture, mounted on
top. View in your mind's eye, a tall gaunt *roanish whitish* horse,
with a big carpet bag dangling on one side of the saddle, with a
bundle of lunch tied a little back of it, and I in my picturesque costume the crowning figure.

On we jogged "through bog, through fen, through brake,
through den," over stumps, through creeks, and forests, up hill and
down hill, right in the heart of the Cascades, a country wilder than
you can imagine. But it was delicious, sheltered from the fierce
mountain blasts, which swept down the river, the air was mild and
invigorating. Every few steps we would meet stragglers from the
boat; some boasting a mule, but the most of them on foot, looking
draggled enough from having to wade through the numerous
streams. Some few were disgusted with the trip; the most, however,
enjoyed it. One lady had a bundle and a cage and bird in her arms,
her husband had a basket and valise; yet she laughingly told me she
thought it was fun. So did the next load we met—a great sled made
of logs drawn by four oxen, packed tight with ladies and children and
two trunks. The cumbersome machine dumped its burden over a
road that it looked impossible to pass over in safety by itself.

I very foolishly gave Jim's sword to a man to carry, who cut across
the woods and got to the boat first; he told Jim I was coming, so
spoilt my surprise. You may imagine his. He started out on the trail
to meet me. We soon reached the boat, and here I am trying to
write, while it rolls like a ship at sea, and indeed the rough waves
and white caps of this Western river bear a striking resemblance to
old Ocean. The Captain thinks we shall lay here all night, and proceed on our journey in the morning.

A NEW HOME

Settling in at Fort Dalles

JANUARY-MARCH 1866

JAN. 10TH [1866].

Here we are at the Dalles!!! The Finis and Ultimatum of all our hopes. We arrived about eight o'clock last evening and found a carriage sent from the garrison for us, merely on the supposition that we *might* come. The largest house burnt down two weeks ago; and there are now only two left. The one which was consumed cost ninety thousand dollars, and was the handsomest house on this coast.[1] The two remaining are very pretty Gothic villas, but all of wood, and as they have the same kind of chimneys which caused the destruction of the other, they may possibly fall victims to the same fell destroyer. The rooms are beautiful and I expect to have a lovely little home.

Captain C[oppinger] of the 14th Infantry is in command of the post, and to his courtesy we are indebted for a sheltering roof.[2] He has most kindly taken us in and really given us nearly all his quarters, reserving only two rooms for himself. I never saw such kindness to strangers! When we drove into the post it was quite dark, but we were met by the Surgeon and his wife, swinging a lighted lantern between them, and waiting to take us to their house to supper.[3] When we arrived, we found their parlor occupied by two hospital cots, daintily made and ready for our use. In the next room which was also the kitchen, we found a charmingly appointed table in the

25

middle of the floor. This house is literally the two rooms and a kitchen, which they tell me will also be our allowance of quarters, so Doctor Steele with his wife and little girl had crowded into one room to care for us. Just think of taking so much trouble for people never seen before! Captain C. came in with us, and seems to be a charming, genial gentleman to whom we were at once greatly attracted.

Our sleep was sweet and this morning we have moved (one valise) into what will be our future home. The rooms are pretty, but you would laugh to see our furnishing. The kitchen is sumptuously supplied already, with a stove, some pans, a wooden chair and table. The parlor has a bowed window on the front, consisting of six narrow sashes with tiny diamond shaped panes set in lead. Hung on the walls at *each* side are swabs, rammers, sabres and other things whose names I have not yet learned, while on the floor with its nose (J. says I must say muzzle) pointing out the window is the dearest brass gun mounted on a wooden carriage. Captain C. says it is a mountain howitzer.[4] A large bookcase built into the wall, a very large mantlepiece and a few chairs complete this room. Our bedroom has a buffalo robe on the floor; a bedstead made by a carpenter here at the post and painted sky blue; a bed sack filled with sweet hay. That is all at present. We hope in a few days to add a little, for we have a promise that we may buy a second-hand carpet and a frame that can be covered for a dressing table.

In point of scenic beauty, I must say a word. You can imagine yourself transported to the crater of an extinct volcano, or as a Californian graphically observes, "to the Infernal regions, after the fire has gone out." For miles nothing is visible but huge masses of rocks and stones, of every size, but of volcanic description, sown broadcast. Trees all seem to have forsaken the land, for with exception of the firs and cedars at the garrison, I don't believe there is as much as a blade of grass for miles. It will look better however when the snow melts. I would like you, Papa, if it is no trouble, please [to] send me some seeds, flowers and vegetables, from the Patent Office, and send them by mail.

Jim sends his warmest love to all his adopted family. I could cry over every letter I send to think we are so far away. I try to be patient and think that all things are ordered for our good, but it seems very hard. I know I can't have everything my own way, and I am very thankful for my darling husband. He is everything I could wish, and I know he feels this order keenly, for he is convinced now that it could only have proceeded from vindictive motives. Yet he bears it patiently, and has never said a hard word against those who have been instrumental in producing it. Kiss sisters and brother for us, we think of you all the time. There are three churches here; a Catholic, Methodist and Congregational; ask Annie which we must attend . . . . We have had no letters yet, no single word from home to your loving daughter, *Julie S.G.*

"FORT DALLES," OREGON,
January 14, 1866.

Dear Mama I suppose you are very anxious to know how we are situated, as my last letter informed you that we had reached our destination. After the difficulty which we experienced in getting here you may be sure we were glad to arrive in safety, and the next question was the settlement of our home. The house is a beautiful little villa in very bad repair. If it were really to be our permanent home we would take great pride in furnishing it, but as we are only sojourners, as much as is necessary for our use. Enclosed I send a sketch of the ground plan, badly drawn, but will give you some idea. We have to let the Colonel have the contiguous rooms, C.C. on the first floor, as his large house burnt down a few weeks ago and there is no other here for him. In fact only two houses are now standing, ours, and one occupied by the Surgeon Dr. Steele. His house is smaller, and his family, consisting of his wife, her sister, a young lady and his little daughter Fannie fully fill it. We have furnished the room D. as a little parlor and a very pretty one it makes. On the second floor we occupy the rooms A.A. marked 1.2. with their adjoining dressing rooms. Only the front one is furnished however. Our furniture is a strange medley; most of it was in the house. One or two heavy, handsome pieces suitable for a mansion, mixed in with pine table and odd chairs. Our carpets are pretty and we bought both of them alike, so in moving from one post to another they can be put together or matched to suit other rooms. This house is Captain's quarters, and their legal allowance is only *two rooms* and a *kitchen*. Look at the plan and see how ingeniously it came within the pale of law. The rooms C.C. communicating by folding doors the whole way across, counts only *one room*; the room D. is the *second* and E. the kitchen is the *third*. The hall B. is not a room, and the second floor is called an attic story which never counts for rooms. The washhouse F. is a frame room added as an outhouse.

The house is Gothic and built of wood.[5] We heard they were of stone which is a mistake. They cost as much money as a stone one would cost at the East. *Everything* is frightfully high here however. Servants' wages range from fifty to eighty dollars a month in gold, and it is only as a favor that you can get one then. Nine out of ten wealthy families living in magnificent style, have to do their own work because there are no servants on this coast. The Chinese are all laundresses and do their washing at their own homes so you can put that out at three dollars a dozen in gold. Even wood with which the country abounds is nine dollars a cord in gold, and no coal on this coast for any price. But I suppose there is more wealth along this Pacific [Coast] than all the rest of the United States combined. Jim's pay reduced to its gold equal is 110 dollars a month, but as we have no house rent to pay and have all our fuel furnished, we can do very well.

Just now we are literally "snowed up." That is, the snow is two feet deep on the level, and in drifts it varies from four to six ft. Fences are covered and almost the houses; the country looks as if a great white sheet had been spread over it with only prominent points of high houses and churches sticking through it. Even the road makes no distinct track for vehicles cannot reach the ground beneath and the tracks remain pure and white, not a discoloration visible. I expect in summer it is pleasanter and there is plenty to interest one in fossil hunting. The fossils of the mastadon are found around here; tell Eddie I will send him one if I find it . . . . Tell Annie to hunt me up that little book of the Opera "Martha" and send it by mail . . . . I have not received any letters yet. But this snowstorm has prevented any mails from coming in. Jim sends much love, he is kept pretty busy now . . . .

Today is Sunday and the churches are closed in compliment to the survivors of the Editor of the Dalles paper, who has just been buried.[6] I do not understand the compliment . . . . When we get furnished and settled I hope to tell you of my housekeeping successes. Till then goodbye. Your ever loving daughter   *Julie*

JANUARY 14, 1866,
Fort Dalles, Oregon.

Darling little Brother   Here I have been waiting for a long time hoping to get a letter from you . . . .

Oh! we have so many birds out here; I do not know where they live for the ground is covered with snow and we have so few trees. This morning I saw five bluejays out my side window; these were fighting, but they generally seem quite goodnatured. They are larger than a pigeon and are a bright blue except a black topknot . . . . How many more stamps have you? I have not been able to find any for you. I do not know of anyone out here who receives foreign letters. I know a lady in San Francisco who has an Album with nearly twelve hundred stamps in it; she has been travelling in Europe and has collected all the stamps now in use and also those that are now obsolete. Give a kiss to Mama, Papa, sister Annie and baby for me.

FORT DALLES, OREGON,
January 28th, 1866.

Dear Papa   Ever since my last letter we have been "snowed up" on land and frozen up by way of the river. It was the most extensive snow that I have ever witnessed, and is disappearing marvelously fast. In a twinkling the snow seemed to turn into a soft rain and a Chinook wind sprang up to aid in the rapid thaw. However of the principal characteristics of this fickle, slippery Oregon is the extreme uncertainty of its weather. In no other state, I believe, is this so apparent. Thermometers become perfectly exhausted with the rapidity with which they have to jump from Zero upward, and then down again, and Barometers are disgusted with their failures in attempting to point out a change before it takes place, and like a fussy little old gentleman who stamps from side to side in the vain attempt to discover which will convey the full extent of his irateness, they are sorely puzzled in which way to turn when it rains, snows, hails, blows, clouds and shines in the same hour.

Yesterday we were veiled in a thick impervious fog that shut out even the parade ground under our windows; last night without a moment's warning, a terrific windstorm shook our house to its very foundation and made the tall trees quiver and bend almost to the ground and the smaller ones to tremble like terrified children. Today the sun rose clear and bright and so extremely clear is the atmosphere that distant hills, the river, town, and even the very floating clouds seem within one's grasp. Out one window I see the sharp snowy apex of Mount Hood clearly cut against the sky beyond as an opal on a piece of azure velvet. Out the other between the sloping sides of two brown hills, whose feet bathe in the river side by side, rises the rounded dome of beautiful Mount Adams . . . . Oh! they are beautiful. Pale rosy tints glow redder towards their peaks, and purple fairies linger lovingly along their shaded sides. This morning when a cloud floated over Adams and hid it from sight, a lovely rainbow spanned the clouded space; one end rested upon its dome, then arched the cloud and lost the other end in the river at its base.

I beg your pardon though, Papa, I am afraid you will only laugh at my rhapsody and think me foolish for so loving hills. These are the only beauties here vouchsafed to us in this wild stony wilderness. The few trees round us here have dropped their loads of snowy blossoms and are green and fresh, but like a laurel wreath, though bright and fair, placed high above the reach of all save one, whom only it is meant to crown. We only in the garrison have trees.

I think the strength of our Winter is gone. We like the "war horse" "snuff afar" not "scent of battle," but violets, which start up in the footprints of the coming Spring. We have been so tossed about that winter has seemed shorter to us this year. Its wings were clipped before we left our home, at sea we found the old greybeard was taking a tropical nap, and though he's paid us up for past deficiencies since we came here, we've been too busy, much to heed his spite. But next week I'll be *lady* of the *house*. (I declare! the sun's still shining, but hard balls of hail are rattling against my windows. Was ever such a land?) I've been waiting till my rooms were well arranged before I undertook to cater for the tastes, or palates I should say. The Colonel has to have his home with us. His house burnt to the ground and there is no other place for him. He's not much trouble or in fact *none*. He has his servant man who also waits upon us at the table.

I am collecting a few ideas of geology. Stray specimens like my fossils that have to be labeled to prevent me from forgetting them. I have some very pretty ones, and hope to have some more.

FORT DALLES, OREGON,
January 28th, 1866.

Darling Eddie   I thought I must write and tell you about my pony. It is a "Cayuse" or Indian pony and only about four and a half hands high. It is the funniest little thing you ever saw, and has a coat of many colors. Indeed the gentlemen here call him a calico horse, which I think is a shame. They want me to name him "Clattewa" which is the Indian for clear out, but I don't like to have him made fun of by everybody who hears his name.[7] . . . My funny little horse belonged to Colonel Coppinger who sold him to brother Jim for enough to get a coat for one of his men, who had his coat stolen from him by the former owner of the horse. The ground has been covered with snow for about three feet deep so I have not ridden him yet. I wish I could put you on his back and see you trot around this parade ground. Tell Annie to ask Fannie Gilliss to lend her a book called *The Prince of the House of David*. I have just finished it and think Mama would like to read it . . . . I have got a pretty little home and a nice chicken house and yard back of it and when the snow melts away we are going to have some chickens, because it is so hard to get eggs out here . . . .

I am having some talks on Geology with Professor [Thomas] Condon.[8] He is the State Geologist, also the minister of the Congregational church, which we attend as there is no Episcopal church here. He has given me some very interesting fossils to begin a collection, and assures me we shall find many after the snow has gone.

FORT DALLES, OREGON,
February 4th, 1866.

My dearest Parents   We are still frost-bound; the river looks clear, but the boats do not yet think it is advisable to resume their trips, so we are not yet in communication with the outer world. Immured in this barren, monastic, rock-girt land we have to take up our daily cross with the utmost patience. The stage from the upper country has not been able to come down here for several weeks, and its preventative, the snow, was supported by a fresh fall last night. So we are into the fourth month of our absence from home without hearing a word, or receiving one of the many letters which I hope and expect are on their route hither. This place is so famous for disagreeable weather that we expect nothing else, which is a blessing, for we should surely be disappointed. We are keeping house now, I do not know with what success. I must leave Jim to endorse my abilities (if I possess any). I shall have to send you the receipts of some of my cooking, I expect. I have one consolation; I have not spoilt anything yet, so that it was uneatable.

Our little parlor looks quite gay with a very large flag festooned across the bay window, a very pretty brussels carpet, bright and flowery, a heavy oak beaufet and secretary, relics of the furniture grandeur that formerly reigned here, several wooden armchairs belonging to the Post, a square table with a red cover on which repose at directly balancing right-angles a few books, while a lamp with gaily painted shade looms up majestically in the centre by way of symmetrical balance. An antiquated lounge of the Cromwellian order of architecture "heaves its huge length along" one side of the room, and a large centre table fills the space between it and the opposite fireplace. The glass doors of the secretary reveal a dozen choice geological specimens dispersed like angel's visits on one shelf; the one above it has a formidable file of eight *Godey's* [*Lady's Books*] while the remainder are waiting for my books that are now on their way. Fortunately the lower half has solid doors which kindly conceal the vacuum within. A cologne bottle, vase, box of matches, china box and a tiny flat iron and rest (the latter two presents wherewith to begin housekeeping) grace the mantel, while a pretty rug, a fox waiting to catch a rabbit just peeping out of his hole, which I know would please Eddie, complete the bird's eye view of this little parlor. Upstairs is a little more pretentious. One good thing, I have no furniture that can be abused, and I am glad of it. For as there is no way of heating the dining hall we have to eat in the parlor this bitter weather and I have as much care as I desire in preserving my pretty carpets from soil.

We are quite comfortable but I should be glad if the house was a little smaller. The halls are too immense to furnish and look rather barnlike in their emptiness. But my bedroom is our sanctum and a blazing fire of logs makes it as bright as possible. We have a splendid view of distance which would be grand if there was anything to see. However it is the only point at the garrison from which you can see Hood and Adams at a glance.

We have sleigh-rides all the time, a wooden sleigh pretty respectable, a pair of mules with one collar of bells which they have to take turns in wearing. It is very pleasant and good for dyspepsia. Then we have a wagon for dry ground but always mules; we disdain horses, on the same principle that Jack would not eat his supper. I would not think of including my calico pony in this condemnation. He is a prince to himself exclusive and (excluded). I am waiting for the snow to melt that I may ride him. I have not yet had that pleasure. I was weighed yesterday and weighed 128 pounds, a gain of nine pounds in seven weeks which I don't believe so I conclude that there must be some slight difference in their weights and measures. Jim says tell you that my pony weighs twenty lbs. less that I do, but I know that is a shameful slander. He, Jim, weighs nearly 170 himself so he wants to make me out as heavy as he is. He is so lazy I can't make him write at all to anybody; I don't believe he has written a half dozen letters since he left home. He makes me do it all by blarneying me.

I have sent you a couple of papers to show you the Oregon style of literature. The Dalles paper [the *Mountaineer*] is printed on *white* paper whenever they have got it. The mail is going out tonight in about a half hour, that is, it is going out from the garrison. I don't know whether it will go much further. However I must hurry to give it a chance if there is one. How does baby grow; as pretty as ever? I wish I had her picture. She will change so much that I suppose I would not know her now when only three months have elapsed. I say *only*, comparatively speaking, for it seems a great deal longer. I suppose this absence from home is my cross of life (and the only one) so I will try to shoulder it bravely and carry it on to the appointed end, though I'm afraid I often murmur at its weight. I feel so anxious that you should know Jim better than you do. I believe you would love him a great deal more even than you do now.

"Necessity's the mother of invention." I've found out how to dress my curls. I want to keep my good ones nice, and I wore the old ones as a waterfall on the steamer and tangled them dreadfully. But I combed them out, dampened them and rolled them up in paper, baked them and took them down, brushed them hard round the stick and rubbed them with a *little* castor oil, brandy & cologne mixed. They looked beautiful. Now I only brush them every day . . . . Your loving daughter,   *Julie S.G.*

FORT DALLES, OREGON,
February 7th, 1866.

Dearest Papa   Your letter of the 29th December arrived yesterday being the very first communication direct or indirect which has reached us from home. I need not say that it was thankfully received, long looked for and anxiously expected; it was the brightest gleam of sunshine that the day brought forth. This morning, Jim succeeded in getting out of the mail which was passing through here on its way to Walla Walla, a letter from Annie written one month previous to yours which I was also delighted to get. I think you have not received all the letters that I have written . . . .

I am not sorry that we are not to go to Walla Walla even though it *might possibly* be pleasanter; it is a few hundred miles further away and the difficulties of communication with the *outer world* greater than they are here. The post is abandoned however, and only used to store old goods not worth transporting elsewhere. This post is pleasant enough to make one as contented as this coast can.

As to the climate, rumors of the perfection of which wafted east-ward give us expectation, like the gold fables melt away at one's ap-proach. I have not seen or heard out here of uniform pleasant weather *anywhere*. San Francisco has *mild* winters very, but it is so sultry one breathes with difficulty and when it does not rain, a thick impenetrable fog gathers in so close that it veils the opposite side of the street. This fog is of daily occurrence and in the eleven days that we were there although it did not rain once, not for one hour were the sidewalks dry enough to prevent your feet from sticking at every step to the black moisture. And the dirty filthy Chinese portion, faugh! I don't like to think of it. No part of the city is cleaner than Washington, and they begin to tremble more in fear of the cholera than their earthquakes. Portland, as indeed all Oregon, is famous for raining all the time, sometimes as in '62, for 100 days without any intermission. Every Oregonian calls himself "Web-foot," for they have to learn to paddle through their land . . . .

Here at Dalles we are higher in the country among the rocks and sand so we do not get rains of water so much but instead have sand-storms Sahara-like. That is a slight improvement. With so much wet everybody gets the rheumatism; mine has all settled in one shoulder so I only have one member to rub every day. But there is nothing like getting used to a thing. I almost forget it except when it gives me an extra twinge . . . .

We would be very glad to have Wash. papers occasionally . . . . I sent you samples of our Western papers. I hope you will not fail to appreciate their merits *if you find any* . . . . I am glad Mama has Aunt Jane to keep her company while Annie is busy at school.[9] It has worried me a great deal to think of her alone with all the care of Kitty baby and the house every day and that has made me wish my-self home a hundred times to help her. We are quite pleasantly fixed getting along nicely and happy as the day is long. The greatest disap-pointment of my life has been this Western banishment when I thought we would be so happy at home . . . . Jim will write when he has time, he is very busy now. Please write whenever you can to your loving daughter   *Julie S.G.*

FORT DALLES, OREGON,
February 7th, 1866.

My dear Sister   Your first letter just came to hand
this morning and you may be sure I was glad enough to get it. You
put me quite to shame with your writing. My letters look like the
schoolgirl's and *yours like the dignified married sister's.* You have
improved wonderfully. I am so sorry you have had sties. They are
difficult to get rid of . . . . Don't try your eyes by studying with an
imperfect light that may irritate and cause them.

I have just been making a cornstarch pudding for dinner and my
fingers feel as if they were beating eggs instead of wielding a pen.
We have a very pretty house and when I can make a sketch I will
send it. I have a soldier for cook. (A girl sent me word this morning
she would like to live with me and would *condescend* to come for
thirty five dollars a *month* in gold if I would take her. But I was not
suited with the amount of wages, so declined.) My soldier cooks
meats and vegetables very well and I do not mind cooking any little
thing that we want. I have taken a great fancy to macaroni and had
to cook it myself 'till the last two days when I showed him how and
he does it quite as well. I go in town to market every morning in the
sleigh or wagon, with two little jerky mules that make one laugh all
the way. We breakfast at 9 (the sun don't rise out here till nearly 8),
lunch at 1 and dine at 5 except Sunday when we dine at 2, and tea
at 7.

Our household consists of the Colonel, ourselves and Jim's clerk.
The Colonel [Coppinger] went away this morning in quest of health.
He is covered with stubborn boils that nothing seems to benefit. So
he is gone for change of air . . . . Jim is at present Captain commanding the post, Captain of Company A, 14th Infantry, Quartermaster,
Commissary, Adjutant and Officer of the Day, with his hands full of
business. My husband, who still holds his rank as Lieutenant of Artillery, was the only available person for these duties. He likes the
extra work, for after four years of constant service with his battery
in the field, it is very hard for him to be in a place where there is so
little to do. With the fierce winter we are having there are no drills,

and the one company here has all its men in the hospital except four-teen, so you can imagine the stagnation of the place.

There is no one else here except Dr. Steele, Surgeon, wife and child, Miss Blackler, his wife's sister, a very pleasant girl, and Jim's clerk.[10] There is a Mr. Porter, a perfect gentleman whom we all like very much. He is very quiet and in bad health . . . . Officers have to mess together out here as it is the only way they could live on their pay while greenbacks have to be sold for gold . . . .

I have learned a new style [of] tatting, very pretty. I will send home a piece in a letter to show you I have really learned how to do it . . . . I suppose you will not be sorry to leave school now when you graduate . . . . I hope Eddie will take the start that you did for when you were his age you disliked books as cordially as he does . . . . I have just heard the boat whistle so I hope it has brought me some more letters. I received one from Papa yesterday dated Dec. 29, one from you today Nov. 29, quite a nice little budget from Mrs. Gilliss, Fannie & Beck, Nov. 19 & 30.[11] None later . . . . I hope you are all nicely fixed at Aunt Jane's and that it will be quite a care off Mama's & Papa's mind and more time can be given to exacting little baby without tiring Ma so much . . . .

How do you like being the young lady of the family, do you find it tiresome? When you do, come out to see me and take a canter on my nonpareil pony. I wish you could all take a peep at me and I at you. I often imagined at certain hours just where you all were at home and what doing, and used to love to think that my imaginings were really true when lo! the picture is dashed away by the facts ar-riving that you are not at home at all but at Aunt Jane's.

Well, I've tried hard enough to bring up some of the vivid pictures that credulous minds believe others to exercise over them at certain times, however great the distance intervening, but it won't do. I guess I'm a tough subject; nothing but everyday practical ones will have anything to do with me. I never hear fairy voices in flower bells, or catch the stars whispering to each other so I have to e'en come down to common sense and real substantial fat people like yourself . . . . write soon to your loving sister   *Julia*

FORT DALLES, OREGON,
February 18th, 1866.

My dear Mama   Although the river is again fro-
zen over and the boat stopped running I will write my weekly letter
that it may be ready for the first opportunity that presents itself. We
always hope from day to day, that each will be the last of the freeze,
for the nightly arrival of the boat is the only excitement we have
here, and the mail it brings, all the news that we receive. We are enjoying very pretty bright weather. The ground is still covered with
snow but the sun is warm, and the air feels so balmy that I was astonished to find the thermometer was only 20 degrees above zero.
We have had it down to 4 degrees.

I went with Jim skating on Friday. The ice was very smooth and
there were a good many ladies on the ice. I'm afraid that I did [not]
make much progress. I enjoy it and did not feel inclined to come
home, but I think I'll require several lessons before I become a
skater. Yesterday Jim took me [on] a nice long sleigh-ride. We found
the country very monotonous, however, nothing but a rolling surface with snow and an occasional pine tree or scrub-oak protruding
through. Before us all the way we had a full view of Mount Hood,
apparently to the base. We all take advantage of bright weather for it
seldom visits us. Jim is still in command of the post, for the river is
frozen again and prevents the Colonel from returning from Fort
Vancouver. I am employed in keeping house and sewing, generally
with intermissions of walks and rides for exercise, but our world like
the Romans of old, is just around us and all that we can see. I am
trying to learn to play the guitar; I have been at it for a week and I
think I make tolerable progress, though I fancy a criticizing audience
would say as Jim does, that the notes are struck so far apart he for-
gets the last before another sounds. However I expect to be able to
do better with a little more practice, and prove myself quite a prima
donna in the evening, rivalling the all absorbing game of "bezique"
which is quite the fashion.[12]

Another fashion which rules here, that I do *not* like, viz., lunch
parties as they are called. They predominate throughout the country, and as much expense and trouble is occasioned in getting up the

lunch table as would furnish a dinner party. *Only* ladies, sometimes forty & fifty in number are invited, to bring their work. No gentlemen are admitted then, and the picture of so many forlorn damsels sitting around, working with fingers and tongues so busily, savors too much of old time country tea-drinkings . . . .

I have nothing very interesting to write about, except that I know anything concerning us will interest you; we live along evenly with nothing especial to break the monotony of our peace or daily life, and having seen one day you have seen all and we are so isolated that I have no news of any other place to communicate. I have learned a little on the art of cooking and have made some plum puddings *nearly* as good as those we had at home, not quite though. I have not been able to find "Miss Leslie's" cookbook yet, but the stationer here in town has sent to San Francisco for one for me. Then I shall be all right, though the market does not produce anything but meat and potatoes during this wintery weather so my abilities are not severely taxed. I am going to make some oyster soup for dinner and it is time to do it so I will leave you for a few minutes . . . .

There is a project on foot to start a line of steam-wagons across the plains very soon, that will render the journey of only six days duration which now takes a stage between thirty & forty days. The capital in hand amounts to six millions, so I hope it will be carried out; then we can run back and forth to spend the day. Jim wants me to go take a walk with him so I will close with much love and a kiss to all from   *Junie*

FORT DALLES, OREGON,
February 26th, 1866.

Dear Papa   Just as our coach and mules drove up to the door to take me to market this morning, I received *five* letters from Walla Walla, among which were two from you. You may imagine the equipage was made to wait while their contents was devoured. The dates were Nov. 30 & Dec. 15 . . . . If I had received my letters in regular order I should have worried, and to no purpose, over the troubles and vexations which were harassing you all at home; I should have probably had a homesick cry over the indisposition of Mama, Eddie and Kitty & done you no good and only spoiled the cheerfulness with which I always try to greet my husband. But as they all came together the assurance that you were all well and quietly housed at Aunt Jane's came before the first written letters.

It is real funny in reading all your letters at once to see the constant digs you always give poor Washington. You think if you were out here you could find something of interest to write etc. But you may be thankful that you live in Washington, and ought to say with all your heart, "The lines have fallen unto me in pleasant places." Be thankful that you are not destined to live in this land, this land of cold, monstrous deeds of wicked men, whose God is Gold, and who has buried deep, deeper than its deepest caverns, all the milk of human kindness and Christian virtues. Not a paper is printed here that does not have a ghastly column of horrible murders and atrocious highway robberies. No one can trust himself without a shudder of fear to walk a mile or two after dark. At home you hear of the salient points which are gilded by this western sun. You do not see the great black shadows cast by these very points. You do not hear of the thousands which the humid air and damp earth send down to a consumptive's grave. Oh! no, such knowledge is carefully withheld, not even the papers here are allowed to publish a mortality list. And why? Because the ruling spirit of the country is the love of gain, because in their eager thirst after riches they would fain deceive themselves that these things are only troubled dreams and must be quickly brushed from the mind. Mine after mine is being discovered, gems and jewels being brought to light, and these poor wretches of mortality bereft of every idea but gold, go from place to place, and clutch all within their reach. A few are fortunate and realize great wealth which is noised abroad; more, far more, lose their little earthly all, and overcome by sickness, despair, sink down into the grave unhonored and unknown. Could the cold earth tell her secrets, many a sad history would be carried to the waiting family at home of the one, long watched for but who never comes. With the great throbbing heart of Nature pulsating audibly in its rushing torrents and bubbling waterfalls, its upward pointing mountain fingers, its carpet of mosses and many colored flowers—with all this grand

and wild to lift the human heart from Nature up to Nature's God, there is more wickedness and corruption than in the crowded thoroughfares of our eastern cities. The very beauties and wealth which is scattered with a lavish hand over the land, brings out all cupidity, avarice, and wickedness in human nature; and again I say be *thankful* that you live in Washington . . . .

Tuesday. It rained yesterday so I could not ride, and today the roads as usual, are deep, deep in a pasty, sticky, slough of despond. But I don't stay in the house much for mud or bad weather, for then I'd *never* get out. Last night Dr. Steele's little daughter, Fannie, brought me a beautiful hyacinth in bloom, planted in a glass of water . . . . Believe in the sincere love of your daughter, *Julie S.G.*

TUESDAY, FEBRUARY 27, 1866.

Papa, I have tried very hard to make a picture of our home, but am forced to give it up. I *never could* build houses, and this atrocious daub, is the *very best* I can accomplish. It is truthful however and will give you an idea of our residence. The beauty of perspective and coloring you must admit. You may be puzzled to find the vanishing point of my lines, but I can assure you it is *somewhere* though how many miles distant I can't say. Then the gorgeousness of the sky will rival that of far-famed Italy. The color of the mansion is truthful though rather peculiar. The only mistake is the tiles of the rooves are cut in hexagons, and I was compelled to make diamonds instead . . . .

Gen'l [Frederick] Steele visits our post tomorrow, on an inspection tour. He has just arrived out, to take command of this division.[13] Jim sends a great deal of love to you all. Don't give Kitty any more arrowroot, give her a slice of pork fat to suck at instead.

FORT DALLES, OREGON,
March 2nd, 1866.

Dear Annie . . . . Jim had to go to Vancouver day before yesterday, and returned last night, bringing me two pairs of beautiful fat ducks which were thankfully received in this town of beef and potatoes (and nothing else yet); we will have fresh fish soon. Gen'l Steele and staff were expected last night, but he has concluded not to visit this post, 'till he has been down the river. We are having a lovely bright day, but the mud is terrible, it exceeds anything I ever saw. The streets in town are running pools from curb to curb and gullies a foot deep are in some places washed down the middle of the streets for a square or two. When you attempt to walk, it is doubtful whether your foot can be persuaded to come out of the deep stickey holes it makes, and when it does you must look to see if your shoe has been left behind.

I am so glad to have my husband back again, I feel like dancing; I felt forlorn without him. Tell Mama when we come home I can cook her all sorts of nice things; I am becoming quite an adept.

Next day, March 3rd . . . . I had to go to market yesterday in a mixed up storm of rain, snow & hail, and had a real funny time. It did me good too, for my cold is almost well. The doctor (Steele) here says I must not stay in the house for colds. They get well in half the time out of doors if you are properly wrapped up. My pony is at the door, I think I will try him. Boo hoo! He's been taken back to the stable as somewhat unsafe. He's developing a naughty character.

(Saturday). Well I'll make one more attempt. I'm so tired that I can't do anything else. Mrs. Steele and I have been tramping over the hills through the deep snow all morning, then I came home and made a custard for dessert, a batch of ginger cakes, and a jelly cake for tomorrow's tea, and I feel sort of finished up for today, especially as I did my Saturday's cleaning before going out . . . .

Now I'll give you a geography lesson. The Humboldt river rises in *mid-land*, flows a distance of about four hundred miles, and *sinks without* warning *into the earth again*. It has no outlet. Its source is pure, limpid and fresh, filled with trout and other fish; while its waters change so much in flowing that near its point of disappearance they are dank and poisonous, killing man or beast who drinks. It has a strong current. I don't think your school books tell you that. Well it's dinner time, I must stop again.

Dinner is over, one cosy little evening chat around our centre table has followed suit, I have been to bed, slept like a log (as I always do), wakened up, bright as a lark, and merry as a cricket, and now it is Sunday morning. A rainy, snowy morning; three inches of snow on top of three feet of pasty black molasses mud. Church today is out of the question, the next best good act is writing home. How I wish I could set my dinner table today for *you all*. It would be the last drop in my cup of perfect happiness. I have a great deal to be thankful for; a darling good husband, and such continued good health as we both enjoy; and so many loved ones at home who will welcome us with outstretched arms when Providence ordains our meeting . . . .

I think I've received all the Walla Walla letters that were written to me. All your repeated news is piper's. Thank you for your commiseration. I'm glad I don't need it. I was not as much sea-sick as others, and it's a very harmless kind of sickness. The only thing is you are liable to lose all you eat at any time and place, so you must be active and get to your room or the side of the vessel quickly. You are well enough between times. I don't mind travelling either. The love of adventure is strong enough in me to make me thoroughly enjoy all I've gone through. Tell Mama not to worry about me; I'm very well, and likely to continue so; the only recommendation of the Dalles is healthfulness. High up among the mountains we have pure air and a wide stretch of country to roam over and plenty of exercise. No news is good news; when letters are delayed you may be sure it is the fault of the mail, for I promise if there is any occasion for worriment, you shall hear in a very few hours by *telegraph* . . . .

I think the more you go out the better for you physically and mentally, for the mind needs relaxation as well as the body. Never mind inclement weather or mud. You will take colds at first. Don't stay in for them, wrap up and paddle out. Put on *men's boots* when the mud is above your knees and *still go out*. That is what we do, and I am getting fat and rosy . . . . I have written you a long letter which I hope you will duly appreciate. When I read them over they sound funny for they are such a mixed up jumble of ideas just as they come into my head. But when I write it almost seems as if I was among you talking. I see you all so plainly . . . . write whenever you can to your loving sister, *Julie*

FORT DALLES, OREGON,
March 4th, 1866.

[Dear Papa,]   Last night I received your and Annie's letters dated Jan. 20, and am very sorry to hear that the delay of mine has caused you so much uneasiness. I hope before this you have received a dozen or so. I hear every steamer from my new mother and sisters, so we always have anticipations of letters from someone when we open the mail bag. Every evening after dinner our little family (Jim and self) assemble around the little red-covered centre table with the lamp, in the middle my basket and work, and Jim's newspapers. I sew and he reads me the news till about eight o'clock when the mail bag comes up from the boat; we assort the mail and have many a laugh over ridiculous superscriptions on some of the country letters. We put back the mail that does not belong to the Dalles, and read over our letters and papers. Then the Colonel and Mr. Day come in to have a little talk and a game of euchre or bezique and then between nine and ten we go to bed. Every day is the same, but we are happy and contented.

I only wish we were near enough for you to come and see my little home. I've got two madeira vines planted in pots each side of my bay window (inside) and I hope to have them grow up and festoon the top. I have a beautiful little round table made by one of the soldiers who was formerly a piano case maker, and though only pine wood it is carved and colored and varnished beautifully. That stands in my window with my full blown hyacinth and a few books on it and makes my little room quite stylish. I have received a very cordial invitation from Mrs. Babbitt to visit her at Vancouver, & I think if Jim has to go down there again for a day or two I will accompany him. There seems to be a sort of fraternal feeling between officers' families, and they never regard any of their number as strangers out here. They feel as if they had a mutual claim to sociability . . . .

Jim is kept quite busy, and has no time to do much private writing. Poor fellow, he never gets any letters. I think it's a shame, nearly every letter from his mother and sisters, is to me; of course he reads them but I know I should like to have some letters *individually mine*, if I were in his place . . . . Give my love to Uncle William and Aunt Jane. Tell her not to let Mama worry about me; If she could get a sight of me, I know she would see how useless it is. The little shadow of separation, is our only one, and I have faith enough to believe that will last no longer than is good for us. And then you forget all my faults and disagreeabilities when I'm away .... I have written more letters in the last few months than I have before in the same number of years 'till I have not an idea left, they have all been sent East. I believe I wrote so much to Annie that I have very little left to say without repeating something. We are well and happy "and hope this will find you the same.".... Affectionately   *Julie S. Gilliss*

Tell Annie, Oregon is a *state*; the postmaster indignantly runs a dash through the "Ter." on her letters.

TRANSITIONS
Adjusting to Country Life
MARCH–JULY 1866

FORT DALLES, OREGON,
March 9th, 1866.

Dear Annie   I have just received your letter of Jan 31, and hasten to answer it because you have not yet had mine with the Dalles address. I cannot understand why letters which I wrote before Christmas have not reached you yet. There is an enormous budget somewhere on the road which I wish would reach their destination speedily for I know Mama and Papa will feel worried. I am sorry you have had such a severe winter; we have not to my mind. I see in the papers where the thermometer stood at an incredibly low figure but it has not felt intensely cold here. We had plenty of snow, and plenty of fun sleighing and running about in it. But it is now disappearing like water ice in August and green grass and shrubs are peeping out, for company for the myriads and myriads of birds.

I had a pleasant ride today and a walk afterwards, and a tramp over the hills yesterday. In fact, not a day passes that I do not spend several hours outdoors with Jim whenever he can be spared from his office, and when he cannot, I have Mrs. Steele and Fannie. Today I got home too late to make my pudding for dinner, so we went dessertless. The pure air of our hills keeps one fresh and well, blows away colds and all other ills. I had another loving letter from young

Mrs. Kip tonight. Jim says it's fortunate she's married or she might want to marry me. She's a very lovely girl . . . .

I think I am progressing finely with my guitar music. I can play several right pretty airs. What do you think I've been doing today? Making hogs-head cheese. I hope it will be nice. It's not a bit of trouble after you get a nice pig's head. You know we live in the country so we must live country fashion. This is splendid, I think, to have all the advantages of country and of city too, which latter is not much more than half a mile distant . . . . I've got another madeira vine growing beautifully but alas! my hyacinth is fading. No matter, I can put away the bulb, and it will grow again . . . .

I wish I could send you some of my minerals in a letter. I have some beauties picked up loose anywhere and everywhere. One which is several *inches* in size is either opal or white onyx and perfectly lovely. I have agates, crystals, quartz, arrowhead flint etc. etc. and a piece of quartz full of gold. I have a mania for collecting them and Jim has procured for me all the prettiest pieces I have. I saw my pony exercising today. He is being thoroughly broken and will make a splendid little horse. He leaps beautifully. I wish I could box him up and send to Eddie, only he would have to keep him in the coal bin. With a heart full of love to you all we both talk of so often, your sister   *Julie* . . . .

FORT DALLES, OREGON,
March 11th, 1866.

My dearest Parents   I have just returned from church, and hasten to write my home letter. We are in the full enjoyment of the most lovely weather—that is, overhead, bright and clear and mild, but underfoot perfectly dreadful. All the accumulated snows of the past winter are running away in streams and rivulets and making this sandy soil worse mud than I ever imagined. It washes out in great chasms from one to six and eight feet deep, and where it remains stationary, the mud is like quicksand and man and beast get mired at a moment's warning, and yet we are considered to have magnificent roads out here.

I had a ride day before yesterday across the creek to see the tower of Drachenfels.[1] It is a huge basaltic pile on the brow of a high hill which bears a striking resemblance to a gigantic castellated ruin. The round towers, the square masonry between the moss-grown roofless top, and its situation on the brink of the bold eminence all favor the delusion. Today I had a walk with Jim along the border of Mill Creek, a turbulent little stream that dashes down from the mountains beyond with many a fall and cascade, over the masses of rock that have in vain upheaved their unwieldy forms to stop its progress. The moss and grass looks fresh and green, and I gathered the first flowers, tiny little white clusters, exactly like, in form and fragrance the sweet alyssum of our greenhouses, only much smaller. It is not a weed, for they never are fragrant. I enjoyed it very much and came home with my cheeks the color of my scarf.

The mail bag has come but nothing in it for me. You ought not to complain of the delay in getting your letters; out here they take from sixteen days up to a month to come from San Francisco, a trip that the steamer makes in three or four days. How is darling little baby Kitty? I am so glad you are going to send me her picture and will watch impatiently for it. Poor little darling! She has a hard struggle with all "the ills that (baby) flesh is heir to," but you remember Eddie was the same and I think most all babies are. I sincerely hope as the Spring opens and the severe weather disappears, that Baby and Mama will both recuperate . . . . I am well and hearty, happy and contented. I have nothing to trouble me except the knowledge that you are fretting about me at home. I know you miss me as I do you, but it may not be long before we can come home again and then you will remember what you now seem to forget, what a troublesome daughter I am.

Papa, Jim received your letter which he was very glad to get, he says he will answer it as soon as he gets time. He is very busy, having a great many duties of his own to perform and in addition, all those incumbent on the commanding officer, as the Colonel is down at Vancouver. He is expected home in a week or so, and then we may possibly go down for a short time. The President of the Navigation Company, who is a son-in-law of Colonel Babbitt, very kindly gave me a free pass up and down the river.[2] I suppose Annie will graduate when school closes. She has worked hard and faithfully .... With much love from us both to you all, I remain as ever your attached daughter   *Julie S. Gilliss*

FORT DALLES, OREGON,
March 18th, 1866.

My dear Parents   I have answered all your letters and have received no others for nearly two weeks, but I feel confident they are on the road somewhere if they could only be coaxed along a little faster. I hope you have got the numerous epistles that I have indited .... I have had many a ramble this lovely spring weather. The snow has all disappeared, and during the last week we have had really perfect weather. Bright clear sunshine, and air as warm as June, have brought out the first venturesome flowers, and cast a pale green mantle over the brown hills. The birds seem nearly wild and the rocks reverberate with their throat-splitting chorus. The deserts of sand have dried and drifted, and thrown up to the surface their stony treasures. I have gathered a pound or two of agates, amber, cornelian, flint and arrowheads, varying in size from a pea to a walnut. Some are exquisitely beautiful, and the glitter of the brilliant colors as they lay in thousands on the shifting sand, is very attractive. I often wish I knew the art of making mosaics, for I have such beautiful and boundless materials for the task. If I have an opportunity I will send you home some Oregon *pebbles*. I have become a regular country girl, and can jump fences as well as any of them.

The soldiers have begun their baseball and their shouts break pleasantly on the still air as their bright colored shirts dart in and out among the green pines of the parade ground which affords them a nice level place to play on. At Vancouver where there are some twenty families (being the headquarters) they have a billiard room, a croquet ground, and amusement of all kinds, and I don't think Dalles ought to be left so much in the lurch. We could easily make a croquet ground here, but unfortunately we have not enough of us to play, and Colonel Coppinger is still at Vancouver, managing by hook or crook to extend his visit ad-libitum, which I think hardly fair, for it leaves Jim so much to attend to, he has hardly time to eat and sleep. He goes to the office before breakfast, and works till breakfast time, and then till five o'clock when he comes home to dinner and brings home any work that he can do in the evening. I protest, but it does no good as the work is obliged to be done.

We expected the Colonel home yesterday, and then we had intended going down on Tuesday for a day or two, but instead of that, we found that though his leave has expired, he had managed to get on a court martial there which does not meet 'till the 26th, and I suppose he will spin it out several weeks longer. Jim never complains a single word, but I can see that he is worked like a pack horse. I wish you could all come out in a letter, to spend this bright sunny weather with me, and let Baby and Eddie roll in the sand and you and Annie keep us company in our roomy house. Tell Annie I would set her to work making ginger cake for I never can get them as nice as hers. Tell Eddie I wouldn't let him ride the mules for they will kick, and can't be taught better manners. He and Kitty puss could play splendidly with Fannie Steele, on the musicians' stand in the middle of the parade ground.

I have a whole row of tin cans full of wild flowers on my window sills, flower pots are a luxury not indulged in, in this country. I have only seen *one*. They look quite pretty covered over the top with moss, which grows in perfection on the rocks. I cannot help acknowledging that the moss and flowers make quite a difference in the looks of the country, but the great dearth of trees makes a dreary, barren looking landscape at a little distance. Two pine trees standing together about the height of the tree in front of our home on "H" street [in Washington, D.C.] we call the Twins, and make them the guiding point from all the walks we take as they stand alone like sentinels just beyond our house. The generality of the trees being a few feet taller than I am, we have not much shade, so we are going to get the largest straw hats we can find to keep off the sun. Mrs. Steele suggests that we adopt the Bloomer costume as being more convenient for climbing the rocks, but I have not yet made up my mind that it would be sufficiently becoming to my style of beauty. It's very fortunate that I have no important sewing to do, for I don't stay in the house when I can help it.

The prisoner soldiers cleaned up our garden yesterday, and brought to view a bunch of hollyhocks which are about six inches out of the ground, which added to a white running rose, a quantity of clematis vines, a bush of spirea for a garden, which I hope to have. We are going to have a vegetable garden here, and we have an ice house nicely packed, so I expect we will flourish this summer . . . . It is much prettier now that we have been dug out of the snow, and I should like it if I could have more of Jim's company . . . . The mail comes in at eight o'clock to be sorted and then tattoo at nine; after which he settles down to writing which often keeps him until midnight. I am trying to arrange a guest-room, for as Captain C. (whose brevet rank is Colonel so I have miscalled him so far) has given me all the house except his own two rooms, so I must be ready to entertain anyone who comes to the post.

We are both well and unite in love to you all, and kisses to Eddie and Baby. Your loving daughter   *Julie*

FORT DALLES, OREGON.
March 24th, 1866.

Dear Papa and Mama   It is almost three weeks since I have had a letter from home; I cannot imagine the reason for the delay as I feel confident you have written. Dr. Steele tries to tease me by saying "it is always the way with people out here, their friends at home write to them for a few weeks and then stop." I don't believe any such nonsense. You would know how disappointed I should be if you failed to write by every steamer, even if it was only a line to say all were well . . . .

I have been busy all day fixing up my spare room; it looks very nice with its pretty green carpet and green shades in the windows; all the woodwork is oak. It has no bedstead in it yet, but I guess I'll have it put up before you get out here to occupy it. My own room is prettier still. I have a beautiful brussels carpet, a rich shaded red ground with bouquets of natural colored flowers in white medallions. My windows are draped with hanging curtains, bunches of rosebuds on a pearl tinted ground; my dressing table has white hangings with a rose colored quilting around the top and a gilt framed mirror. The bedstead which is a fixture here at this post, is unfortunately painted *pink*, and wash stand and towel rack mahogany; bureau walnut.

After I had finished my work this morning I took a walk after flowers to deck my parlor for Sunday. I found an uncountable number of these yellow bells, called here wild tulips. They have a delicate perfume and are very pretty, and together with my little wild alyssum and a few yellow meadow stars, and little pink flowers that I can find "no name" for, and bunches of green fern, I succeeded in making three vases full . . . . We have had a semi showery day, but I noticed rifts in the clouds at sunset. When it dries off thoroughly we are going to attempt a croquet ground, if we can get the rules from Vancouver. Won't that be a dissipation for Dalles . . . .

Sunday Morning, March 25th. The rain clouds of yesterday have passed with the night, and given birth to the loveliest of Spring mornings. Very fair and beautiful are the green hills and moss-covered boulders, the "fir tree and the pine tree," in their most vivid garments with the glad sunshine breaking into a hundred arrows of gold through their branches, the little cottages nestling at the base of the huge rocks, and overhead, the bright blue canopy of Heaven with a few pure fleecy clouds floating in mid-air. With a grand swelling cadence like the lingering notes of a rich refrain I hear in heart & mind continually—"Oh! that men would therefore praise the Lord for all His goodness, and declare the wonders that He doeth for the children of men." It is the keynote to the grand choral symphony of the birds and breezes, it is the text to the "sermon" that the morning teaches not only in stones, but in the green grass and springing flowers, the merry tinkling music of the stream and the soft murmur of the zephyrs through the pine tops. A little bird outside my window whistles back to me as I chirp to him and with his head on one side and his black eyes sparkling seems to say no one could harm him amid such beauty. Tell Eddie we have a bird's nest on the top of our front door, and yesterday the bird made a mistake and flew in our vestibule, but he went out pretty quick when I went there to look at him. I have a box full of wild tulips outside my window.

Mama, I am braiding a white marseilles dress and cloak for Baby Kitty so don't get her one. Let me know when it arrives safely. I shall send it as soon as finished. I wanted to make a merino suit but after two months' fruitless search after materials I relinquished the idea. This town only produces Miners' outfits, Tobacco Pipes, Whiskey of course, Beef and Potatoes. I went everywhere to find a common penny stick of cotton cord; half the stores did not know what it was. I send you another sketch of our house, it is very poor but will give you a better idea of general appearance . . . .

I wish you could see our blankets. Jim bought me two pairs in San Francisco which are the prettiest I ever saw. They are so thick they look as if made of eiderdown or little wooly lambs or curly puppy dogs. I never saw any so perfect before. Captain McKibbon of Phila. came down from Colville last week and brought a small lump of pure gold just as it was found which he said he had destined for the first Army lady he saw which fortunately happened to be me.[3] So I am in possession. I hear dishes clattering which reminds me it is nearly dinner time and I must go watch a Tapioca pudding which I have in the oven. *I have found Miss Leslie's cookbook.* At least the bookseller sent to San Francisco and got it for me. Love and a kiss from both to you all, your loving daughter   *Julie* . . . .

FORT DALLES, OREGON,
Easter Sunday, April 1st, 1866.

Dear Papa & Mama   After waiting over three weeks almost in a state of despair at the non-appearance of home letters, and when the last lingering ray of hope had been so spun out and attenuated, that a breath would break it, your welcome letter came. It is postmarked Feb. 20, read March 28, and your last previous to that was Jan. 20, overland, so you missed writing by one steamer (of Feb. 12) or else a letter is lost. I think my letters take their time on the road also, for you had just received my letter from Cascades written about the 1st Jan. Do you notice the numbers to see if they come in regular succession?

Today is Easter Sunday. Dull, dark and gloomy, fitter for the sad emblem of Good Friday than the glorious resurrection morn. Yesterday was bright and clear, but today has a raw damp air and leaden sky. I hope you are through the severity of our eastern season and Mama and Baby can begin to go out with the crocuses and young grass . . . .

Jim is very thankful for scraps of political news and we would be for any paper that you think worth sending. Our literary world out here is limited and badly supplied with re-hashes culled from old papers, mostly with only *one* point, bitter, raucous condemnation of the President, served up without even the polish of refined language to hide the venom of their sting. I rarely read the paper we have; if there is anything interesting Jim reads it to me but there is so much I do not care to see, that I feel no inclination for closer perusal.

We have had several rainy days lately and the mud renewed so I have been a prisoner except when I ride to market and I do long for a real dry sunny walk again. I have made one discovery, that is that I like the country better than city, though I think somewhere in New York state would suit me decidedly better than here. One thing I can't learn to like, It makes me fidgety—the incessant singing of the frogs. Day and night those energetic songsters of our neighboring ponds make the air vocal with their efforts, till it has become a perfect dinging in my ears. Jim says it is cheerful, I think it dolorous. As we are well and still jogging on "the even tenor of our way," I have no interesting news to offer. Your loving daughter   *Julie*

FORT DALLES, OREGON,
April 22nd, 1866.

[*Sister Annie*]   You graceless Nan, how much longer are you going to make me wait for a letter from you? I suppose you are busy preparing for examination and think that is sufficient excuse. Perhaps it is, and I will write on the strength of the supposition . . . .

Our boxes which were shipped around the "Horn," have come safely to hand, and their contents uninjured, with the exception of a little mould and mildew which is fast disappearing on exposure to air. Tell Papa "Martha" arrived safely, *one week after* the letter which announced her .... Tell Eddie that we have a tiny little puppy, either a pointer or setter I forgot which, also a Maltese cat and two kittens. Mr. Day has a puppy like ours, and is going to have a tame raccoon, so we have no lack of pets.

My floral department has received reinforcements in the shape of two lovely rose bushes (a tea rose, and a full pink rose) and two small rose geraniums, all presents from Miss Blackler. The sweet scented syringa grows wild all along the banks of the creek. I have wished very much to paint a group of wild flowers, but I left my Chinese White at home and cannot do it without, and cannot get any out here. I have finished Baby's dress and will send it off this week. Tell Mama the button holes are "unique," that is the best I can say for them, but after working one, I was compelled to work all, that they might possess the merit of uniformity and anyhow, for I am convinced no one else could have worked any to match them. I have been trying to arrange some seaweed on paper, but the "modus operandi" is all that I have as yet mastered. When I succeed in *artistically* preparing it I will send you a specimen. I have some that look like very delicate painting: truth compels me to say mine is not of the number ....

The town here is swarming with Indians, of every "sort, kind, class and description." They have been permitted to leave the "Reservation" for the purpose of selling salmon & game, but "niver a bit" of either have they brought in yet, except one or two lovely pairs of blue grouse. They are lazy and dirty and lay around the street all day, only moving enough to follow the sunshine like a dog would do. I have missed church so much since I've been out here, but especially during Lent. The Congregational church which I generally attend is unfamiliar. It is almost the same as Presbyterian but as I was only in that church once, it seems strange. The minister always extemporizes and though he is a well read man and has some fine ideas, he has no command of language whatever and his frantic efforts to find a missing word or phrase to express his ideas at all, sometimes border on the ludicrous, and you forget what he has said in waiting for what is to come.   *Julie*

FORT DALLES, OREGON,
April 26th, 1866.

My darling Mama   At last Mr. Nicholson has arrived bringing the package of pretty things from home loved ones. Most thankful am I for your eagerly waited for letter. I have not felt slighted Mama, for I knew you would write to me when you could but I wished so very much to hear from you. Baby's picture is lovely, just as cunning as can be . . . . For your kind thoughtful care and beautiful presents, I so not know how to thank you, so I will not try. You will surely guess how very full my heart is. Tell Annie I highly prize her handiwork; I think it lovely and Brother Jim says she deserves a great deal of credit for the neatness and beauty of the work. The muslin dress is just what I intended to get this summer on account of its utility. The puffed waist and all the other pretty things I shall look at occasionally to see how nice they are. Kiss Eddie for his butterfly, the salt air turned it bronze but I think I can brighten it up again with whiting.

Mama please do not think of getting me an opera cloak or indeed anything. I have all I want and can't begin to wear what I have because it is not suitable to the country. I have not even peeped at my nice dresses since we left San Francisco. We live in the country amid sand heaps and pine trees . . . . Our house is a decaying remnant of grandeur incongruously set down in the wild woods and with its nine gables lording it over the log cabin and frame huts in Robinson Crusoe-like fashion with neither furniture nor surroundings suitable to it nearer than San Francisco. The "city" is a very short distance but its elite is composed of Jew tradesmen & bartenders, and I *never* go into it except to market. Even the "haut ton" of fashion has a very low tone. I sometimes regret that my trunk is not filled with calicoes and delaines; then I should not look regretfully at my pretty things. However they will be fresh when I get home. So you see I really would not know what to do with an opera cloak, and if you will send me something let it be a linsey woolsey dress, a gingham sunbonnet & a strong green cotton umbrella.[4] Mama dear, I am *perfectly well* and happy and nothing is wanting but the consciousness that you are also . . . . I think sunshine makes one feel better in spite of oneself. Not a window in our house possesses shutters, and the sun will shine in everywhere, and I think does a great deal towards keeping us well. I read an article the other day on the subject, which endorsed the idea and said the revivifying influence of sunlight was wonderful, even restoring to health and vigor paralytics who were exposed to its rays without clothing. Tell Papa I think his Capitol [photo set] is a great success, and we heartily thank him for it. Jim is having a set of frames made for the whole set so you must think of us surrounded by glimpses of Washington. Frank Dodge was up to see us today; he is here at the Dalles connected with the Navigation Company.[5] Tell Eddie we have a sheep and two little lambs added to our livestock. Jim sends a great deal of love to you all, as also does your loving daughter   *Julie*

FORT DALLES, OREGON,
April 26th, 1866.

Dear Annie   I must write and thank you for your successful efforts in my behalf. You have done wonderfully well. One thing I am very sorry you sent me; your collar & cuffs. It seems like robbing yourself for I have a dozen times as much as you. I expect too that they fitted you but they lack an inch on me. They are a new style that I never saw before. I expect the new way of wearing your hair is very pretty if one could make it out; it looks wonderfully like anything you choose it to be in your drawing. You see I am paying back some of your saucy speeches. The fashion will reach here the next century. I astonished the natives when I arrived, I was a new importation, and actually the first wearer of rats & waterfalls. Many ladies here had never seen them before. My poor little velvet coat was also a subject of comment the first time I went to church . . . .

You think I made a mistake in regard to my pony's size; not a bit of it. I have never been on his back; firstly because I'm afraid my toes will scrape the ground, secondly, because he's too lively & Jim's afraid he'll break my neck, which he is not quite tired of yet. In spite of your prohibition the Congregational church is the only one I attend, I do not like the Catholic & the Methodist. Oh! Oh! I went in it once and moved about all the time, for fear if I were long in one position I should stick fast to the dirt. Floors, ceilings, walls, pews, everywhere perfectly filthy. I breathed freely when I got out in two feet of snow and I have never ventured in since. The church I attend is a neat, nice little building, and the sect differing from the Presbyterian only in the fact that it is governed by the whole congregation instead of a presbytery selected by them . . . .

I thank you very much for your pudding receipt & would gladly try [it] if I could get the materials. Lemons can't be had here for love or money, the storekeepers say they are never brought up so far. As for gelatine, I already had made a tour of the town in quest of it, but did not find anybody who *knew what it was*. I succeeded in getting some isinglass.[6] . . . Fannie Gilliss sent me a beautifully made spool wagon filled with cottons & needles of all numbers. A very nice present isn't it? With Mama's hooked eyes, card & working cotton, I am quite set up. Tell Mama I've been wearing canton flannels this winter so have not thought about my cotton undies. I will go to work on them soon. Jim is reading some Washington papers which arrived tonight from Papa and are thankfully received. He sends love. Kiss everybody for me & believe me as ever, your loving sister   *Julie*

FORT DALLES, OREGON,
May 1st, 1866.

Dear Papa   Although it is a bright clear sunny May-day, our peculiar wind is blowing in such a hurricane-like manner, that one feels small temptation to go in search of the myriads of flowers, that have been gathering their forces in anticipation of this, their special season. Returning from market this morning the unruly zephyrs seized my basket, whirled it out of the wagon, over our heads, rolled it backwards down the road, then finally turned a somersault & alighted on its head (i.e. handle) in a pond by the wayside. Luckily its contents which were few, preferred remaining on the floor of the vehicle like respectably behaved articles instead of riding through the air, Mother Goose fashion. You may be sure after I got in the house I was well content to sit down and hem kitchen towels.

Not that I stay in much for windy weather, I have become a firmer advocate for fresh air even than you, and I never allow myself to remain in the house twenty-four hours at a time & whenever I leave a room, I open doors & windows. We have open fireplaces & wood fires in every room and *never* shut any doors. I think our good health may be attributed much to it & I have not had a cold in my head for so long that I am afraid my handkerchiefs will fall to pieces in very disgust at never being used. I have a fancy, from the nature of this disease, that plenty of open air is a preventative of cholera, & I intend to act accordingly.

We were very much pleased with your large picture of the Capitol. It is excellent. I am so fortunate as to be surrounded with such accurate glimpses of home . . . . Tell Mama my puffed waist fits very well except that it is a little tight across the shoulders. I think I can easily remedy it. It is quite becoming. Tell Eddie that a little whiting on a piece of rag worked a wonderful change in his little butterfly & made its wings shine resplendently silver . . . .

So Secretary Fox has resigned.[7] When his line of Steamers begins running, you & Mama & the children can take a run out to see us. To use old Mrs. Gillette's simile, I should "jump about like a chicken on a hot gridiron" to think of it.

Apropos of kitchen utensils, I'm sure it will be a great gratification to know how I am assisted in the culinary department. I think I am very fortunate. I have a woman, a Mrs. Kelly. She is Irish but rather above the ordinary class. Her husband was a hospital steward, & after his time [in the Army] expired, kept a drugstore in Dalles.[8] They have a small farm & two or three houses, but her husband has sold out his store & with three thousand dollars, part of which belongs to her, he has gone East, she says to make a fortune, but Dr. Steele the surgeon says he is a grand scamp and he has got hold of her money & she'll never see it again. Her houses here used to rent for thirty dollars a month, but now bring only twelve, for the "city" seems to be falling off. She has a little girl three years old and she did not like living alone, so sent to me one day to know if I wanted a cook, that she would like to come, as she wanted a home more than the wages. She agreed to come at very reasonable terms for this country & I took her. She is as clean and neat as can be, and has a full appreciation of her superiority to servantism, but she understands her work & does it, & seems like a housekeeper more than a lower servant. She does no washing; no house out here knows what a wash-day is. Laundries & laundresses are as thick as blackberries & I have not seen or heard of a single family who have their washing done at home.

To a stranger all this would sound like a very queer topic for a letter but I know it will interest you all to know just how we are living. We have very little society & sometimes feel a little isolated, but it is very pleasant here notwithstanding. I have no objection to go East, however, at the earliest opportunity. I made somewhat of a bull the other day at dinner. Lieut. Toby of the 14 Infty. was dining with us, and he is disgusted with this coast.[9] I said very innocently, that I would be willing to stay out here if I had all my family & friends around me, but on no other condition would I be content always away from home. He said it was an Irishism for in that case I would have no home but this. But I don't know about that either, for as an American I recognise nationality anywhere within its border, yet with the Switzer's love of fatherland, I recognize only that portion around which cluster the memories and haunts of childhood. Tell Annie everybody out here says either & neither, so I can almost imagine myself at St. Mary's Hall . . . .

The wagon is at the door to take me to town so I will close with the warmest love & kisses to Mama, Annie, Eddie, & Pussy, from your loving daughter   *Julie*

Jim is busy at the office or would send his love.

FORT DALLES, OREGON,
May 6th, 1866.

Dear Papa & Mama   The same mail that brought me letters from you & Annie dated March 28th, brought one of eight close pages from Ella McKean & one from Clemmie Kip in San Francisco, so I am very much in debt and thankful for it too. It is needless to say how very glad I am always to receive your letters and how eagerly I look for them. It will require no imagination to strengthen the knowledge. The *Godey's* were welcomed as coming from home, but not as strangers. I thank you very much for them but you need not send them to me, I have them all for we get them here almost as soon as you do. They reach San Francisco the 20th of the *month previous* to *the one* for *which* they are *issued*, and are brought up here in the Steamer . . . . I got the *May* number a *week ago*. The newspapers arrived, we are much obliged, especially Jim. I believe he reads all the advertisements. I expect next thing to see him turn the paper backwards after once reading it to see if anything escaped his notice. We get all your letters regularly. I do not think any are lost except the one you wrote to New York; that was never received. I am afraid that Steam Wagon train has been crushed into nothingism, I have seen nothing more about it. You must all come out in the first steamer run by Captain Fox line. Going to sea is not half as bad after you get used to it. I'd be willing to make the voyage again at a day's notice . . . .

I sincerely hope when this reaches you it will find you all happily settled in our old home. There is no place like it, even if it is ever so tiny. My trouble is too *much* house though, I don't like to see so many unoccupied rooms. We try to fill *three* that communicate on the second floor. The large front room is chamber proper, the small one a dressing room, the back room contains our trunks, a box of wood for the fire and other unused articles. But that still leaves plenty of room for visitors. How glad I am you have seen [Albert] Bierstadt's "Storm"; now I want you to see his "Mt. Hood." It has been severely criticized, but falsely I believe. His pencil has too mighty a power to fall short here where everything else is so fully furnished. By his past success I know he can truthfully & beautifully depict the slender mountain in all the symmetry of its form, in all the changeableness of its moods; whether it is standing boldly defiant and purely white cutting its azure background, or as I often see it, like a dream, only the dim outline of its summit gleaming ethereal & heavenly through the opaline atmosphere surrounding it. It has a majesty of beauty amounting to sublimity which it only shares with St. Helens. Adams is too roly-poly, Jefferson & Rainier rugged and frowning. Hood & St. Helens alone possess the exquisite delicacy, perhaps in the latter, which makes one look upon them with reverence and almost awe, as it they were the outpost of those pearly gates which open on the New Jerusalem. Bierstadt as a man has a delicate sensibility, a refinement of feeling which will make him appreciate the subject and lend a finer point to the brush of the artist.

Tell Eddie I have never mounted my pony yet, and do not expect to. A side saddle of moderate size can't be persuaded to stay on him. He slips through it easily. I know very well, Papa, how high *four hands* is and knew all the time that I was being quizzed, but as everybody had combined with Jim to tell me that was his height I did not dare to offer opposition to such an overwhelming majority. I knew you would know better than to believe it. He is the smallest horse I ever saw & is four or five years old, so will not grow . . . .

It is barely possible that Walla Walla will be our final destination yet. All the troops have been removed from here to Fort Boise. Jim now commands the post, but there is some talk of its abandonment & the reoccupation of Walla Walla. I don't know what will be the termination of it all, but will let you know as soon as we do. We expect to go down to Vancouver for a visit of a few days next week, and we may have a hint from Genl. Steele as to what he intends doing. The bill has finally passed Congress for the establishment of a Mint here which will be a great benefit to the town.[10]   *Junie*

I forgot to say we are both perfectly well, so you need not imagine that we are sick.

FORT DALLES, OREGON,
Sunday after Ascension, May 13th, 1866.

Dear Annie   As I promised in my last letter home that the next should be to you, I now fulfil the same intention. I hope you will not expect this closely ruled sheet to be as closely written for that would be next to impossible with the small share of news and events that fall under our notice.

By the way of a little variety, Jim and I steamed down to the Cascades last Monday morning, for a day's fishing, rising at *three* o'clock for that purpose. It was just light then but the sun rose soon after *four* and the day was as lovely as could be. If I had the pen of a poet, I could tell of the beauties that my feeble power would never attempt, of the mighty river chafing and foaming like the ocean in its imprisonment & between its two narrow shores. Its depth in some places is immeasureable and such is the combined power of its waves and winds that many persons cannot ride upon it without a fit of genuine seasickness, and its turbulence has wrecked two or three steamboats. The hills and mountains that slope down to the water's edge are covered with a soft delicate verdure like emerald velvet, and as the river "like a winding ribbon" in and out, these hills close together as we pass and melt away into that rich purple haze so well depicted by Messrs Bierstadt and Leutze.[11] As the sun rose, Mt. Hood burst upon our view through an opening, glowing golden pink on its bright side while the other was thrown into a pearly shade. The scenery though beautiful is monotonous and often you watch for miles a chain of hills so like in form and color that you scarce can tell the difference of landscape [and] you weary for some little change.

We reached Cascades at half past eight A.M. I seemed to have lived a day already and could scarcely believe it was not afternoon. Cascades is beautiful. A few poor little deserted houses are all the town, but the wild entanglement of flowers, trees, everything green, flowery and beautiful made poor rocky, sandy Dalles suffer by comparison. At the former as well as the latter place, the Columbia gathers the spread forces of its waters and dashes with mighty leaps through a channel almost a hundred feet wide from shore to shore. It roars and grumbles with a deafening sound. The Indians have a legend that at some remote period there was a gigantic natural bridge over the river which was then wide and smooth at the Cascades. But the two mountains who stand like sentinels on either side got into a fierce quarrel, they hurled at each other all the great rocks they could find but they all missed their aim and fell into the water. At length the bridge with its vast masonry, its trees that for centuries had gathered their strength of life upon its span, was madly seized by both sides at once and neither gaining it, fell with a great earthquake into the waters below. The destruction of this bridge calmed in a moment the fury of the antagonists and they have stood peaceful ever since.

The shattered bridge formed the half dozen beautiful little islands that fill the river here and the rocky missiles are now the cause of the succession of rapids and cascades which give name to the place. Here in this perilous position the Indians stand and with a net, dip, dip from morning till night with commendable patience for salmon. Some days they catch hundreds but on others they are rewarded only by two or three. Jim and Johnny Andrews in a little muddy boat went up to a lake for trout, so Mrs. Andrews and I walked down to the Indian village about a mile and a half below her house.[12] We were well repaid. The village which is the blot on the scene, consists of two or three large huts, in which are Indians of every "sort, kind, class & description," cleaning salmon. With a true eye for the picturesque they have pitched their summer camp here on this lovely spot. A narrow level green belt with the river rushing at its feet, the range of Cascade mountains on the opposite shore frowning down and seeming almost to overshadow it. On this belt are the huts, back of it is the Indian Lake. That is all I can say of it but I wish Mr. Bierstadt would paint it. It is a perfect semicircle like this ⌒ , still clear and pure. It has no outlet unless a subterranean one. There is no marsh around it but hard solid earth and myriads of flowers to where they are kissed by the waters. The plane is toward the belt, the arc beyond is bristling with an army of pointed pines beyond which rise again the "everlasting hills."

There are several lakes in this vicinity of considerable size with no outlet, and *no bottom*, though the latter contradicts the former assertion. They are curious for being high up among the mountains and keeping their waters pure and fresh by some agency down at the center of the globe for aught we know. They are full of trout, of which Jim only got fourteen when his bait was exhausted, but they were large enough for three breakfasts. He bought a trout for dinner yesterday which I think was three feet long. Don't imagine we ate it all even though we had Major Myers to dine with us.[13] He is in command of a company of cavalry which arrived here Friday night en route for Boise but will probably remain here a week or so.

On Wednesday Jim and self accompanied by Mr. Day (Jim's clerk) and Mr. [Henry] Catley who was vol. quartermaster here when relieved by Jim, and a basket of luncheon, hooks and rods, rode up the creek some seven or eight miles. We came home in the afternoon with the firm conviction that we only went for a picnic for nobody had caught any fish. Mr. C. dined with us. Thursday we had Colonel Dick O'Beirne and Capt. Weeks from Vancouver to dinner.[14] It seems real pleasant to have a company of soldiers here again, to hear the bugle calls and see the men on the parade ground. Major Myers is very pleasant . . . .

We have had fresh salmon twice as it has just come but I expect we will get a surfeit. The farmers expect to have green peas & strawberries in two or three weeks. Tell Papa there is an article with woodcuts of the "Yosemite" valley in *Harper's Magazine* for May . . . . Tell Mama my cook continues elegant, I only wish she had her; it would save Mama a great deal of trouble. She could keep house without any care for Mrs. Kelly could take care of everything. We have lettuce and radishes out of our own garden now . . . . Yours affectionately,   *Julie*

FORT DALLES, OREGON,
May 19, Saturday Evening.

My dear Parents   The papers sent by you by the last steamer (postmarked April 8th) arrived safely, but to my great disappointment there were no letters. I do not know whether they were lost or not. Jim heard from his mother & Fannie and as they said nothing to contradict the hope that you were all well, I will think that you were too busy to write . . . . We are in the midst of housecleaning, and the whole house is redolent of fresh paint. The walls of the parlors and dining room have been painted pale blue; the ceilings to be white. The floor of the vestibule was first done in blocks of black & blue with a heavy white line between; the front steps were nearly red so Jim said he could not make up his mind whether it was the entrance to a Dutch barber shop or a Lager Beer saloon. It is in process of being remedied. I propose the floor to be in imitation of black & white tiles, but the only objection is the impossibility of keeping them so. The sand blows in solid masses almost, and dumps itself down everywhere.

Whitsunday, May 20th. Last evening after I had written the above the mail came in bringing me letters from Mama & Annie; so my grumbling is at an end . . . . All letters that are not marked (per steamer) go by the overland route, so you see that is the way most all of mine have gone . . . .

We have had two or three days of showers, quite a rarity, for since the snow melted we have had continued sunshine. Our little garden is springing up. One rose bush has two flowers full blown. A white rose that has run up all over the bay window has hundreds of buds, and everything else is ready to burst. I have made some tatting which I intended sending home to show my ability but it really looks so *dirty* I'm ashamed to. It *did not come off my hands*, the cotton was soiled on the spool . . . .

We are both very well. Mrs. Kelly is still with me, as good as ever . . . . Tell Eddie all our lambs are *eaten* all except one, and he is too great a pet to be killed. He kisses me right in the mouth sometimes. With love to you all from us both, I am your loving daughter   *Julie*

I had a present from Major Myers of a large jelly cake, iced all over with red roses & green leaves and a purple grape with gold leaves, quite a crumb of civilization, but it was better made than even civilized cakes generally are.

WHITSUNDAY, MAY 20TH, 1866.

My dear Annie   I cannot resist the temptation of writing to congratulate you on your accession to my old purple dress, with the hope that you may fill it as gracefully as I did. Also allow me to state that I was neither cross eyed nor in love when I made it. I expect you stretched it out of shape when you ripped it up. I expect your ash-of-rose silk must look quite pretty & stylish. Mama speaks of the extravagance of prevailing fashions; if they combine every hue & color, mixed with tinsel, they are also raging out here. The bonnets cap the climax. I have not seen *one* that I would wear, so I made my own which I think the neatest in the place. It is the Pamela shape; the front to the first wire is fine white straw, the crown a soft one of white silk with illusion[15] puffed over it; a folded white ribbon covers the juncture of the two, & a little to the left side on top is a pretty bunch of flowers. Loops of narrow white ribbon fall over the tiny cape, white strings & inside flowers. The "style" here is a green or yellow crepe, puffed over the Empire frame, pink strings, purple flowers across the cape, a large bunch of red roses fasten[ing] a yard or two of black & white lace veil on the left side, yellow & blue flowers with gilt leaves inside, and a large cameo, to balance the veil. Now my taste may have degenerated, but I can't appreciate them. Jim thinks my bonnet requires a red bow on one side & a blue one on the other to redeem it from oldfashioned plainness. Fannie & Rose have both informed me of the increase in Harry Whiting's family. Sallie spent the evening at her mother's, ate a *whole lemon pie*, went home and ate some fried oysters, went to bed and her son was born before morning. Pretty well for her . . . . Your aff. sister,   *Julie*

FORT DALLES,
Trinity Sunday, May 27th.

Dear Papa   On Friday evening your letter dated 19th April, addressed to Jim came safely to hand, the newspapers preceded it by three days. I believe we receive all papers & letters now regularly, or at least within a week of the time that they are due. Your letter is the only one so far, that came by this steamer, but I am sure that one or two more will come straggling along in the course of the week. I am very much obliged for the flower seeds; they are in the ground already, for my beds were all nicely dug by Jim and had a good many seeds planted before. They have just appeared above ground, & I expect to have quite a garden in the next few weeks, though to be sure it is not necessary to cultivate a garden, for you can gather a most gorgeous bouquet of sunflowers anywhere on the hills.

Day before yesterday we had the most magnificent view of Mt. Hood which has been afforded us since we have been here. I went up on a knoll outside the garrison, where I could see much better. It was grand. I see by the "chronicle" you sent that Mr. Bierstadt's picture of it is on exhibition. I hope you will all see it. These Oregonians have an artist who has painted Mt. Hood, which the press affirms to be far superior to Mr. Bierstadt's. I saw one of his pictures and I'm sure with a very little teaching I could do quite as well.[16] But the Webfeet do not know anything about colors except yellow. They complain that Bierstadt's has too much foliage, that it is not truthful as trees are as scarce as can be out here . . . .

Major Myers with his cavalry is still here, & we are daily expecting another company commanded by Col. [Eugene M.] Baker but they will both proceed on their journey in about a week.[17] We also expect a visit from Gen'l Steele & Staff on the 3rd of June. Captain Lafollet with his company of volunteers will probably come in tomorrow to be mustered out of service.[18] The Army on this coast is constantly on the move . . . .

Our farm is progressing slowly. We have our own lettuce & radishes and once had Kale; the other things will be ready sometime this summer. Peas are in bloom, but we get them from San Francisco. Salmon are becoming plenty. I wish we could transport a fresh one to you. The salted ones are not nice. I went to the Indian village and saw them putting them up. Ugh! I'll never eat any but fresh ones hereafter you may be sure. Mr. McMurtrie talked so much about the fat oozing out like pork.[19] They are quite the contrary; they are as delicate as any fish I ever ate when boiled, which is the only nice way to cook them because they are so dry. The salt salmon are soaked for a week before boiling. The river has fallen a little since I wrote last.   *Julie*

FORT DALLES,
May 27th.

Dear Eddie   You have not yet answered my last letter so I concluded I would have to furnish a reminder to your memory. If you are very busy at school I can wait, but if you don't have many lessons I want more letters. I want to know all about little sister & all she learns to say & do; how many teeth she has, and when she takes the first step. In return I'll tell you of my kittens & puppies, birds, flowers & lamb. The birds over our front door grew large and flew away, as brother Jim took the nest down about a week or two ago. Well, yesterday we found there was another nest right in the same spot with three little white eggs in it. I was walking up a hill the other day and I saw what I thought was a little scrap of blue paper right before me. I very carelessly stepped on it and crushed it! It was a tiny blue egg, as blue as the sky. I was very sorry . . . .

No one ever disturbs the birds, consequently they are very tame. Cats & dogs are all quite well and would no doubt send their love if they understood that I was writing to you. They are getting so familiar that I have my hands full trying to keep them out of the house; as soon as a door is opened in they rush, then the cat & the dog look all sorts of cross things at each other but the kittens & puppies behave better. I have to carry them out again for they won't go otherwise. I have not been able to find you any stamps lately, but hope [I] will soon. Kiss everybody for me and be sure to write soon . . . .

FORT DALLES,
June 3rd.

My dear Ann Tipodes   I have had no letters during the past week, consequently have nothing to write about, and as I am ashamed to write a letter full of nothing but nonsense to Mama or Papa I concluded to make you the recipient of my weekly favor . . . .

The stream of Dalles conversation all sets in the same channel at present, namely: the rise and fall of—not the money market—but the Columbia river. It has overflowed its banks and is filling up the main street of the town. Two or three stores have been flooded out and the hotel and Railroad bridge piled with rocks to prevent them from taking a sail. Merchants are fast packing their goods and abandoning their stores. The water is only four feet lower than it was in '62 when the 1st floors of the houses were immersed and the steamboats sailed up the middle of the street. As the water is still slowly rising, there is every reason to suppose it will attain its former height. However it affords some excitement as an equivalent to the trouble that is caused. People are providing themselves with canoes and small boats so they can sail out their second story windows.

Mrs. Kelly, who has lived here ten years, says in previous floods a great many houses went down the river. She is a character. Perfectly respectful and good tempered, but very strong minded; everything that surprises her brings forth the exclamation "For the land of Goshen!" Now where the said land may be located I haven't the faintest idea. She has a mania for scrubbing the kitchen floor. Whenever I want to go in there to make cake or pudding I have to request beforehand that she won't scrub the floor 'till I get through. Yesterday I found her on her hands and knees with a great jackknife scraping out grease spots. She exclaimed, "Oh! Mrs. Gilliss, if you would only get me a plane I'd have this floor clean once, for I'd plane all the dirt off of it." I'm afraid to accede to her request, for fear that like the old lady in Holland, she'll scrub us through into the cellar, and with the assistance of a plane I'm *sure* she would.

Apropos of domestics, there was one little incident of our voyage that I believe I forgot to tell you. There was quite a pretty girl on board, small and graceful, with large dark eyes, black hair and olive complexion. She was lady's maid to Miss Hovey whose father was on his way to Peru as minister plenipo' and all the rest of those long titles.[20] Well this young Spanish girl was remarked by the whole company for her modest manner, and great taste in dress. She very rarely spoke probably on account of her imperfect knowledge of English. When we reached Aspinwall, General Hovey and daughter were invited in our "special car," where we had a "special party" and a picnic basket and lots of fun. Miss Spanish, carrying her mistress' cloak, was brought in also. She was in a seat in front of me, and received quite gracefully all the little civilities offered her by the gentlemen. They brought her lunch and ice etc.; whenever the cars stopped the nouns masculine all got out to pick flowers, guavas etc. for us, and she was also the recipient of them. At length an old white-haired gentleman sat down by her to talk. In a kind fatherly manner he questioned her about herself. To his surprise he learned she was from *Washington, her name was Annie,* she did not *understand* a *word* of *Spanish* etc. Several Africanized words betrayed the fact that they had all wasted their attentions on a *mulatto.*[21] Imagine the disgust when it was talked over on the other steamer, after the General & his party had left us for Lima. I enjoyed the whole thing hugely, for I had recognized her as soon as they came on board at New York and knew from the very beginning that she was the daughter of a not-to-be-mistaken-darky-mother. Many a hidden laugh did I have at the expense of my fellow passengers, when they were discussing the mystery enveloping the dusky beauty, and I would not have been the means of dispelling their insueing illusion, for a dollar.

Our post will again be deserted tomorrow. Col. Baker, Major Myers & Lieut. Bernard with all their cavalry leave for Boise.[22] Capt. Babbitt dined with us on Thursday last, on his way to Boise.[23]

Paint & whitewash are at length dry and carpets down. My flowers are coming out nicely, those that escape the ravages of cows. We have no less than *seven* gates opening into our garden on all four sides, and it keeps one on the qui vive to keep them all shut, and there are always so many cows roaming around that take a fancy to my nice green bushes. I had a present of two very pretty plants from one of Jim's employees. The leaf is the shape of a currant leaf with flower bells of a bright salmon color, clustered all along the stem from the root to the tip. I have forgotten the name of it; the flowers belong to the class "Fritillaria," I think. We have a great profusion of wild flowers, some of them beautiful . . . .

Don't send any more letters by Steamer, they are too long on the way; the Overland now comes in twenty-five days when they don't get lost; of course the Steamer is safer. Our river is higher on account of the Portage. We have fifteen miles of railroad between Dalles and Celilo,[24] and as it is built mostly on trestles over the rapids, it would be submerged in an unusual rise. The cars are as fine as we have at the East. Dinner waits so I will stop . . . .   *Julie* . . . .

FORT DALLES,
June 10th, 1866.

Dearest Mama   During the past week I have received a nice letter from Annie which I will answer in due time. This Sunday I will devote to you. Two days after the receipt of Annie's letter, the papers from Papa arrived . . . . The people out here say the world is *turning over*. I begin to believe it, for certainly all its inhabitants are being turned topsy-turvy. The little churches here emulated their brethren at the East. Quiet humdrum little congregations are in turmoil and confusion. The members of the choir have quarreled and seceded, the melodionist won't play for any new, indifferent singers, and when the congregation will sing they have music, and when they won't, they don't. So it goes. Politics are fierce and party spirit runs high, and I never saw such a constant flowing tirade of bitter falsehoods as emanate daily from the press. Frank Dodge is the Democratic candidate elected to the Legislature.

The weather does not seem to cool the exuberance of their spirits in the least, although it is as windy as March and chilly as April. Not a single day yet has been warm enough for a cambric waist, and I have to wear my *beaver cloth coat* every time we go riding, for the mountain winds are so keen. Flowers and fruit are consequently backward; if you could drop down on us today with our bright wood fires indoors and early Spring-like appearance outside you would think you had gone back several months. The sun is warm, and if the wind could be coaxed to lull would be very pleasant. I picked enough gooseberries off our bushes yesterday to make a batch of pies and after dinner Jim and I picked a basketful of pease, of which there is enough to feed a regiment. Isn't that doing pretty well?

On Monday last we had a visit from General Steele, accompanied by Major Glenn and Lieut. Strong.[25] They left about noon on Tuesday en route for Boise. They will return about the middle of July together with General Halleck and Staff. I was very much pleased with the General. He is about fifty or more perhaps, small and rather wiry in appearance, but a thorough gentleman as also were his attendant officers. As Jim is the only officer here and we have this big house all to ourselves, we keep open house for all the officers that come here nearly. Gen'l Steele insists that on their return here we shall be ready to accompany them down to Vancouver. He is a bachelor and being commanding officer of the department has a large house. He says Jim and I shall have a suite of rooms on one side of his hall which I must consider mine as long as we will visit him. They have parties, dinners, hops, billiard and croquet matches and all the fashion outside of San Francisco. There, according to all accounts, I know I shall enjoy it very much, and the Gen'l says he will give Jim as long a leave of absence as he wants to stay there.

I have got my house fixed up finally and I think it looks pretty well. Not wishing to buy more furniture than we can help in the uncertainty of our remaining here we have rented a very pretty parlor set, mahogany and haircloth, and a walnut extension dining table, from Mrs. Kelly. She had stored them away on breaking up, and asked me to use them for the sake of taking care of them. To this of course we would not consent, unless she would allow us to pay for the use of them. She stoutly and indignantly refused, but as I remained firm she at last agreed that the sum every month should be put away for her little girl. Jim saw a beautiful marble top centre table which he wants to buy if I like it, so I am going down town tomorrow to see it. I see Mr. [William] Faxon has been made Assistant Secretary of Navy and Captain Fox talked of as *second* assistant. Is it possible that he would see Mr. Faxon in his old place and accept a position subordinate to him? . . .

Jim sends a great deal of love and also does your loving daughter   *Julie S.G.*

FORT DALLES,
June 15, 1866.

Dear Papa   I am very happy this evening, this week seems almost too good to realize I have had so many letters. Day before yesterday we received your Steamer letter (which we enjoyed in partnership) of May 9th. Yesterday I had one from Mrs. Gilliss and Fannie and one from Clara Haight; today your nice letter with its "Overland" sign illuminated the mail-bag for the Gilliss mansion, and here I am two hours after its receipt sitting on the verandah answering as requested. The sun is just dipping behind the hills, and a faint breeze has sprinkled the parlor floor with a snowy covering of rose leaves, from the climbing bush that has latticed itself all over the bay window and is covered with hundreds of creamy blossoms. The sweet orange flowers are nodding like timid brides under the green shelter of their polished leaves; my pet lamb "Dick" is strolling leisurely around nipping an occasional tuft of grass or clover that comes in his way; a robin is sitting on the edge of a water barrel taking a drink, and this is the way I like the country and Mama would like it too. I would not like an ugly, uncomfortable house or unsightly surroundings at all. We have nothing here to offend either eye or ear. Inside the house looks comfortable and cosy and if I could have you all here I would have nothing left to wish for.

Bright and early on Monday morning we went down town to see that centre table Jim liked so much, and as I was delighted with it he bought it, also a beautiful little pair of antique vases. The table is round and the marble slab has a fluting an eighth of a yard wide all round the edge. My vases are lemon-colored lava with a wreath of green ivy leaves painted on them and mounted in gilt racks or stands.

Our chest of books has finally arrived and [they] are in a fairly good condition considering their long voyage around the Horn; only a few are warped and mildewed from dampness. Did I ever tell you of the kindness of Captain C. when he left us?[26] He gave me his rocking chair; it is a lovely thing, looks as if it came over in the *Mayflower*; also a pair of old-fashioned brass candlesticks. We miss him very much out of our household; he was always so genial and pleasant.

I've killed six mosquitoes so far, I'm afraid there will be nothing left of me to finish this letter. I boasted too soon of our cool weather, the last three days remind one forcibly of the tropics.

Colonel & Capt. Babbitt dined with us, and spent the evening on Wednesday; Thursday morning they returned to Fort Vancouver. We get letters quite regularly now, and the papers you kindly send arrive constantly. I am so glad to think that you are home again now.[27] I think you will all be much happier; it will be better for

Mama and little Kitty Puss. How I wish I could see her glorious little babyhood . . . .

Tell Eddie my kitten is playing with my foot and the old cat rubbing against the side of my chair and purring to have her head scratched. I am offended that you say my little flowers smell like salmon. Ugh! get within a mile or two of an Indian encampment when in the fishing season and conclude if flowers smell like salmon you are content to be without them. I have no less than six bouquets in the parlor, for Jim brings me one nearly every time he goes to town. Salmon we get in abundance from the Indians, from ten to fifty cents apiece. I wish you were near enough to say to them as I do, "Six Siwash nika ticky mika choco tomollo, ipscum tenas salmon."[28] You might get tired of so much of it, but just now you will be ready to eat anything after your starvation winter.

Tell Mama if she wants a nice dessert to take a quart of milk leaving out a cupful; in the former put a small cup full of white sugar and set it on the fire. In the cup full of cold milk stir six tablespoonsful of cornstarch and when the warm milk is ready to boil, stir it in and boil till it thickens. Flavor with lemon or vanilla and pour in a mould. We have it quite often and are all fond of it, but I make half this quantity; it looks very pretty in my pineapple mould . . . . I have made another progressive step in guitar music. I have learned all the chords, so that I can play an accompanymant to most any song, but I'm afraid the singing thereof will match the frogs . . . . Jim sends love. Your affectionate daughter,   *Julie*

FORT DALLES,
June 16, 1866.

Dear Anxiety [Annie]   I hope I will be pardoned for leaving your nice letter so long unanswered, especially as you waited to get *two* from me before you wrote. I sincerely congratulate you on your graduation. You must write me an account of your emancipation from the school room, and what prizes you took, etc . . . .

What an extensive improvement *Grant Avenue* must be. Does it extend through an *entire* square? I see in the papers which Papa frequently sends, that many of the streets [in Washington, D.C.] are being paved and the Canal is in process of improvement; a bridge built across the foot of 17th street, numerous & sundry other improvements, which I am very glad to see.

All the morning Sunday though it is, wagons loaded with masculine and crinoline are passing through the Post to the country beyond, for fishing and frolicking. It is a terribly wicked place. When one church is open the other closes as *two* congregations can't be raised at once. So the one church has service in morning & the other in evening. We have had very warm weather the last few days. Now the wind has risen again, but I don't know if it will blow cool. I rather think it will be a sort of Sirocco blast in the middle of the day, though now in the morning it is pleasant ... Your loving sister,   *Junie*

FORT DALLES,
June 24, 1866.

Dear Mama   I had written to Annie last Sunday when I heard that Lieut. Catley would leave next morning for Washington, so I gave him the letter to carry. He goes by Steamer, I will send this by Overland and see which wins the race though he is one week in advance.

Last Sunday was so warm that I was dressed in white muslin. Monday we had to have fires, the rest of the week was mild until yesterday, when fires came in again. We have had some pleasant rides this week. Once we went up the banks of the river for four or five miles, passing the last tree that can be seen; beyond the country is desolate in its barrenness. We reached the point from which Mr. Bierstadt painted his Mt. Hood. I do not wonder Papa calls it a quiet picture. The mountain is there to be sure in all its grandeur, nothing else. Not a stick or stone, shrub or single tree, to break the monotonous wave of bare brown hills. And now I can see where to an Oregonian eye the falsity of the picture comes in. You cannot possibly imagine such a desolate scene, and a single leaf of green introduced into the picture is put there as an artistic addition, and this same Sahara-like view seems to extend to where the horizon meets the land. Even the river here is prisoned between two stone walls less than a hundred feet wide, and flows so low between the hills that it is lost from the landscape. When we were down on its banks we saw a seal with head erected, swimming along; the river is said to be full of them.

We had a nice ride on Friday in the opposite direction [west], and the prettiest I have seen out here. The road crossed the stream called Chenowith creek, and winds up the side of a steep hill.[29] The scrub oak grows thickly on its banks and wild flowers in the greatest profusion, the sweet-scented orange blossom and wild roses, covering nearly every rock. It was something like a ride on Rock creek, but such drives as we have around Washington would set the people here crazy. They go in[to] such ecstasies if a road happens to have a tree or blade of grass growing through the sand.

We jog along day after day, each one the same as the last, so I don't have anything interesting to write about. Jim goes fishing sometimes and brings home a few tiny little trout for breakfast. I look after my house, play with my pets, and make cakes (and eat them); when the wind don't take me off my feet I take a walk, but one can find few such times during a summer on this coast. In my letters from Clemmie Kip she says it is terrible in San Francisco. She never saw such blows in her life. They have had another earthquake; there have been four or five in as many months. I should be uneasy at so many "shakes" . . . .

Oh! if I could only get you all out here in a few hours, though the way the wind is howling at present would somewhat startle you, but we could stay in the house and build a bright fire, Baby Kitty could roll on the floor and play with her namesake and we could have such a nice happy talk. Papa & Jim with Eddie could go to the stables or fishing. Well never mind, we may not be here much longer, and we will sometime be near enough to have a visit from you, so I will wait with all the patience I can muster. I have turned my blue silk and it looks as good as new. My white muslin made up beautifully with the pretty worked trimmings . . . .

I see by the papers that Captain Fox is going to Russia in a Monitor to congratulate the Emperor on his escape from the assassin, so I suppose he would not accept the *second* assistant secretaryship. I have not had any letters during the past week, but I know the steamer mail is in so I daily expect them. Mr. Day had one yesterday from New York. Tell Annie my last letter from Clara Haight announces the marriage of old Miss Kitty Haight, that real old maid teacher at St. Mary's Hall . . . . Tell her also that Lieut. Bernard of the 1st Cavalry out here is a semi weekly correspondent of Ginnie Smith's, who used to go to Miss Brooke's school. It's queer how I find little connecting links with the old home life everywhere I go . . . . your loving daughter   *Julie*

FORT DALLES,
July 1st, 1866.

Dearest Mama   Your letter mailed May 23rd arrived here June 24th, which is the quickest trip yet made by any of my letters. In it you tell of darling little Eddie's sickness, and you may imagine how worried and anxious I was to get another letter to hear how he was getting. On June 29th I received Annie's mailed May 27th, in which she says Eddie was able to sit up for an hour. Oh! I was so glad . . . . I wish I could send him some of the currant jelly that I made yesterday, for it was a decided success. It is as clear and pretty as can be and so firm you could cut it with a knife. Tell Eddie we have seven hens and a rooster, and we found two eggs the next morning after they arrived, for we bought them down the river. They are nice pretty little speckles. I will have to take a pencil; these pens are so poor they wear out in writing a line or two.

The weather is intensely warm today, and mosquitoes and flies perfectly tormenting. I am nearly eaten and really look as if I was covered with a rash of mosquito bites. Snakes, beetles, sand-flies, ants half an inch long, spiders & May flies & fleas abound, not to speak of a certain obnoxious insect which at home confines itself to beds, but out here prefers every other place. I have only found three in our house; they (two) came out of the hall near the front door, and the third upstairs, but I keep a vigilant watch, for Mrs. Steele says every crack in their house is full of them and the house that burnt down was in danger of being carried away by them . . . .

They are making very extensive preparations here for the celebration of July 4th, a picnic during the day and fireworks at night and popping in between from our mountain howitzers which they will borrow after we have fired our national salute for the edification of the garrison, which consists of Capt. Gilliss & wife and ten or fifteen private soldiers .... We have made an ice-house in the stone foundation of one of the burned houses, filled it with good, solid ice, and had it and all our fences whitewashed, so this forlorn place looks clean at least.

We got quantities of green peas from our garden but nothing else. There is no fruit planted there. It is quite plentiful but commands exorbitant prices. Strawberries, cherries & raspberries are now down to 50 cts. coin a quart, and that is considered a low price. In Boise apples sell from 25 to 50 cents *apiece*. The Salmon season is over but Jim has packed down a barrel of them in salt. Poor fellow; he's got another one of those toothache spells, which kept him awake all night; it seems a little easier now so he is trying to get to sleep. The tooth is apparently sound so we can get nothing into it .... Your loving daughter,   *Julie*

FORT DALLES, OREGON,
Tuesday, July 3rd, 1866.

My Dear Mama & Papa,   Yesterday (July 2nd) I received Mama's letter mailed May 31st, while Papa's mailed May 30th has just reached me this evening and I am sitting out on the verandah writing with a pencil because I have no convenient place to put down my inkstand. I am deeply grateful for your constant letters .... It has been a very severe trial to me that I have been unable to share your nursing of my dear little Eddie, but I know it must be all for the best though it is very hard to bear unmurmuringly. I was very much distressed when I found I had been kept so long in ignorance of his illness but I am glad now, for I might have worried myself sick without doing any good at all. I am still very anxious about him and always shall be, but I know everything I could desire in your constant letters. I am so glad you have found so many kind friends ....

We thank you very much for the two budgets of papers . . . . It is one month now since you went to our dear old house; I hope my next letter will be able to tell me that thanks to Mrs. Nichols' kindness and her carriage little brother was safely moved. But the grey twilight is creeping around and as that is the time when I get homesick fits I have adopted the plan of keeping myself busy about something that will occupy me fully. As this cannot go tomorrow (as the new mail regulations only bring letters on alternate days) I will leave it till then to conclude, only remarking by the way that we (enjoy?) the hottest weather here I ever experienced. There is no degree of *warm* that will express it. The Thermometer ranges from 98 degrees upwards; yesterday it stood 110 degrees in the shade on the north side of the house and today is still worse, though I have not heard the gauge taken. I hope tomorrow will not be higher still or I will surely melt.

July 4th. Well! we have survived through the hottest night I ever remember. Not a breath of air and every article of furniture in the room so warm you do not like to touch them; the pillows & sheets felt as if a warming pan had passed over them. Jim did not sleep at all, in fact did not try, he walked through the rooms all night stopping at every window to see if it was getting any cooler. Just about daybreak a little breeze sprang up and though not at all cool we were very grateful for it. Just as the sun rose it stiffened considerably and when Mt. Hood was gleaming like a molten ruby, it increased into a gale which has been blowing ever since. I do not suppose it is many degrees lower than yesterday, but the wind is refreshing after such a desert-like stillness of atmosphere. I am very sleepy today and have not quite recovered [from] the "stunning" effects of the national salute which has just been fired in front of our house. The whole town is out en masse about a quarter mile back of us, on a grand picnic. The wind blows from us so we do not hear anything but [the] monotonous thum, thum, of their drum; all the wind instruments do not reach us. There are groups of children and girls, firemen & boys constantly crossing the parade [ground] in their wanderings, and I do not envy them under this vertical sun . . . .

About an hour ago Jim received orders to proceed immediately to Walla Walla to adjust the A.Q.M. property there that has remained since the Post was abandoned, and send it to other Forts where it may be needed. We will go early tomorrow morning and expect to return home in about a week so I must hasten to close my letter for it is nearly dark now. We will arrive at Walla Walla on Friday, being two days in transit.[30] Give a warm kiss to my darling little brother and take the enclosed and buy him something for a birthday present that he will like. I had intended doing so myself but added to the difficulty of sending it home is the finding of *anything* to send. I will write to him pretty soon. Give my love to Annie and be sure not to forget to kiss Baby Kitty. Mrs. Gilliss wrote to me what a lovely baby she is. And with hearts full of love from us both believe me as ever your devoted daughter   *Julie*

CONNECTIONS

On the Way to the Next Post

JULY–SEPTEMBER 1866

ON STEAMER IDAHO,
July 12th, 1866.

[Dear Papa,]   On July 5th at four o'clock in the morning we left the Dalles for Walla Walla where we arrived safely on Friday evening. The first day & night of our journey was spent on the river through rocks and rapids you can scarcely imagine, with the same "low, barren, bold" country on both sides. The second morning we reached Wallula so early that the whole town was still asleep; here we were to take the stage, and as we numbered fifteen hungry passengers, we determined to rouse up the Inn people and get some breakfast. The gentlemen of our party pounded on all the doors and windows with such success, that in about ten minutes we were all seated in a long room like barracks, at a table covered with a clean cloth but nothing else in sight. We were sleepy and hungry, but certainly had learned patience before breakfast appeared. You may judge if it was worth waiting for. A plentiful supply of hard fried ham that no knife could go through; one small plate with very few slices of bread; another containing three potatoes, a small dish of six fried eggs; plenty of thick black coffee, and *no* butter nor milk. A sleepy looking damsel with her hair in curl papers drawled out with a nasal twang, "Thems as has bread can't have no 'tatters, divide 'em twixt yerselves." After this sumptuous meal we mounted

82

on top of the stage coach and travelled through alkali dust and sage-brush, and not until we reached the Walla Walla Valley did we see a tree or any sign of fertility.

The valley is beautiful comparatively. It would look quite poor in New York or Pennsylvania, but the soil is rich and the fields of wav-ing grain compensate for the *total lack* of *trees*. It is a plain one thousand feet above the level of the sea, surrounded by the Blue Mountains and watered by a perfect network of streams. The garri-son is very pretty & the town much larger & more important than Dalles . . . .

On Sunday we went to the Episcopal church & heard Bishop Scott who went up with us on the boat.[1] In the evening General Halleck & Staff arrived from Boise but left in a few hours.[2] We made some quite pleasant acquaintances there and attended quite a company on Monday evening . . . . The society there is very good. Tuesday morning we left there and arrived home last night, General Steele & Staff accompanying us. Today we are on board the steamboat on our way to Ft. Vancouver, so you see I have to send you this scrawl written during the trip in order that you may not miss a weekly letter . . . .

When you write, Papa, please tell us something about the Army bill, we get very few scraps of information in regard to it but feel quite interested. Mrs. Gilliss wrote that she would tell us if she knew but that you understand it better. I will try and get Jim to write a nice long letter soon, for I am ashamed of these apologies for them written with lead pencil but ink is not to be thought of on such a rolling boat even if I had it; there is almost as much motion as if one was as sea. I had a letter from Fannie Raymond brought up by . . . one of Genl. Halleck's Staff. She says she had written three to me but I have never received them. With a kiss all round I remain your loving daughter   *Julie*

IN WHARF HOUSE WAITING FOR THE LOWER BOAT,
July 12th, 1866.

Darling little Brother   Here we are this far on our journey. We have passed over the Cascade portage in the cars and now we are at the lower wharf waiting for the boat which is very late. Most of the passengers are strolling around the country and Brother Jim and some other officers are fishing with a line made up of all the string they can find to tie together. They have not caught any fish yet. We were home last night long enough to find that our chickens are laying eggs every day and doing very nicely. One egg was found that is only as large as a walnut and perfectly round. When I was at Walla Walla a Mrs. Noble told me she would give me a turkey if I knew any way to carry it down, but it was impossible to take it on the stage.[3] My pet lamb Dick has been sheared and looks so funny. We have a perfect menagerie out in the yard and have to whip all our animals to keep them out of the house; we don't whip very hard though . . . .

Well, here I am on board Steamer *Cascades* a beautiful boat with mirrors, walnut furniture & velvet carpets all new and bright.[4] In a short time we will be off toward Vancouver where we will arrive about three or four o'clock this afternoon . . . . Kiss Mama & Papa, Sister Annie & Baby Kitty and just imagine that you are getting a dozen kisses from   *Sister Junie* . . . .

FORT VANCOUVER, [WASHINGTON TERRITORY]
July 15th, 1866.

Dear Annie   Here I am still at the pleasantest Post on this side of the Rocky Mountains, except for the constant rain. It has been bright and clear ever since we arrived but they tell me that is something unusual. Friday Capt. Babbitt took me [on] a long ride through the country around for about eight or ten miles and it is perfectly beautiful. Great trees interlace their branches overhead and make a continuous green arch to drive through. Ferns & undergrowth attain an almost tropical luxuriance, and not a rock is to be seen, and all this less than two hundred miles below the barren desert region of the upper country. I had a drive with General Steele also, behind a pair of spirited bays, which I enjoyed vastly.

The Fort here is beautiful; the houses are heavy log buildings more remarkable for strength than beauty, but they all have their little gardens filled with flowers and some fruit. They are handsomely furnished and the interior & exterior are somewhat incongruous. Almost all the officers and their wives are under thirty years of age and consequently full of life and spirits. The band plays every evening for an hour and then we walk about the grounds or go down to the billiard hall. Some of the ladies are very excellent players. I am perfectly charmed with the society at the Post.

Today we are having half-hour guns fired and flags at half-mast, in respect to the memory of General Scott.[5] The order just reached here, and consequently the salute is so much behindhand. I have done nothing but ride, visit and receive visits since I have been here. I had a beautiful bouquet sent me on Friday by Lieut. Strong.

We have just returned from church. The Chaplain (Episcopal) is very ill so his church was closed and I went with Mrs. Babbitt who is a Catholic, to mass. Of course I should never say anything in disrespect of their religion to Catholics, but the more I saw of it, the more I wonder that intelligent minds should become so weak as to bow to the mummeries & hollow mockeries of the Romish service. It is blindly done, which may account for it, for the mass of people cannot fully understand even the church service which is all Latin & French. The gorgeous robes of the Priests and the flashing ornamentation of the church with the never ceasing gesticulations impress one with the idea that it is some splendidly gotten up tableaux at which you are simply to look till the acting is over. I do not say this in a spirit of narrow minded bigotry but in simple wonder that anyone should believe in it.

Just at present (noon) it is very warm but until ten in the morning and after four or five in the evening it is almost cold enough for fires so we have to put on a thick dress until the middle of the day; then we melt in a thin one for a few hours and then shiver wrapped up in a shawl. I never saw such a climate. With the greatest possible care you can't help catching cold not in your head, but in the form of neuralgia, rheumatism etc. Several Infantry officers have been ordered East on recruiting service. I wish we were among them. We are both well and send a great deal of love. Your loving sister   *Junie*

FORT VANCOUVER,
July 22nd, 1866.

Dear Parents   Here I am still at Vancouver and having such a nice time that I don't want to go home. I expect however we will return there next week. Jim went up for a day last week to send off his papers and to see what letters were awaiting me. There were none from home and I have not had one since the day we arrived from Walla Walla. I expect they will soon arrive. I send all letters overland as it is much quicker; it is next to impossible to find out when Steamers sail we are so far away from them.

Last Wednesday night we had a "Hop" here and I enjoyed it very much, it was my first dance since we left home. I have also learned to play Croquet, tell Annie. Yesterday we had a long ride out in the woods as indeed we do almost every day, but this time we took a lunch and went out to join Jim and Captain Babbitt who had been out all the morning fishing. Captain Weeks drove his wife, Mrs. Babbitt and myself out in a barouche. I have not gone to church to-day for none are open except the Roman Catholic. Mrs. Weeks and I went down to Portland the other day to do a little shopping and to see Mrs. Ainsworth who is her sister. Just think how nicely that family is situated. Old Colonel Babbitt and his wife are stationed in San Francisco, Mrs. [J.C.] Ainsworth, their eldest daughter, is in Portland, Mrs. Weeks and Captain Babbitt, who are twins, are both stationed at Fort Vancouver. Their parents have both been up here on a visit and the whole family was united for the first time in ten years, and their children are all quite young.

We had a very pleasant visit to Portland and returned the same day. The boat runs over in the morning and back in the evening. Mrs. Ainsworth & her husband gave me a very pressing invitation to come over and spend a week with her, but I do not expect to do it. They are very wealthy and live in grand style.

I found this little photograph there and as I think it a very good likeness of my pet mountain I send it to Papa. The photographer said that it was next to impossible to get a picture from nature and had never been accomplished. He was going to try this summer to take some pictures of the scenery in the Columbia river but did not know whether it would be practicable. I have one of the Horse Tail Falls which I believe was taken from the steamboat, but it looks to me as if it was copied from a picture, although it is very true to nature. . . .

Are you all well and happy in our home? How does Baby Kitty like her new carriage? Mrs. Weeks has a darling little girl just the same age of our baby and I pet her for the sake of my little sister. The plague of my life are the fleas. Oh! there are shoals of them, and I have not learned to be very expert in catching them so they nearly set me crazy. They are worse here than at the Dalles. Jim had a letter from Uncle William's brother [John Thomas] last week introducing a Capt. [Ephraim W.] Baughman (his son-in-law) . . . .

General Steele has just told me that we will probably be sent to Fort Stevens as soon as Jim has closed up the business at Fort Dalles, which will be abandoned.[6] I am very glad, for to be in touch with the Steamers will seem like being nearer home. It will be an anomalous position for Jim for he will be in charge of Engineer's work, mounting guns on the ramparts, and building a long pier out over the water. He certainly has varied duties; he is still a Lieut. of the 5th Artillery; also a newly appointed Captain and Quartermaster and now will have Engineer's work.[7] Well, he seems to be able to do it. Jim goes back to Dalles now and I remain a little longer to visit the wife of the Ordinance officer here. Your loving daughter,   *Julie*

FORT DALLES, OREGON,
August 4th, 1866.

My dear Parents   We arrived home on Monday evening last after a most delightful visit and found a letter from Papa, one from Fannie and Mrs. Gilliss . . . together with two bundles of newspapers from Papa . . . . I am very sorry to hear that little brother continues so weak. Why don't you give him Cod Liver oil; I'm sure it would benefit him. I am glad Baby Kitty is getting fat again. How I wish that I could see her! I sincerely sympathize with you Mama in your perplexity in regard to servants. I am particularly blessed and am only sorry that I am not able to turn Mrs. Kelly over to you. I am well and strong enough to get along with the trouble and yet it falls to my lot to escape it, while you with a sick household have to do the battling . . . .

Mrs. Kelly will go to Stevens with us if she can make a satisfactory disposition of her property, and I certainly hope she can, for Mrs. Dr. [Alden H.] S[teele] who has been at Stevens since February had not been able to get a servant yet. We expect General [Frederick] Steele in a few days; there is trouble brewing with the Indians, therefore the troops are being massed at Fort Boise. I am continually in fear of Jim having to go there too.

Jim has been and is still very busy packing and sending off all the Government property at this place. He is really sick but will not give up an hour while there is a stroke of work to do. Mr. Day, his chief clerk, will go with us to Fort Stevens and Dr. and Mrs. S. are already there. It is almost incredible to see just the goods packed in the two warehouses. He expects to have it all sent away, and the buildings sold in about a month, and then we will take flight again.

Last Tuesday a large party from Fort Vancouver came up the river on an excursion trip and spent the evening with me; we took the train and went over the Portage to Celilo to see the Falls, then returned in a couple of hours & had supper on board the Steamboat *Oneonta*.[8] They all returned to Vancouver the next morning. Captain Babbitt and his lovely little wife are coming up next week to make us a visit. I expect Colonel O'Beirne will be here at the same time, for he with his command have been ordered up to the Boise district, to his supreme disgust, and they will have to come here for Jim to furnish the transportation. We do have the most remarkable weather here, one day you roast with the thermometer at 115 degrees, next day a wind arises that takes you off your feet if you dare to go outside the door, the third day the heat is almost stifling during the few hours near midday, while in the morning and evening you can wear an overcoat comfortably. I never saw such a climate in my life.

This city of Dalles is dying, the sale of this Post will be its death knell and in a few years the houses and streets will—not be overgrown with grass, that is impossible, but they may be scattered to the "four winds" which beat about them. All the Jew merchants are packing up and moving elsewhere, a sure sign that its glory hath departed . . . . I will quote the usual sentiments of those leaving this place.

> Knowest thou that land that was formed for the savage,
> That land so prolific in ponderous rocks,
> Where soil was discovered that once grew a cabbage,
> The land of the otter, the marten and fox?
> 'Tis the land of the mist and the home of the drizzle,
> The Ultima Thule, half peopled with Scots!
> The finest of countries from which one can mizzle
> - Provided at least you can sell your town lots!
> Where the food is a mixture of seaweed and salmon
> Alternately changing with bacon and beans,
> Beans and bacon repeated without any gammon
> With occasional tastes of inferior greens!
> Farewell! Oh Town Council without any function;
> Adieu! Great Assembly without any brain.
> I leave thee, Great Humbug, with "halo"[9] compunction,
> To thy mists, to thy pork, to thy beans and thy rain!"

FORT DALLES, OREGON.
August 12th, 1866.

My dear Anastasia [Annie]   As I have been to church, and since I came home eaten a hearty lunch I will write to you as next on the order of good things. I have this week received a lovely little letter from Eddie and very proud I am of it. He is improving very much. Tell him I will answer it soon. I also received on the same day letters from Mrs. Gilliss, Beckie, Fannie and from Clemmie Kip in San Francisco. I have before me now yours of June 24th which I will endeavor to answer. Here I am talking . . . as if you were still a little school-girl when it has just entered my head that you are a *Graduate*. I am very glad indeed that you were successful in gaining the prizes you have so long and faithfully worked for . . . .

You give some descriptions of new bonnets; the last "style" out here consists of two broom straws of equal length crossed in their center and tied there with a blue bow, red tassels depend from the four points, and this elegant and tasteful little affair can be purchased for the moderate sum of $45. I don't think I shall get one, I'm afraid it will not be becoming to my style of beauty. I've got a "Sundown" hat which I consider the most sensible of all.

Col. O'Beirne has been here for nearly a week; he leaves tomorrow for Boise to fight Indians. I am sorry for anybody that has to go after those bloodthirsty Indians. We expect General Steele up tomorrow . . . . When I was at Vancouver I saw Laura Ainsworth have some tiny aprons that were so cunning, so when I came home I made one while I remembered them, and about an hour after I had finished it Lieut. Bernard came down on his way to San Francisco to sail for the East, so he took it for me. He is going home to marry Ginnie Smith I believe. That one who lives on the corner of 19th & I streets . . . .

I do not think the Dalles will be illuminated by our presence much longer. Jim is getting through his business as rapidly as he possibly can, but he has worked himself sick, and won't give in. He's a little bilious and has a bad cold in his head and is out of sorts generally, but I never saw anyone so unwilling to confess it; he still holds out that he is not sick . . . . Give our united love to Papa and Mama and write when you *have time* to your Affectionate sister,   *Julie* . . . .

FORT DALLES, OREGON,
August 19, 1866.

My dear Parents   With a sadness equal to your own I have received your letter announcing Cousin Harry's death.[10] And even though his enfeebled frame proved that the end must soon come, yet the descent of the Angel of Death seemed like a sudden swoop at last. To his family the loss is immeasureable and I know it will be great to you Papa, loving and living as brothers as you have been. What a strange fatality seems the connecting link between Cape May and our family.[11] There grandfather lost his life; there years afterwards Cousin MacDonough's[12] first wife's breath went out on the receding tide; there, now has passed away the spirit of him who years ago assisted you in rescueing Mama from the treacherous undertow . . . .

I am very sorry Papa dear that you have been so sick, but I think mountain air if it be like that up in the Cascades will be no recuperator. We have hotter weather than Washington summers can boast of, and no alleviation. Since the *first week in May* we have not had a *drop* of *rain*. I do not think we have had the sun obscured for one day. On Friday last for about two hours we had thunder, low mutterings and growling from the direction of Mt. Hood, but unaccompanied by any visible lightning or rain. The alkaline earth is dried and baked, and the poor feeble flowers and grass that in the early Spring struggled up into the light and life, have withered away into the grey dust that stifled them. Even the wind comes over the hot sand fierce as the rushing of the Fire Angel's wings. Thunder showers are unknown, the only rain being the incessant falls during the Autumn which continue till frost-bound by the Winter . . . .

On the 25 August will be sold at this Post a long list of articles enumerated in the advertisement and thus ends the history of Fort Dalles. Shortly after, we will bid farewell to its smiling sand hills and fair rock piles, its warm zephyrs and sunny skies, to see what jewels we shall find on the framing beach of old Ocean's mirror. I think Fort Vancouver is doomed before many months pass over its fresh green face to fall back and take its place among "the things that were." General Pope is ordered to this Department, and the Headquarters to be removed from Vancouver to Portland and the needless expense of maintaining posts with no use for them must be curtailed.[13] General Steele stopped here one night this week on his second journey to Boise; I think he is much disappointed at losing his confirmation as Major or Brigadier General which rank he only holds by Brevet. He is a pleasant affable gentleman and I shall be very sorry to see him superseded by General Pope of whom I know nothing. I believe General Halleck would order us home if we desired him, if he had the power, but I think the War Department alone possesses that. He is of course all powerful in his own division but I believe his authority extends no farther. If I could make friends with Secretary [of War, Edwin M.] Stanton, for a little while I would ask him so sweetly, he could not have the heart to refuse. It is so intensely warm and the flies so annoying that I beg you will please take the will for the deed and believe that I will fill out this letter when the Thermometer can be coaxed down from its altitude. With love from us both and a kiss all around I remain your loving daughter   *Julie* . . . .

FORT DALLES,
August 26th.

Dearest Mama   I was very very glad to receive your letter this week even though you do call it an old one. I get so few from you that I rather enjoy their being a sort of journal from one week into the next. The last date on it was July 15th. We leave here tomorrow for Fort Vancouver where Jim will remain doing duty for Colonel Hodges during the two weeks he is in Boise, before we proceed to our destination.[14] We have been quite busy the past week taking up carpets, boxing furniture, etc. and today, the last of our residence here, if you could look in on us you would laugh. Old tattered flags hang from the windows instead of the curtains, all the furniture we have left is the old wooden stuff which has been made here in the carpenter shop. The dinner table groans under the weight of its pewter kitchen castors, tin dishes, cracked plates & pitchers and all the old trash not worth taking away with us. A tin wash basin and bucket of water replace the toilet set on the washstand, and the pile of boxes and bales on the verandah show pretty conclusively that we are soon to be on the wing.

I would have written before but really have not had the time, and I know you will pardon me for you have had some experience in moving and know that a transit from one city to another takes more time because everything has to be boxed up, and out here where they charge from 15 to 20 dollars per ton by *measurement* you have to economize space on a small salary. However we get along happily and comfortably and when greenbacks go down low, we find our wants decrease until they go up again. Tell papa we are very much obliged for the package of newspapers which arrived last night. I must go and finish packing my trunks. This letter can't go before I do, so I may finish it at Vancouver.

Monday, August 27. Poor Dalles has all its misfortunes come at once. Heretofore it was always supposed to be a healthy place and now a sort of epidemic diarrhea has broken out which few seem to have escaped not even excepting the *dignitaries* at the Garrison. On Saturday and Sunday I had my little portion of it, but by a prompt course of treatment I feel today almost as good as new. Jim would not let me go down the river this morning however, he thought I had better keep quiet today so I am writing on the lounge although I feel quite well. I'm afraid Jim will get it next, so am anxious to get down to the cooler air of Vancouver. He was not perfectly well this morning when he went to the office, but he don't have time to get sick though he takes time to wait on me. He's just as good as he can be, and I can't possibly see what right I have to be so happily married . . . .

Wednesday, August 29th. I will add one more piece to this patchwork letter. Here we are safe and sound at Fort Vancouver, after a journey of twelve hours yesterday. All the dogs, horses, mules, wagon, furniture and trunks came safely and we will remain here a few weeks longer before going down the river. Our friends at court want to get Jim special orders so he will rule the Quartermaster's department at both Fort Stevens and Cape Disappointment *independent* of *the Post Commanders*. This will be very pleasant for him and will give us the choice of residence on either side of the river we wish. We have most favorable accounts of the advantages of both places.

We are both quite well again and very pleasantly situated at Capt. Weeks. His wife is Capt. Babbitt's twin sister. Mrs. Weeks has given me a quantity of crabapples and we are both going to work today preserving. They grew in the post garden here . . . .

We could not get any photographs taken at Dalles. There is one establishment there but their productions are rather clouded and mixed up. We will go over to Portland and have them taken for you the first favorable opportunity. Today it is raining, the first that we have seen for nearly four months. Hoping you are all well and happy, we send all the love that is in our hearts and a kiss to everybody from your loving daughter   *Julie* . . . .

FORT VANCOUVER, WASHINGTON TERRITORY,
September 2nd, 1866.

My dear Anaspasia [Annie]   I have just returned from church . . . . During the few days that we have been here it has rained most of the time. We have had one nice ride. I expect Jim will go down to the mouth of the river tomorrow morning to visit the two Forts. He will return in four or five days by the next boat. I will remain here . . . .

Capt. Babbitt and his wife have gone to San Francisco, to my great sorrow. They left here before we arrived but I hope will return before we leave. The Capt. has had a very serious spell of illness, and the Doctor ordered him down for his health on a sea voyage. I think a great deal of them, and their sister Mrs. Weeks also. I won't say anything in favor of the latter, for she has just informed me this morning that she and I are exactly alike in appearance, character and disposition. I think there is some slight resemblance, for many others have noticed it, but the preponderance is so greatly in her favor that I only seem the ugly shadow.

I have not a particle of news to tell you. I am making a very pretty sofa cushion for my lazy husband. It consists of stripes of Afghan knitting and will look quite Persian when it is finished . . . . Tell Eddie we brought our dogs with us except one which was lame and we left him behind 'till he recovers . . . . Jim sends love. Your affectionate sister   *Julie*

FORT VANCOUVER, W.T.
September 9th, 1866.

Dear Mama & Papa   Last night was most delightful. The mail brought me a letter from Mama, one from Annie, a coat pattern with scraps from you all; then the evening boat brought back my husband after a whole week's absence. He visited both Forts and says there is no comparison between them, Fort Stevens possesses nearly all the advantage. He brought up the plan of our future home . . . . I think it is very nice, and have already settled in my mind how nice it will look when I get our stock of worldly goods in their places. I have just been to church; it is a very hot day, and the flies bit me into a perfect fever, and gave me a little headache. I cannot tell, Mama, how glad I was to get your nice letter of August 6th, especially as you are all well again . . . .

Capt. & Mrs. Babbitt are expected home tomorrow, I shall be very glad to see her. Well! the Army bill has arrived out at last and all the good it does Jim is to put him a dozen files further up, but as he is still 24 from a Majority I suppose he will remain a Captain the rest of his life.   *Julie*

FORT VANCOUVER,
Sunday, September 16, 1866.

Dear Papa   . . . . We leave here by daylight tomorrow morning for Fort Stevens, so all future letters must be addressed to Astoria, Oregon. I have this week received a compound letter from Mama, Annie and Eddie mailed August 19th, less than a month en route. We will only have two mails a week down at Fort Stevens. Papa, dear, I think if you were a Quartermaster in the Army, you would be always well, for you would be kept travelling around all the time, and that would just suit you. I am becoming a perfect adept in the art of packing and unpacking trunks . . . . Tell Annie she need not be so conceited about her preserves, since I have been at Vancouver I have put up three jars of crab apples and two of Bartlett pears and they are all delicious; and by the way I forgot to pack them up yesterday so I will have to do it today. Tell Eddie I intended writing to him today, but I have been to church all the morning and am a little pressed for time, so will defer it. Please give Mama the collar as a little birthday reminder. I'm afraid I have not made it very nicely but it is my first attempt. How does Baby grow? Is she fat and well? . . . We had a letter from Jack this week written from Sacramento.[15] He was well and expected in a few days to go out on the railroad up in the mountains. Joe Raymond, the brother of the gentleman Beckie is going to marry, came out with Jack, and is now up here travelling with Genl. Ingalls.[16] I wonder how many more officers would like to come out on Inspection tours. The number that have passed by the same route have become almost too many to count. It is very nice, no doubt, to travel over so much country and draw mileage.

We have received the Army Bill and we *are not* a Major. Well Majors and Brigadiers are common; we'll be uncommon as a Captain, and would not care a bit if they had not cut thirty-six dollars per month off our pay . . . . Isn't it most time to have some cooler weather? I shall be delighted to reach the sea breezes although it always gives me a headache, even to walk near its influence, but I hope to become accustomed to it. We will see all the ocean steamers come in.   *Julie*

ON THE COAST

Astoria and Fort Stevens

SEPTEMBER 1866-APRIL 1867

ASTORIA, OREGON,
September 21st, 1866.

Dear little Brother   Last Monday night we arrived here, and expect we will leave tomorrow for Fort Stevens. The officer who is living in the house that we are to occupy will move out today. He is ordered up the river.

This is a queer town built on the slope of a steep hill, on the site of old Fort George.[1] Our post-office is here, and the ocean steamers stop at this pier once a week. We have a tiny mail sloop which plies between Astoria and Stevens and as it is the only vehicle by which we can leave our post we will feel as if we were living on an island.[2] I never saw such large trees as grow here; I hid behind the trunk of one this morning, and although I had my arms outspread, I could not be seen from the other side. These are charming people here and I am enjoying this week of waiting very much. On the opposite side of the bay is a very high hill covered with ferns which are so tall that a man on horseback can ride through them without being seen, except at intervals.

When we left Vancouver with the last of our baggage, brother Jim's little black horse got frightened at crossing the plank to get on the boat and fell off into the river. She swam down a long way and we were afraid she would drown, but three men went out in a small boat and drove her on shore on a narrow ledge that she could not get off and held her while the steamboat ran down to her and got her on board. She with all our furniture has gone down to the Fort. It is very cold here, we have fires and wear shawls around us in the house.

Tell Mama and Papa that perhaps they will receive their future letters irregularly for the steamboat only takes the mail twice a week, and letters can only come up here from the Fort in a sailboat depending on the winds and waves. We have a very nice schooner belonging to the Fort. Brother Jim had to go down yesterday to receipt to Lieut. Barrowes for the Quartermasters property and I am expecting him up this evening.[3] He wanted to get our bedroom furniture unboxed and put up before I got down there.

Tell Mama we had our photographs taken day before yesterday, I will send them home as soon as we receive them. The operator got me to sit for a picture to hang in the gallery, what do you think of that? . . .

Write whenever you can to your loving sister,   *Junie*

FORT STEVENS, VIA ASTORIA, OREGON,
Sunday, September 30th, 1866.

My dear Parents   A week ago we arrived at the above named place, our new home till we are whisked off somewhere else. I wish you could have seen the manner of our arrival; I laughed until I could scarcely stand. The steamboat brought us to the point where our pier is to be built, but where its substitute is now a rowboat. However, this small boat was absent, and as the steamboat could not get near land, it being high tide, we began to fear that we would have to swim ashore. A mule, with a dump cart behind him, was driven to our rescue. We climbed into the cart, and with the water up to the top of the wheels and the poor mule nearly submerged we drove up the beach until we reached dry sand. Did any dignified officer, with his bride, ever make such an entry to his station before!

I think it is destined to be a very pretty place and that at no distant period judging from the strides that have been made during the past twelve months. One year ago where our houses now stand was a primeval forest of spruce and hemlock; and a few miserable huts on a sand stretch still stand to show where the officers lived last winter. Tree after tree has bowed before the woodman's sturdy stroke and mingled their ashes with the native soil as the resistless fire swept them down. Mignonette and cabbage, corn stalks and roses mingle in delightful confusion where erst the tall fern and wild clover reigned supreme. Residences, stables, warehouses and wharf are rising like mushrooms and the sea gull and wild goose have not had time to forsake their former haunts. Between us and the beach lies the Fort proper, a beautiful little earthwork bristling with guns and neat as a model, the gravel walks as precise and the grass as green as if they knew they were expected to do their best. The ditch with its smoothly cut borders is filled with water and the iron entrance gates as black and forbidding as if their clanging hinges closed on a prison.

Standing on the parapet and looking off to sea the misty outlines of Cape Disappointment loom between and the white surf dashes in breakers at its feet. The never ceasing pulsation of old Neptune's heart comes throbbing on the still air, now in low wailing murmurs, anon in the stillness of the night in loud angry roarings to show his power. Then the sea fog comes rolling in thick, heavy and murky, the sun and sky seem suddenly blotted out of existence; it sometimes advances to our very doorsteps though somewhat cautiously, and generally stops at the fence. Just now the sun has burned it off and it is rolling away like a leaden curtain, and my little garden looks fresh and bright with the patch of blue sky above it. The charm of Oregon clings lovingly to its old domain, I mean its army of fleas, those omnipresent never-to-be-caught little vampires whose name is Legion. I am becoming expert for I caught four today, but six jumped away. How they do bite!

We are nearly "fixed" in our new domicile. I like the house very much and will like it more when the extension gets a coat of whitewash. I have a cunning little garden laid out by Lieut. Borrowe who lived here before us. It has a good many flowers still in bloom and a center mound covered with mignonette.

I am settling down here as if we had no expectation of leaving for ten years, in hopes that a contrary rule will then send us home. It is real heathendom. The only church (Presbyterian) is seven miles and a half distant, and the roads on the beach can only be travelled at low tide. Mrs. Kelly came down with me and as she is a Catholic misses her church very much. I am glad that you have a nice girl for a cook as Annie wrote me. I hope she is still with you . . . .

Much as I want to see you all I would not like you to come out here. There was 7 1/2 feet of rain fell here between last Fall and July, and the dew and mists water the flowers every night. There is not much chance to go outdoors. Tell Annie every useless piece of silk or velvet she can get that will cut the enclosed pattern please to send me in her letters. Mrs. Babbitt has just finished a silk quilt for her bed, it is a perfect beauty; Mrs. Weeks is just beginning one and I am ambitious of having one too, but have so few scraps on hand to begin with . . . . Jim sends love to you all as also does your Loving daughter   *Julie*

For Annie,   DELICATE CAKE. 1 cup white sugar and half cup butter beaten to a perfect cream; stir in gradually the beaten whites of four eggs, lemon, 1 cup of sifted flour with a small teaspoonful of yeast powder. It is nice and can be made when you have used the yolks of the eggs, for other things, and if your flour is very good it does not need the yeast powder.

October 1st . . . . For two days we have been on foraging expeditions with very little result. We got very little as the prices are so high, and our greenbacks are now down to sixty-five cents. As a slight offset, we get our meat, the few times that there is any, from the Commissary at six and a quarter cents a pound. We are mighty glad to get it, and it adds to the interest that we have to guess what it is. We are told that it is always beef, but such shapes and such bones, I never saw before. Nothing like a steak or a roast exists, but the animal appears to be all cut into even chunks. Now of course, this is very impartial and therefore has its good side.

We came home in a cold drizzling rain, only to find the house dense with smoke from the chimneys which won't "draw" at all. I think they were built inverted, as they always draw downward so we do without fires whenever possible. We brought home a large variety of carnation plants, which we bought from a farmer, who is also going to sell us strawberry plants as soon as our ground is ready.

FORT STEVENS, OREGON,
October 12th, 1866.

My own dear Mama   I have just received your nice letter dated August 26th . . . . Our rainy season has set in, and one would think by the way the water comes down in sheets that the clouds would soon be exhausted but the fashion of the land is a continuance of just such weather 'till the sun comes out again *next May*. They don't know how to build chimneys either and they smoke so badly that I feel like a mummy this morning. Today is the first anniversary of our wedding day and more antipodal in externals it could not be, but the thoughts and feelings of a year ago, strengthened by time, makes it very easy, to take one little step back into that sunny October day in Washington.

We get along pretty well here. It is somewhat isolated and all our meat and produce has to be brought from quite a distance and at intervals. The farmers are a grasping, sordid, tight-fisted set who will not sell you anything unless you pay exorbitant prices, but . . . we get meat (*when we get it*) for six cents per lb. while at the Dalles we always paid twenty-five (coin). Our time is divided into feasts and fasts and Jim thinks Friday comes very often. For when meat won't hold out we fall back on dried salmon and mackerel . . . . We are trying hard to find a cow. These Clatsop plains for miles around us are famous for their dairy products, but the very lowest prices for which they will sell is 45 to 50 cts. lb. for butter, and 10 cts. quart for milk (coin) and they won't send it to you then, and very rarely can [one] get anyone here at the post who has time to go miles away for such things. When we get our cow, we will be set up. I am very sure you will think the enclosed scrap of my new dress is pretty. We need bright color out in this grey country   *Julie* . . . .

My own dear Papa   I have received this week your very welcome letter of Sept. 11th which arrived several days before Annie's of the same date. It is the first one I have had from you for a long time so I thought you must be very busy . . . .

Thank you for your interest in my husband's Brevets; they do not increase his rank however, so the accumulation of honor does not rest heavily on his head. I will have to scold a little bit if you call him Captain so formally. If you can't screw your mouth to say Jim as I do, please call him James as do all the rest of his family. He belongs to you just as much as I do, and wouldn't you laugh to call me Mrs. Gilliss. Wait till we get home and see what a model couple of children we are . . . . I am in constant though I'm afraid very frail hope of receiving orders to the East. Every mail without them seems to strengthen my belief that they will come next time. So we hope from week to week . . . . Lovingly,   *Julie*

Give Eddie the stamp.

Many, many thanks my dear parents for my darling little sister's picture which safely arrived yesterday. I was becoming a little uneasy for fear that it would be lost. What an intelligent, splendid looking baby she is. She looks two years old instead of one. I am much obliged to Mr. McMurtrie for saying she looked like me but I am convinced he knew he did not mean a word of it. Why her great black eyes would make two or three pairs of my little grey peepers. I suppose he thought as I was so far away from home it would please you to have him say so. Apropos of the gentleman I have seen those little Savoy Cabbages he spoke of. It was not all a yarn, though not all strictly true. They do not grow singly as he represented, but their first appearance is like a cabbage head or a cauliflower, but strip off the two or three large leaves which envelope the whole and you find the size of a tea-cup growing thickly like buds all over the stalk. I *believe* when they are cut off singly and the stalk remains that in course of time new ones will grow on it, but I am not *sure* of this part of it . . . .

He [Jim] seems well and insists that he is perfectly, but he is getting thin as a rail. I believe I told you that Mrs. Kelly came down here with us. She is perfectly disgusted with the incessant rain (it has rained *twenty-one days* since October 1st) but says she is glad to get away from the Dalles for awhile as she is tired of hearing the constant gossip and tattle there in regard to her husband's desertion. The word "delicacy" is not in Oregon vocabularies, and people thinking themselves ladies, do not hesitate to ask all the questions which their natural Yankeeism increased by Western residence, can prompt . . . .

I almost forgot to tell you the most important news of the day. We have got a *cow*. Don't I feel proud like a real country girl. But cows have to be kept shut up in stables here so you could just as well have them in a city. The country is full of wild cattle and cows run away and sometimes join these bands. We had a present of an immense winter squash from one of the farmers who furnishes the Post with beef. Mrs. Kelly's little girl is very much taken with Baby's picture, she wants to look at it almost as much as I do. She says "dats a nice little chile, what a pitty jess and yibbons." I think that's the vernacular as near as I can render it . . . . Mrs. Steele has gone to Portland on a visit and left her nice sewing machine with me. I am having a splendid time doing all my sewing, it almost takes my breath to think of the railroad speed that has characterized this week. I can manage it very easily. It is a perfect Wheeler & Wilson, it only cost *one hundred* and *seventy five* dollars . . . . Your affectionate daughter,   *Julie* . . . .

FORT STEVENS,
November 11th, 1866.

My dear Parents   . . . . It has been raining all the week, my pretty little garden is blackened and water soaked, and the flowers and leaves have rotted and fallen off from so much moisture. Jim brought me a nice flower box yesterday, I am going to take up a few plants that have the most life left, and bring these in the house . . . .

Our friend Captain Weeks has been ordered to Arizona. I am so sorry for he will have to leave his wife & children in San Francisco; and Colonel Babbitt has been ordered from the latter place to Fort Vancouver so that Mrs. Weeks will not even have her mother with her in San F. I never saw such an unstable department as this; they seem to do no work but changing officers. I think it's a pity they can't draw mileage, they have so much travelling to do. Jim is at present commanding this Post; Capt. Janes is absent with recruits and had been for two or three weeks.[4] Mrs. Steele is in Portland where she will be joined tomorrow by her husband, so Jim and I will be sole monarchs of Fort Stevens for awhile. He certainly can't complain of monotonous employment; added to his duties of Quartermaster, Commissary, Fort builder & ordinance officer now he commands a company, makes out muster roll, and is sort of "Jack of all trades." Besides being wood chopper, for he and Dr. Steele have been trying to clear a road through the woods, which is quite dense, in to our back door. They find cutting down trees and grubbing up stumps pretty hard work for inexperienced hands. As we get mail only twice a week we can't keep much reading matter on hand, so we have to fill up our evenings with chess . . . . Mrs. Steele is a first class chess player so I have not had the courage to try it with her, but with the others I can win about half the games we play. I go into my little spare room (which I think very pretty) every day and wish that we were in some sunshiny region and you were in my little room . . . .

We have a new mail route from Salt Lake to the Dalles which will take almost a week off the usual time in summer, but I doubt its efficacy in winter. If it had been established a year ago we would have reaped the benefit during our sojourn there . . . . It is Sunday but like Robinson Crusoe we shall have to cut a long notch in a stick to find out when it comes. The only distinguishing feature we have is the cessation of the workmen's hammers . . . . We have just had an arrival of six more guns for our Fort, so Jim had the long tedious task before him of mounting the monsters. I am perfectly surprised at the immense battery they are taking the trouble and expense to mount on a perishable earthwork; the guns are worthy of an Ehrin-vertstein.[5] The lumber has all arrived for our fences and we will feel much more civilized when we get nice white palings around our houses. We are very cosy and comfortable inside. The only eyesore is the parlor mantle which Jim is going to have repainted. It is a grey color speckled all over with black and white supposed to be in imitation of granite, but looks in fact as if it was suffering with an aggravated attack of smallpox. I hope this letter will find you all well and happy as it leaves us . . . . Your loving daughter   *Julie*

FORT STEVENS,
November 18th, 1866.

My dear Sister   Two mails have arrived since my last letter was written, but they brought nothing for me, from anyone at home. Is anyone sick? for Mrs. Gilliss and the girls have not written for the same length of time. I have hoped on from day to day that it was the remissness of the mail but yesterday a packet of Washington papers from Papa arrived and still no letters . . . .

It has been raining and storming during the past week, and I think the name of this place should be changed from "Point Adams" to "Stormy Point," the latter being much more significant. Dr. Steele with his wife, daughter and wife's sister arrived yesterday from Portland so we have a house-full. Captain Janes also returned so Capt. Gilliss no longer commands the Post. If the former gentleman was only as pleasant as he is disagreeable we should like it much better. He has not yet attempted to interfere with Jim, but he is of a quarrelsome turn of mind and generally contrives to make this place too warm to contain other officers who are here. He was reproved privately by General Steele for his conduct, but I do not know that that will be the end of it for General Halleck has been informed of his behavior. But I never saw such a mixed up Department; they don't seem to know what to do. All the summer they have been busy breaking up and abandoning posts, selling off at sacrifices, and transporting property at great costs and now they are refitting the same places; I should not wonder if we brought up at the Dalles or Walla Walla yet.

I suppose this will reach you about Christmas, so I hope you will all be merry and happy. I wish that I was with you to dress the Christmas tree. I've got such nice little pictures & ribbons etc. to make cornucopias . . . . You know how much trouble we had to get the right kind when we trimmed the last tree when I was home. Well, I hope next Christmas will find us more united; with us Christmas will be quite solitary, for our community is very small and we are so cut off from the rest of the world, that we have hard work to get materials for a plum-pudding. I suppose our turkey will be the everlasting piece of beef as that is the only thing we can get. We did hope to have a little eggnog but as far as I can find out, there is not an egg within twenty miles. Well, we'll have "praties" anyhow . . . .

Tell Papa he must have a country rice-pudding, so I will tell you how to make it. I think it far superior to the usual kind. Wash a cup of rice and put it in your pan, sweeten a quart of milk and pour in on it with a small lump of butter and lemon. Bake it for fully *two hours* in a steady oven. *Do not boil* the rice first. Jim can't bear rice. He says it is very good of its kind, but a very poor kind . . . . I am working on [a] hanging bracket, and Jim has cut me a nice shelf to hang it from. He is quite a nice hand at cutting out shelves. He sends love to all and so do I, with plenty of kisses too and will close with a "Merry Christmas and a Happy New Year." Your loving sister   *Julie*. . . .

FORT STEVENS,
December 2nd, 1866.

Dear Nannette   I am very sorry that you have been afflicted with toothache; I hope it is entirely recovered without the loss of your tooth . . . . We have had a constant storm of rain, wind, thunder and lightning for a week past; the rain of course still continues. They have had an earthquake at the Dalles so we escaped just in time; I hope it won't visit us next . . . . Dr. Steele and family are still staying with us; their house is not yet finished . . . .

I have been making some little mats out of white darning cotton which are very pretty but I will call upon you to do a little knitting for me which I cannot do myself. When you have nothing else to do, if that time ever comes, please make me a *pair* of *little socks* like those you made for kitty puss. I shall be very much obliged. You promised to make me any "little articles" that I might need. How do you like the prospect of being an auntie? Tell Mama I have learned to do hem stitching at the tops of hems and tucks. I am becoming quite learned you see. It looks quite pretty. The hem stitching I mean, not the learning. Please ask Mama to cut in tissue paper the pattern (natural size) of an infant's linen shirt. I can't get the idea of the sleeves at all. I have nothing to judge of size by either.   *Junie*

PORTLAND, OREGON,
December 9th, 1866.

My dear Parents   Here we are in Portland; arrived last night, one year to the very day since we first stepped ashore in the same place. We will stay probably about a week or ten days. The storm that has been prevailing so long has broken away and the past two days have been lovely and as it is somewhat cold I hope it will remain clear. I never saw anything so beautiful as the mountain peaks yesterday. Just before sunset we reached a point from which we saw Hood, St. Helens, Rainier and one other which I do not know whether it was Jefferson or Adams. They were all covered with a new fall of snow and looked as smooth as if [not] even a stone disturbed the crest. The long range of connecting hills were veiled in that rich purple haze peculiar to mountain scenery, and the snow peaks were a brilliant rose color deepening to violet in the shadows, but almost instantly with the setting of the sun they changed to an icy steel blue. The atmosphere was so remarkably clear that it did not seem a long walk to reach them.

We had a race with the ocean steamship *Montana* on her way up from San Francisco. She left Astoria about twelve hours before we did, but owing to some delay I suppose, we overtook her and soon ran ahead. She kept in sight of us but that was all she could do. We had to stop at all the way stations and twice to take in wood while she ran steadily on and passed us. All the passengers on both boats were interested and collected on the decks waving handkerchiefs and hats. But her triumph was short lived. In about fifteen minutes we came up with her and although she turned and shot across our bows we gracefully glided ahead of her and kept our place. She ran up sails in addition to all the steam she could carry but we reached Portland wharf nearly an hour before she did.

It is Sunday and nearly church time and I mighty prize the privilege of attending church of which I have been deprived for so many long months. We saw Col. & Mrs. Babbitt last night; they have just arrived from San Francisco .... The roads here are in such bad condition that I do not think it advisable to send any more letters "overland," especially as an arrangement has just been completed to bring them from San Francisco to Portland by steamer in three days, which otherwise came from there overland in twelve days to Portland, shortening the time fully a week. The mail goes out in the morning and I will close with much love from us both.   *Julie*

ARRIGONI'S HOTEL, PORTLAND,
December 16, 1866.

My dear Nancy   Behold us returned to the city of Hebrews and mud. We have had a very pleasant little visit to Fort Vancouver, Jim has received his last two months' pay (we don't have visits from paymasters down at Ft. Stevens very often) and we will take passage at six o'clock tomorrow morning for our seaside residence. Our trunk is rather full, with the addition of boots, shoes, bundles etc., that we were deputed to buy for our unfortunate friends down the river who didn't come up with us. I have to sit on top of it to get it locked. General Steele insisted upon us spending a couple of days with him and while there he had a very delightful "hop." He is a bachelor and says he feels lost in his large quarters. We came over here on last evening's boat, as also did Mrs. [Captain] Weeks and the children. Her husband's orders have been changed and he will remain in San Francisco instead of going to Arizona as intended, so his wife will join him. I haven't a single bit of news to tell you; we just jog on day after day, and I expect if it were not for the trouble of dressing every morning we would not know whether we were one year or one long day here. Even the raindrops fall in the same spot so long that they fall asleep and still keep it up from habit. Mrs. Weeks has been here with me for the last hour or two; she is so pleasant. It is getting too dark to write any more . . . . I hope you all will have a "Merry Christmas." Your affectionate sister　　*Julie*

> FORT STEVENS, OREGON,
> December 27th, 1866.

　　My dear Nannie　　We left Portland on Monday morning of last week after enjoying a very pleasant visit and having a delightful little party at Genl. Steele's. We reached Astoria the evening of the same day but owing to the stormy weather we were not able to reach this place till Wednesday. We seized the first lull of the elements to come home and it has been storming ever since. The steamer has just come in, overdue, and I am told her wheelhouses are considerably broken but they did not look so from my window. I found two letters from you and expect more from this steamer so I must get my mail ready to go out on her . . . . I don't remember feeling sad since I have been married except when I am worried about some of you at home being sick. I think we are a very cheerful, happy couple, and I generally feel as merry as a cricket. You must keep up your spirits and think as I do that every day shortens the period of our exile.

　　We had a very quiet Christmas, marked however by the inevitable plum pudding. Stormed all day of course. Dr. Steele has gone to San Francisco, and expecting to be back by the 25th, he was deputed to buy all the Christmas presents. Jim has just gone up to Astoria in the sloop to see whether he has arrived in this morning's steamer. So Christmas is yet to come to us. Fannie Steele hung up her stocking and got 14 presents. I had a mince pie and a loaf of nice cake and a chicken sent me by my wash-woman. Give the stamps to Eddie . . . .

　　Tell Mama dear I am so sorry she has the rheumatism. Mine has all gone long ago. All I did was to rub well with volatile liniment and when it seemed to be in any particular joint to paint that joint with Iodyne every morning until the skin dried and peeled off. But the only way to permanently get rid of rheumatism is to *persevere* in the use of your remedies. I used the liniment morning & night for several months until I thought I would turn to grease. Dr. Steele's house is finished; they talk of moving in, in a week or two. I forgot to say we had some eggnog. Jim got some eggs in Portland. You have not the faintest idea what a splendid brother you have . . . .

I stopped and ate some lunch, now I will proceed. You don't know, yes you do too, what enormous eaters we are; well, we are still of the same "corn-crib pusswasion" only more so. I am really ashamed to go out anywhere to dine; I never get enough to eat. Dr. Steele has arrived and brought me a beautiful soup ladle ordered by my dear husband; it was just what I had been wishing for. It was all a mistake about the *Oriflamme* having her wheelhouse broken, she is all right. Lovingly,   *Julie*

FORT STEVENS, OREGON,
January 6th, 1867.

My dear Parents   I have just come in from a pleasant walk and must write my weekly letter. Yesterday and today we have the loveliest weather that I suppose Fort Stevens ever experienced. At least nobody who is here now remembers it. The mild air, the blue sky and bright sunshine seem almost like a glimpse of the East. The river and bay look as calm and blue as the sky and several vessels ran in this morning, thankful no doubt for such a propitious moment to cross the terror inspiring waters of Columbia bar. Cape Disappointment looks as if it had crept several miles nearer than usual and the misty blue hills beyond stand out today bold and clear against the sky. I can see each individual tree on Scarborough Head, a point said to be seven miles across the river.[6] This atmosphere is very unusual, we are generally glad to see outlines of the opposite shores. We had a heavy white frost this morning almost like snow; I suppose that had something to do with it. Yesterday I picked a pink daisy and several heartsease in my garden that had just come out, but I suppose now the frost has nipped all future buds for this winter.

Another Steamer came in this morning. I hope we will get some letters by her. The date of our last home news is in November. I have not had a letter to answer for a long time and all my original remarks are exhausted . . . .

FORT STEVENS,
January 13th, 1867.

My dear Parents   Another steamer is in but not one letter. Four packages of Washington papers arrived the steamer before this one but that was all. I am trying to be very patient now till the *Oriflamme* arrives, which I expect will be some time this week, and then I hope we will have a whole budget which have been collecting ever since the last one which was a month ago, and consequently written the middle of November. In one of the papers which Papa sent me [I] see an account of Beckie's marriage which is all the news we have had of it.[7] . . .

The sun is shining a little now, and the ground is whitened with a faint attempt at snow and hail, but the latter makes as much snow as the former, however it looks white and cheerful and I like it much better than the rain. We succeed in getting a little walk almost every day running out between the squalls. It has only been cold enough down here to freeze once. I suppose salt air makes the temperature equal . . . .

Speaking of the Drama, Fort Stevens has its share also, though the nature of the entertainment was somewhat promiscuous as [Petroleum V.] Nasby would say.[8] It took place in the soldiers' quarters on pay day of course. The man called himself "Herman the Wizard," but I believe negro jigs and songs made up part of the performance. The audience was select, composed of soldiers & workmen and graced by the fair proportions of the laundresses. Officers and ladies of course would not spoil it by their presence . . . . We amuse ourselves by reading when we can find materials. Tell Annie I have begun [James D.] Dana's *Geology* which I like very much, and I think she would find it equally interesting as she used to be fond of Physical Geography. I have a number of minerals and geological specimens which will make the accounts doubly entertaining. Captain Janes, who commands this post, sent me a splendid double white hyacinth and an iris savonia and ranunculus. I do not exactly know the two last, but I have planted them and will watch them carefully. They are house flowers.

How I wish I could see you all, and hear how disgusted you are with the progress of the political world at Washington. What do you think of the passage of the suffrage bill, and the novel chance of a sable mayor and city council, perhaps a Congressman, and who knows but what a noble specimen of the same dusky hue may sometime fill the Presidential Chair, and wield his sceptre of power, as he erst did the cart whip, or make speeches in the same stentorian tones that once cried "He-yah goes yer nice fresh oysters oh!". . . I see that Bierstadt has married and built himself a residence on the Hudson, with a studio eighty feet long. What does Mr. Leutze think of that? . . . Your loving daughter,   *Julie*

FORT STEVENS, OREGON,
January 20th 1867.

Mama darling your letter makes me so sorry that we are not home. The only time such repining feelings come over me [is] when I think of you all struggling through sickness when I am so well and strong [and] could be so much assistance. I was afraid someone was sick from the long silence. Your letter of December 2nd, which has just arrived, being the first one for more than a month. And now our Nannie must get sick. She must take a strengthening tonic and a long walk every day, rain or shine, and when I get home, like a firm physician I shall enforce my prescription so she better begin at once. There is nothing like outdoor exercise. To it I attribute my remarkably good health. Though we live on the stormiest point in the whole United States according to actual statistics, yet we manage to have a walk most every day, running out between the squalls. Since we have been here Jim has picked up again and now weighs 160 lbs. and I 128 lbs. I always feel like a streak of sunshine, so I never take the trouble to make a long face out the window at the raindrops. We are very comfortably fixed, so nicely in fact that I wish you could drop down on us unexpectedly, and see us just as we are.

It would do you good to see us, a pair of overgrown, frolicing children keeping house as lovingly as two kittens. Our parlor is nearly square with two front windows looking out on the verandah and one at the side into which Jim has fitted a nicely painted shelf and on it stand my flower pots. My hyacinth is coming up splendidly; two great thick, strong stems that look as if they could weather the outdoor air. They (the windows not the flowers) have yellow shades with crimson tassels, to make believe sunshine. Opposite is a large open fireplace piled with blazing logs. Diagonally across the front corner of the room is a crimson damask lounge with my sofa cushion showing off finely at its head. Between the windows is a little octagonal table with chessmen and books on it. Against one side wall stands the curled maple sideboard, the beauty and glory of our Dalles house, far too handsome a piece of furniture for the dining room where there really is no space for it. In the middle of the floor is our pretty marble top table with a lamp, books, my precious picture of Mama, Baby and Husband (I wish I had all the rest of you) and a little Chinese plate, full of visiting cards. The mantlepiece is flanked at either end by a pair of tall, old-fashioned brass candlesticks given to me by Colonel Coppinger, and my pretty little lava vases, with a cribbage box and a pile of geological specimens in the middle. Add to this half a dozen oak chairs and a large folding chair cushioned with flowered reps,[9] and you have our parlor, not forgetting the crimson ground Brussels carpet, and Papa's photographs of Public Buildings on the walls. The hall floor is painted in blocks of black and white to represent tiles, and Jim has a large pair of elk horns which he is going to fasten to the wall for a hat rack.[10]

Now please walk upstairs and I will show you our bedroom. It is over the parlor and the same size with a dressing-room opening into it. The floor is covered with a three ply carpet of green and orange; the shades at the windows are dark green with a twisted gilt band around the edge. A cottage set of veneered walnut (smaller pieces, all painted of course) makes up the room except the stove which I greatly deplore. I have become so attached to [an] open fireplace that I dislike stove heat, but the chimney is built up solid and it can't be helped. We have a ventilator over the room door, however, and we keep it always open. Our spare room is a little smaller with carpet like the parlor, yellow shades and flowered chintz hanging curtains. Bedstead and chairs stained like walnut, but no bureau; this deficiency is remedied by a splendid closet, and a crimson covered toilet table with a gilt framed glass hanging over it. In one corner is an hour glass table covered with white muslin and belted in at the middle by a red band. Now ain't we stylish? And just as happy as possible to be except when we think how you all at home are worried about us . . . .

I am afraid my letters may reach you very irregularly, for the mail matter has collected in immense quantities at many points on the road where I suppose it will stay until spring. The bad roads and inclement weather interferes greatly with overland travel, so that now I always mark letters for the steamer as that is the only hope for their punctual transition . . . .

[Jim] and Mr. Day & Mr. DeRussy went up the river yesterday on a deer hunt, but it rained in torrents of course and they came home without having seen any sign of venison.[11] We get elk meat and venison quite often from the farmers, but it is a miserable dry-as-a-stick apology for good roast beef. One consolation, it don't cost anything . . . . Your devoted daughter,   *Julie*

FORT STEVENS, OREGON,
January 25th, 1867.

Dear little Nannetticot   I cannot think of letting you get so thin. You must fatten up, eat plenty, walk plenty and drink *no coffee*. Dr. Steele says young people never should touch it, it ruins their complexions as well as makes them nervous and bilious. Tea is much better if not too strong. I drink nothing but milk and water though it is a sore deprivation to abstain from coffee. In my old copy-books, I had a sentence, "To be happy, you must be good." I change it a little and say "To be healthy you must be happy." Now I have vanity enough to believe that you fret a great deal because your good-for-nothing sister and brother are making a trip through this western country. It is always good and brave to look at a point from all sides, but my dear little sister, *never forget the bright side*. If you look for it, you will *always* find it, and soon the habit will teach you to find it *first*. I believe our prolonged separation is for some good and wise purpose, and in my daily prayers for a reunion with those at home, I never forget to add a supplication for patience to wait the will of Him who works all things together for our good . . . .

There; now I suppose you will say Junie has preached long enough in virtue of her seniority, and truly I feel so much younger than I ever did before that I begin to think I am the child to be lectured. Miss Stellwagen was twice as much a woman as Mrs. Gilliss is. The *dignity* that belonged to the former I am sadly afraid is of a mystical character now. I feel an intense desire to be mischievous all the time. I have to pinch Mrs. Gilliss sometimes to make her remember she is not a school-girl, but the august personage she is supposed to be.

I declare I forgot to grumble at the mails. Well, we have had no steamer for two or three weeks; no overland mails on account of the snows; the telegraph lines are all down from the same cause; and "we don't hear nothin from nobody." This is a "goak" as Artemus [Ward] would eloquently observe.[12] Dr. Steele and family have finally moved into their new house. I am very glad, for they are nicely fixed and so are we, and it's refreshing to feel your house is your own, and then we can go visiting now, which we could not do before . . . .

We are both very well. It still rains hard here, but the air is mild and three little trees near our house are full of birds that sing very often. You ought to see your lazy brother Jim stretched out full length on the lounge reading one of Cooper's novels. Your loving sister,   *Julie*

FORT STEVENS, OREGON,
February 3rd, 1867.

My dear Papa   . . . . The last Steamer treated me splendidly; in addition to your letter I had one from Annie, two from Mrs. Gilliss, one from Mrs. Beck Raymond, and a short one from Fannie, so I did not grumble a bit . . . .

I appreciate the kindness and love of you all which prompts the desire to send me pretty things but please do not do it. It will make me cry and I don't look handsome with red eyes. Besides we have got just as much luggage as we can carry in our tramps through the wilds . . . . We can't get anything here but potatoes and apples so if you want to send us something a few potato bags or an apple basket would be the most acceptable. Wait 'till we come East . . . . We are both in excellent health. Steamers have just gone up the river. Hurrah for some *more* letters. Jim sends love. He has just put up the Elk horns in the hall. They look quite ancestral.   *Julie*

FORT STEVENS, OREGON,
February 10th, 1867.

My dear [Annie]   We have been on quite a voyage since I last wrote. We were invited to tea over at Cape Disappointment, only across our Bay and in plain sight of our point. We embarked in our little sloop, "The Bluebell," quite early in the day, and in a short time were on the shore looking at our Fort from the other side. The Cape is a very high promontory and we had a steep climb to reach the lighthouse on the summit. At its feet the beach is washed by heavy breakers, and the surf dashes high and breaks in spray almost to the top. A life-saving station here always has plenty of work. The post, Fort Hancock, lies back of the point, and is very pretty but quite isolated. We had a charming afternoon, a lovely tea, and started home by the light of the moon, but alas! we had taken no thought of tides, and we were not halfway back, when the tide ebbed, and our little boat was turned around and around. The three sailors put up all the sails, but we were so close to the Bar that we were slowly going outward. The roar of the Bar was terrific, and we were surely drifting into it. The men shipped their long oars, and two men to each oar worked with all their strength all taking turns except myself, who sat a forlorn, sleepy heap flat on the deck. Hour after hour passed in the same place, and there we were with not a moment's letup of the hard rowing, until the turn of the tide which carried us back to our beach at three o'clock in the morning. We were *so* cold and hungry. Fortunately, Mrs. Kelly could see us all the time, so she had the house warm and lighted, the table set with bread and butter, cold meat and milk, and I assure you we did full justice to her thoughtfulness, before we remembered we were sleepy . . . .

I am very busy all the time, I do a great deal of sewing, my art of hemstitching comes in very prettily. Let me tell you young lady, what I said about Mrs. Weeks' knit shirts was *strictly true*. The rumor that you heard from Mrs. Gilliss, who got a letter from Beck, who heard from Fannie Raymond, whose brother had just come from Oregon (there; let me take a breath, I wonder if that is all right) was a premature news entirely. At the same time I had a letter from Clemmie Kip saying such a report was going the rounds of San Francisco. I can't trace it to any particular source; everybody heard it from somebody else and like the three black crows, I suspect the original was something very different. However it was "coming events casting shadows before." I can't deny it now and don't particularly want to. Won't it be fun to call Mama grandma . . . .

Tell Mama please not to send us any valuable presents. Our pay is about the same as Papa's and by mathematical calculation the same amount will divide more largely between two people, than five or six, so we are much better able to get things than you are and we will do so when it is convenient to carry them about.[13] I don't want nice things till we get home. That is, any more than we have now, that we would not want to dispose of in packing and risking the loss in travelling . . . . I have learned the art of making old silk and ribbon "look amaist aweel's the new." Take a lump of *Sal Soda*, dissolve it in about a *large pint* of cold water. Wash your silk or ribbon by rubbing it *smoothly*, while wet iron quickly. It starts some colors so you better try scraps first. The same solution makes combs and brushes look beautifully new. We are both perfectly well; I am remarkably so. Jim sends many thanks for Dec. papers just received. Your affectionate sister,   *Julie*

Jim unites in love to you all.

FORT STEVENS, OREGON,
February 24th, 1867.

You dear delightful papa for writing me such a nice long letter with all its pretty scraps of home news . . . . Many thanks for your kind New Year's wishes for us both. I assure you that they were warmly reciprocated. We had eggnog and plum pudding on that festive occasion, which I am forced to confess was the only way of making it different from other days, except my birthday . . . .

While I think of it I will repeat my oft reiterated wish that you should send all letters by *"Steamer."* The overland route is now irregular and altogether too much mail matter that way falls into the hands of the Snakes,[14] much to the edification of their Indian wisdom and cunning I've no doubt. How very pretty the opening of that new street must be. I think with all its natural advantages that Washington could be made a beautiful city, if it could only be purged from the effects of political warfare . . . .

It is perfectly dismal outdoors. We have had a pretty heavy snowstorm, it is raining on top of it and dirty piles of snow alternate with slushy black pools. All the buildings are perfectly black with water soak, and the sky is scowling above the plenitude of its tears. However it's nothing remarkable, except the snow. Jim, Mr. DeRussy and Mr. Day made a sledge out of an old box, hitched in two mules, with one string of bells, but their ride was short, the runners cut through into the mud and made the pulling too hard, and the riding too, I imagine.   *Julie S. Gilliss*

FORT STEVENS, OREGON,
March 3rd, 1867.

My dear Mama   Having just eaten an apple, two ginger cakes and some English Walnuts you may tell Annie that for once I have lost my appetite. It's sure to return by dinner time though. Yesterday I received your letter of Jany 18th, and though the Steamer which is to take this has not yet arrived I thought I would write a few lines in answer to yours while it was fresh in my memory. I am very, very much obliged for the little shirts and socks but they did not come with the letter; however I expect them tomorrow. I had already made three little shirts; I hemstitched the sleeves and flap pieces and trimmed them with narrow edging, one valenciennes, and two with thread. They look real cunning I think. Having so much leisure I have learned to sew quite nicely I flatter myself. I guess you will be glad to learn this. I have finished all my little wardrobe but two dresses, and I am perfectly delighted with my success, as I did it all by myself. It has been such a pleasure to me to do it that I really pity Rose who will have everything on hand ready made when she needs them. Indeed I don't think she is to be envied anyhow; she has everything she can think of and like Alexander will have to set down and cry because there is nothing else to get. I think half the pleasure is in anticipation of getting things one at a time and you enjoy them so much more afterward. I have made half dozen flannel skirts, same number white ones, three night slips and eight day slips and dresses (some of them real pretty), six flannel bands, a couple dozen *etceteras*. I bound a square of flannel with white ribbon for a shawl but I intend to work one with white silk. I have a cunning little brush, sweet soap and powder. There! won't I do for the first attempt without any assistance?

I have been just as happy through it all as possible to be. I have been and am still perfectly well, was not even nauseated for more than a week. The only thing I am heartily ashamed of was fainting once. We went to church in Portland and as it was a cold day the building was shut closely with hot fires; it made me feel a little sick so we went out, & I fainted. It was all over in a few minutes and I was perfectly well again, but I am so ashamed of it, that I am very glad I never did it a second time.

I expect to be sick some time in the middle or last of May. Dr. Steele lives about a hundred feet from us and we see him every day. I expect that's the reason I'm so well. The Dr. is so handy to get at, that I don't get sick for spite. There are plenty of physicians and nurses in Oregon, in fact they are the most profitable profession. I never saw such a *productive* state in my life; twins are every day occurences, and three and four at a birth are quite coming into fashion—please destroy this letter quickly, that looks dreadful in black and white. I have learned a good many little medical secrets by living with Drs. always at our elbow.

Yesterday was bright and clear and I took a nice walk and Jim gave me a very pleasant ride afterwards. I am out of doors whenever the weather permits and the Doctor says that is one reason I keep so well. He thinks it will do me good to get a little weaker, just enough to feel lazy all the time. I am more energetic than usual .... Did I tell you that one beautiful little shirt had arrived in Annie's letter? I have a new flower on my window sill; Capt. Janes sent me a fuchsia; it is not in bloom yet so I don't know whether it is purple or white . . . .

March 4th. The mail has just arrived bringing me a letter from Mrs. Gilliss and one from Rose. The little shirts have not come.

March 6th. A steamer has arrived; Jim has gone up to Astoria to see if she brought any mail. What a water rat he is, he takes to it as naturally as a fish. Jim has just returned from town with a letter from Papa and one from Annie and the package of the little shirts and socks. They are lovely and I am just as proud of them as I can be. Tell saucy Nan she need not make the socks of extra size for my feet are getting quite small. I only wear three's & a half. Isn't it funny, the shirts I've made are exactly like the one of Rose's. One dress I've finished I think quite pretty; it is fine jaconet with a deep clump of tucks above the hem, and Cluny lace about 1 1/2 inches wide all round the bottom. The waist has a front piece of alternate rows of Cluny insertion and little tucks, with lace belt and on sleeves. That's the prettiest one; then I have a cambric with embroidered waist and deep worked band round the skirt with five tucks above it. Another cambric has plain skirt, the waist made of worked insertion bands running up & down with puffs between; edge on neck & sleeves. A nansouk one is plain with only insertion belt and worked edge on neck & sleeves. One linen dress has the hem cut in vandyke points upwards, the waist plaited and trimmed with only little worked points. Then I have brilliante and plaid muslin made with three and four strings round the waist & necks with only little trimmings on the sleeves.[15] One flannel skirt I braided [in a] very pretty pattern but only scalloped all the rest. I made everything by my own inventions. I did not have patterns for anything except the shirts . . . .

We are really having some sunshine but it is quite cold. I have not missed taking my daily walk for a week. It is wonderful that the weather has allowed it. I think Baby will look very pretty in salmon color. I saw one in Portland last summer braided with the same color only a darker shade; it looked very rich. I am sorry to hear that Fannie Gilliss has had a slight attack of diphtheria. Is it prevalent? It is quite an epidemic in San Francisco . . . Jim joins me in love to you all. We are both quite well, and think longingly and lovingly of you all at home. Your affectionate daughter   *Julie S. Gilliss* . . . .

The stormy weather has at last ceased. We have just come in from a charming ride up the beach towards Tillamook Head. Several of our friends have been lost off that treacherous point and I never want to go really to it. We found some jellyfish, plenty of clam shells and starfish, some kelp, nothing pretty. Our flotsam and jetsam are rather funny, for we are continually finding lumps of beeswax. This was a great puzzle to me, but when I asked an old resident of Astoria for a solution of the mystery, I was told that years ago a Chinese junk laden with beeswax, had been wrecked on the Columbia Bar, and the wax had been coming to land ever since.[16] I do not know if this statement is true, for I find I am often imposed upon.

Last week I had a royal find. The little Steamer *Fideliter* came in from the Sound, while the wind was blowing a gale, she came over the Bar on a breaker, which nearly stood her on end, and washed from her deck a number of boxes and barrels.[17] Several days later, I was on the beach, when a wooden box was carried in on a big wave and fell right at my feet. It was in good condition and full of fine apples. We notified somebody, a salvage company I think, but I was told to accept it as it was clearly mine. We certainly did enjoy those apples; we had so few luxuries, that we never even noticed if these tasted of the sea.   *Julie*

FORT STEVENS, OREGON,
March 10th, 1867.

Dear Nannie   Although there is no steamer in to take letters I think I may as well begin one so that it will be on hand when the mail is ready to go. You remember my old school fashion of having letters in progress for a week and adding bits day by day, so you will be at no loss to understand the discrepancy between the interior date and that on the outside at the time of mailing. I have just returned from a nice ride down on the beach with Jim. We saw a large reddish looking jellyfish and plenty of empty clam shells, but old ocean don't throw up many pretty playthings at this point.

The past week has been charming; the snow has entirely disappeared, the sky is clear and the sun bright and warm; the air is a little keen, but makes walking bracing and pleasant. I have been out every day and thoroughly enjoyed it. Tell Eddie that yesterday I found on the beach a little crab that the waves had dashed high and dry and the sun had dried and stiffened with all its little feet outspread. It is perfect and could lay on a silver half dollar. It is up on the shelf of the sideboard in a bird's nest with some speckled eggs. And now I must thank you for my beautiful socks. I think they will shrink in washing; if so I will pardon your impudent reflections on the pedal extremities of your brother & sister . . . .

Sunday, March 17th. A Steamer arrived last night bringing Papa's letter of Feb. 8th, with your little socks number two. I am very much obliged . . . . We had a pleasant visit yesterday from Col. Mendle and wife and Mrs. Welcker, daughter of Genl Adair, who are visiting their parents at Upper Astoria.[18] They spent the day and went home on the evening tide. What would you think at home of going eight or nine miles on a schooner to make a call! It's nothing out here. People take a trip of one or two hundred miles to take dinner sometimes. At least that is *almost* true, for it is quite customary to go down to San Francisco and return on the same steamer just for the trip. It's a miserable old coast though; I don't believe it was ever intended that a white man should put his foot this side of the Rocky Mountains. It is a rough uncouth region and its principal charm consists in freedom from social restraint, on the basis that "when the cat's away the mice will play," or as Mr. DeRussy observed the other day, 'he enjoyed being out here because he could go in his shirt sleeves when he felt too lazy to put on a coat, for even at balls & parties that garment was not absolutely necessary,' and that is just so. Everybody thinks it's a fine place to wear out old clothes and save themselves the trouble of shaving their faces. People who come out here instead of bringing all their own refinement to bear on the moral tone of the country, immediately become rough in order to adapt themselves to what they find here, and this is so general that it is almost impossible to withstand its influence.

I have just eaten a hearty lunch of bread and cold ham and pickles, so my ideas are not very ethical. I feel altogether matter-of-fact and practical, and that reminds me that I lost my walk yesterday because we had company and today I had forgotten it 'till now, so I will say adieu, and take a stroll if this sharp wind don't bite too hard . . . . I remain yours affectionately & sisterly.   *Julie S. Gilliss* . . . .

FORT STEVENS, OGN.,
March 24th, 1867.

My dear Papa   Your kind letter of Feb. 8th arrived a week ago. That day we also had a "tough old goose," a wild one, but his heart was very nice, and I made the rest of him nicer by chopping it up with celery and making salad. He didn't pull our "tops out," and I am very sorry for yours, especially as my teeth are breaking so easily that they don't require any assistance. Just because we are more than a hundred miles away from a dentist. I am sincerely sorry that you had *a rainy day*; how dreadful it must have been. We have a few out here . . . .

Astoria *is* growing really though. It is now the oldest town on this coast . . . and has *its first church* nearly completed.[19] A tiny little wooden church that requires all the fairs, beggings and donations of the country around to erect. And this too at the greatest commercial spot above San Francisco. Tis true nature has something to do with it. Its little wooden houses are clustered at the base of the "everlasting hills," and half the town nearly is built on wharves out over the river. When they sell water lots there they don't mean those on the bank, but the right and privilege of building a wooden lot out over the water. In fact from the inaccessible, impassable nature of this country I don't believe it was ever intended to be civilized and belongs so legitimately to the red man and wild animals that a white man can scarcely get a firm footing.

I am so much interested in Congressional proceedings on the "Legislative, Judicial and Civil Bill," but I can't learn anything. Sometimes the wires are down and we don't get any telegraphic news and although I have watched the papers closely I have seen no action taken upon it. What has been done?[20] . . .

All the winter our cellar has been full of water up to next to the top step leading down there. The whole front yard was a pond that could have water dipped up with a pail. I saw a cart drive through when the hub of the wheel was under the moist element. We have had two weeks since March 1st of clear weather with *very few* showers and the surface has dried off but if you dig two feet down you find plenty. The post holes for the fences had to be bailed out . . . .

We are very much obliged for the constantly arriving papers. They are very interesting. It is scarcely worth while to send ones in return, they are all made up rehashes of those from the East. The sun has just peeped out so I will go take a walk and finish this afterward. There, I've come home again and made a nice pudding for dinner which I know my husband won't like. He's as anti-Chinese on the rice question as you are the other way. But my list of desserts soon runs out for lack of materials .... Your affectionate daughter, *Julie* ....

FORT STEVENS, OREGON,
April 7th, 1867.

My dear Mama   I have just received another package containing three shirts, two pairs of socks and a darling little sack which I suppose is Annie's work. They look so pretty and cunning, but I shall have to cry "quits" unless I am to furnish wardrobes for all destitute babies. Fannie Gilliss has sent me four pairs of socks, four knit shirts that look almost like Yak lace; and says she is knitting me some sacks. So I have *nine* prs. socks & *twelve* linen shirts and I won't know what to do with so many things. I have just finished embroidering a little flannel shawl with one corner gathered up into a hood like yours. Jim says Annie ought to be married, she makes little things so beautifully. But you will think me very foolish to talk of nothing else, but it's the truth. I open the bureau drawer several times a day to see how pretty they all look, though it is so full I can scarcely shut it again. I am still very well and go out every day, enjoying very much the Spring weather.

Jim is busy making a garden, sowing seeds etc. for amusement when not busy in the office. He took me [for] a ride down the beach on Thursday to see the soldiers and Indians "hauling a seine." We saw the seine arrive safely several times but no *fish* in it. They have caught salmon three or four times but no spectator has succeeded in seeing them. We are having very nice weather, the showers are only sufficiently numerous to keep grass and vegetation growing ....

We have living near us an old Indian named Toastern, who with his really pretty daughter often brings fish and berries for sale.[21] We were always glad to hear the musical call "Olallies" [berries], at our door, but we have now set out a large strawberry patch and planted so many currant bushes that we hope to supply our demand. The Indians bring us the Sal-lal and the Buffalo berries and we find in our woods the beautiful salmon colored raspberry which is larger and finer than any other of its kind.   *Julie*

FORT STEVENS, OGN.,
Palm Sunday, April 14th, 1867.

Dear Nan   The *Ajax* has arrived and I did not get any letters .... Well the *Oriflamme* is expected on Tuesday so I wait for her mail bags. I have nothing especial to communicate except "gardening." I guess Jim and I have got a garden mania. He gets along splendidly. He has put a nice green sod border all around his beds, and plants quite artistically. He has just set out one strawberry bed which looks beautiful, and is waiting for the rain to cease to set out another. I suspect we will have a real pretty place this summer. Above is a rough sketch of my flower garden in front of the house, the "mound" is banked around a clump of young spruce trees, which are full of robins. Whenever it gets dry enough again I will go outside the front gates and try to sketch something that will look like the place. We have had a month of lovely weather but it is now raining hard again. However I expect it will clear up soon, it can't possibly rain here *all* the time. Don't you congratulate us on the passage of the Army Pay bill? It gives us about $180 back pay ....

April 16th. Your letter of March 9th and Mama's of Feb. 27th have both just arrived this morning. They were brought in by the last Steamer, and although we have had *two* mails since, my letters have been laying in some Post office all this time .... I am determined my baby shall have nothing more solid than milk and water 'till it is six months old anyhow. I have been reading a good deal on the subject, and that is the sum and substance of medical advice. I think I have learned a great deal of theory and if we are both spared, hope to make practical application of the same. I am in excellent health, everyone remarks how well I look. Abandoning the use of coffee has been of wonderful benefit to me, and *very perceptable* to my complexion. Everybody says, "why! you must have been sick last Fall you were so yellow and sallow and now your skin looks whiter and clearer." But I'm awfully *freckled*, I suppose they wouldn't show before.

Jim is very well and *ugly*. He's grown a horrible beard on his chin that adds ten years to his appearance. I'm going to show him that last remark, that's the reason I wrote it. Another steamer is expected in today, and he has gone up to town, to try and catch her mail, otherwise it will not come down 'till next Friday. He says he is going to buy me a new hoop skirt, I wish I could peep in the store and see him. He's a first rate hand at shopping . . . . Jim thanks for the papers.   *Junie*

FORT STEVENS, OREGON,
Easter Sunday, April 21st.

My dear Mama   I was very glad to receive your letter of February 27th. I had been anxiously looking for it to learn how darling baby was getting. I was quite worried to find there was so little improvement in her, but fortunately Annie's letter of a later date arrived by the same mail saying she was better . . . . I hope by the time that you receive this, that I will be a proud and happy mother. Pray for me Mama darling, and for my husband. If God should see best to take me to Himself it will be a severe blow to him. He has been perfect devotion to me always. I do not feel afraid, I believe God will take care of me and I almost feel assured that He will spare me to train my little one. I pray earnestly that I may not make idols of my husband and child; I know that He is a kind and loving Father and will not take from us the objects of our earthly affection unless they come between our hearts and Him.

If I am taken, teach my baby to be a Christian, and love my husband doubly for his loss and for his love for me. I have been mercifully kept in excellent health, and preserved from all preliminary suffering which almost makes life a burden, and I hope it will have the effect of making my baby healthy and strong. How I long for its little form alive and well. My nurse is a very experienced one, but I feel as if no one however careful can think of all the comforts and necessities for a little stranger as a mother can. It seems strange that I should have thought of all the little things that I have done without experience or in fact any reminder but an innate feeling, a sort of instinct that such would be needed. I can more fully believe in the promise that "as our day is, so shall our strength be" when I find how quickly thoughts and feelings change to suit different circumstances, and although *now* I look forward with a slight dread mingled with the fluttering of hope and joy, yet I have no doubt that in the hour of my trial grace will be given me to bear it.

Oh! if you could be with me Mama. But I must not think of that, I ought rather to feel glad that you would not be near to see me suffer, for I believe it would be worse for you than for me. The month of May is expected to usher into the world a great many arrivals out here, that I have heard of. My favorite doctor in Portland, Dr. [Rodney] Glisan, says *every one* of his nurses is engaged for that month.[22]

April 26th. We are having very fine weather now and I hope it will continue. It is so pleasant to have sunshine . . . . I am enjoying a very pleasant little visit from my friend Mrs. Babbitt; we are just the same age and very excellent friends.

The Steamer is in but I received no letters so I must send this without having heard any further news from home. I am hoping today's mail may bring an overland letter. I received a week ago from Fannie a beautiful little knit sacque, white with rose color border. It looks lovely with Annie's blue one long side of it. I have lined and trimmed my baby basket with white muslin and blue quilled ribbon, with pin-cushion to match, and filled it with all necessary things. It looks quite pretty. Mrs. Babbitt says I must give you her love for she knows me so well that she hopes to know you also. She is sitting by my side embroidering a cluster of grapes and leaves in my baby's flannel shawl. The mail leaves very soon, so I must see about some lunch for Jim who is going over to Astoria on business. With hearts full of love from us both to you all I remain your devoted daughter   *Julie*

We are both very well.

FORT STEVENS, OREGON,
April 28th, 1867.

My dear Mama & Papa   The last mail brought us a nice lot of letters and newspapers, dated variously along the first part of March. One was from Annie to me and a brief note from Papa to Jim. The news contained in the letter relative to the Army bill we had already learned, and are delighted to see in one of the papers that Papa has had his salary raised to eighteen hundred, and the good fortune to get the extra three hundred beside. I don't know of anything that made me feel so glad, not even our own extra pay, though that is very nice too . . . . Mrs. Babbitt is going home tomorrow but I hope she will be able to come down again during the summer if I am well enough.

Junie has asked me to finish this letter for her but I did not find it until I had already written the letter enclosed with this [writing of James Gilliss, Julia's husband].

A WELCOME ADDITION

The Arrival of Baby Julia

MAY-JUNE 1867

ASTORIA, OREGON,
May 5th, 1867.

My Dear Mr. Stellwagen   Last Tuesday (Wednesday?) I sent you a telegram announcing Junie's confinement and birth of a daughter which I hope has reached you before this. I know how anxious you all are to know full particulars and also how she is. Since the advent of the little stranger both have done splendidly, and Junie is less sick than I could possibly have expected. The Doctor comes every day but says that no medicine is necessary as nature is doing everything to restore her to her health and strength again. We came up from Fort Stevens last Monday, not expecting the event until the early part of next week. On Tuesday morning Julia went out for a walk, but feeling an unusual weakness returned again in a few minutes.

In the evening I went for the Doctor as Mrs. Brown (an experienced nurse) at whose house we are boarding, told her that she would probably be sick that night or the next day.[1] Dr. Trunhard came about ten o'clock at which time Junie was suffering considerably. From twelve o'clock until half past five in the morning the pains increased, but since the birth of the baby which took place at that time she has had exceedingly little pain and no fever whatever. I am thankful that both are getting along so well and I trust that before long Junie will be up on her feet again. Our Nurse (Mrs. Raymond) was to have come up on Friday (yesterday) but as the event took place long before I expected, she was a few hours behindhand and arrived at nine o'clock, three or four hours after the baby was born.[2] Mrs. Brown however had done all that was to be done so that we were not without assistance.

As soon as Junie is able we will go back home again but in the meantime we are very comfortably situated here. I am so near the Post that I can go down in the morning and come back in the afternoon, so that I have ample opportunities to attend to my duties and be here at night too. As yet we have not attempted to say who the baby looks like and the only description that I can give of her is that she is of medium size, has large dark eyes and dark hair, is very fat and knows how to squall when she gets the cholic. I can't say that she is the best baby I ever saw as I have never been very observing of them. When I get better acquainted I will endeavor to tell you more about her.

I must write another letter tonight and as it is bedtime, everybody in the house having retired long ago I must finish. With much love to all from us both I am Yours Most Truly,   *James*

ASTORIA, OREGON,
May 11th, 1867.

My dear Mr. Stellwagen   I wrote by last Steamer about the new arrival in our family and how Junie and the baby were progressing. They are still doing equally as well as last week. Junie sat up yesterday for the first time and today was up also. It is ten days today since the baby was born during which time she has had no fever or bad symptoms whatever. The baby appears perfectly healthy if I except its having cholic occasionally. This I suppose is perfectly natural. We have almost concluded to call her Julia and you may therefore consider her mother's name will be hers.[3] We are anxious to get back to Fort Stevens again and will go as we can. Although very comfortable yet it will be far more pleasant to be at home. I go down every other day or whenever I imagine there is anything to be attended to but always return at night to this interesting village.

Our weather since the 1st of March has been magnificent. Scarcely a single day of bad weather during this time. As yet it has not been very warm but it never becomes uncomfortably hot. The northwest wind which blows every afternoon prevents much heat. I hope that I won't be disturbed this summer unless to go East, but shan't be surprised if I am moved on only a short notice.

Junie unites with me in sending a great deal of love to all. She is very proud of her baby and would be delighted to make an exhibition of her to her mother. O hope it won't be very long before we will have a chance.

It is quite late so I must close this hastily written letter. I hope Junie will be strong enough to write next week. I am Yours Affectionately, *James*

ASTORIA, OREGON,
May 18th, 1867.

My dear Mama & Papa   I am only permitted to write a very few lines to tell you that I am sitting up and to say how nicely baby and I are getting along. God has been very good to me. I have had very little suffering, and the presence of my husband during my sickness which I was afraid I could not have; and now our darling, fat, dumpling of a baby. I must not begin to say a word about her for I would not know where to stop and I have already written as much as I ought to. So I will leave the rest of this sheet for Jim to finish. With much love to all from your affectionate daughter,   *Julie* . . . .

My Dear Mr. Stellwagen   As Junie has written the above to tell you of her condition I will only add a few lines. Nothing of interest has transpired since I last wrote. Junie gains strength slowly and I hope will be able to go out of doors early next week.

I won't attempt to say anything about the baby, as that is out of my line of business and to tell the truth I don't know what to say. As long as she keeps fat and grows to be strong and healthy, I care but little about looks.

The Steamer for S.F. leaves tomorrow morning and will carry this letter. With much love to all I am Yours Most Truly,   *James*

ASTORIA,
May 25, 1867.

My dear Grand *Papa*   I have wished to write a nice long letter full of our *baby* of course, but my head has ached all day and by deferring until it was better, I find myself now on the dim edge of evening and the mail leaves about daylight tomorrow. We are very happy and proud of our little daughter as you may imagine, but she is still too young to be very interesting to strangers. She is the fattest little butterball, and grows every day. Her eyes are very large and dark blue; her mouth is very pretty but her nose prevents her being a handsome child. It is long and broad, and fat and flat and sizable in every way. I have hoped its growth will not keep pace with the rest of her body. Tell Nan she *has* got *long feet* but very narrow, but as a compensation everyone remarks the beauty of her hands. They are *very* small & her fingers almost pointed with the most beautiful shaped nails. That is certainly no inheritance from her mother. It seems just as natural to see her little brown head (with hair an inch long) nestled in my arms as if she had always been there. I thought at first it was so funny.

I have just received a letter from Mrs. Gilliss saying you and Eddie had been to see her. She paid Eddie quite a compliment; I expect he behaved very nicely. Give him a kiss for sister and his little *niece*. It is too dark for me to write more at present. Tell Mama we are getting along nicely; I will write to her soon. Baby is crying. Your loving daughter   *Julie*

Julie has forgotten to say that for the past three days she has been out walking a little each day.   *James*

FORT STEVENS, OGN.,
June 2nd, 1867.

My dear Mama   In spite of this atrocious pen I must seize this opportunity to write a few lines while the baby is asleep. I find my time is not my own, for little Miss Gilliss is constant and decided in her demands. So far we have been unable to get a nurse for her for the "helps" of this country are fond of society and cannot be persuaded to isolate themselves at Fort Stevens, though I have learned to think it a very pleasant place. It looks quite pretty now and I shall be glad if they do not remove us from it while we have to remain on this coast.

The above was written several hours ago; baby waked and filled my hands and arms (for I am writing with her in my lap now). I have so much to say and the mail leaves tomorrow morning so I will not be able to write much. I have just received a package with a worked waist and pink and white crochet sacque for which I am very much obliged; they are so pretty and useful . . . . Tell Annie I have just received a pretty knit sacque, scarlet & white from Rosalie Ferguson, so baby will be quite set up. She is so tiny that we will have to wait till she grows into them.

June 3rd. I had to give up yesterday for baby got the colic and wouldn't let me write. We came down home here last Friday from Astoria on the steamboat which plies between the latter place & Portland. I was very glad that the Captain would bring us and so avoid the sailing vessel of which I am very tired. We are quite well. I have become such a toper; I drink two glasses of Stout Porter a day. Baby is ugly, fat & very healthy except the colic which I hope she will outgrow as it makes her very restless. You must not be disappointed if you do not get so many letters from me now for I don't have the time to write that I did. I just seized this moment while Mrs. Steele holds the baby. I will try and write to Annie soon. I am sorry that she has a sore throat. Give Nannie the enclosed ribbon to wear with her new dress; I think the latter is very pretty indeed. Jim joins me in love to all. Kiss baby for me, Your affectionate daughter   *Julie*

FORT STEVENS, OGN.,
June 8th, 1867.

Dear Nannie   My baby is asleep and I will take advantage of the brief time to scribble a few lines. She is a miserable sleeper and has been since she was two weeks old; previous to that time she would sleep like a log for three or four hours, but now she is never free from colic and has that irritating baby-rash all over her body worse than ever. She is very nervous in consequence and jumps and twitches so that she can't sleep but a few minutes at a time. She is very restless and just as much like Mama's baby as two peas. She is so fat and healthy looking that the Dr. thinks she will outgrow these troubles in a few months. She is five weeks old, and cunning as she can be. They laugh at me for getting frightened about her so much, but I am so ignorant and inexperienced that I distrust myself probably more than I need to do. My nurse, Mrs. Raymond, lives only two or three miles from us; she remained with me constantly for a month and now comes here every other night and takes care of the baby so I can sleep soundly and more rapidly regain my strength. I am getting along quite nicely; go out walking every day and am getting strong again. I get a little tired holding baby for she *will* stay in my arms, and cries to be held all the time, but we have sent to Vancouver to make another attempt at getting a nurse. One of the laundresses here has lent me her baby's wagon to pull mine in. I rode it about this morning out in the garden till she fell asleep. They don't have those nice little gigs out in this country. I won't complain though, for I heartily wish you could all be here with us from the present time till fall.

The weather is charming; never warm enough for a white waist; in fact we are comfortable wearing poplins & alpacas. Everything looks so green & fresh, and the sea breeze makes one long to live outdoors. All our houses and fences have been whitewashed and a large old building which was the sutler's store converted into a church, where we have service and Sunday school. We are dependent on any minister that comes along, so the service is at intervals and of various denominations, principally Presbyterian & Congregational. I think it quite pleasant enough now to compensate for the past dull winter and more fully endorse the poet's maxim, "beware of desperate steps. The darkest day live[d] till tomorrow will have passed away." Of course I have a care on my mind now, never felt before but which will always remain, but I hope I will be able to fulfill all duties faithfully, and I feel amply repaid by a flash from my darling's bright eyes for they almost talk . . . .

June 12th. The mail leaves tomorrow so I will close this scrawl. You can't imagine how often I have thanked you for my breakfast shawl; it has been & still is so very useful. The balls are quite dirty, I am sorry to say. Our garden looks so nice now; everything is coming up. We will probably have green peas ripe by July fourth. Love and a kiss to everybody from   *Jim & Julie*

FORT STEVENS,
June [probably 30th, 1867].

My darling Papa   Your letter of May 19th has just arrived, enclosing a nice little one from Eddie; and by the same mail I received one from Annie enclosing a letter from my old teacher . . . . It seems real queer to be addressed as Miss Stellwagen while I am rejoicing in my maternal dignity. I don't think the past two years have made me look very ancient, however; I am continually told that I do not look more than eighteen, and I am sure I feel almost like a "cat lugging a kitten" when I have my baby in my arms. Don't you feel funny to be a Grandpapa? She is a tiny little lump of humanity but as fat as butter and healthy as possible. She looks around with her great blue eyes, taking many a stare at the new world she has entered. We weighed her when she was six weeks old and her weight was twelve and a quarter pounds . . . .

This still quiet Sunday with its cloudless sky and golden sunbeams, its soft winds whispering through the forest, and the distant murmur of the "rising tide, whose waves are kneeling on the sand as kneels the human knee," seems very near to Heaven. It makes the thought very sweet that we are being guided by a loving Father's hand through our infancy in this world, up to the full glory of our manhood in the reality that He who has bid "all who sorrow to come unto Him" has fitted our backs to our burdens and whispers in our troubled hearts, "Peace, peace." Our strength is to sit still and accept both blessings and troubles as gifts from a wise Hand. My constant prayer is that I may train my little one in the way that she should go, and I have no fears that my prayers will be unheeded. She is a dainty little flower in our pathway, and I now realize the depth and tenderness of a mother's love. Not that I think a father loves less, but there are a thousand little ailments, and an ever-growing sense of its perfect helplessness, together with the great responsibility that deepens and intensifies a mother's affection. I earnestly hope that your precious little one may be spared to you, and we may sometime show the little aunt and niece to each other . . . .

Jim planted corn, potatoes, tomatoes, peas, radishes, lettuce, cabbages etc.; all are doing finely, though we have no soil at all except made land. It is late; baby is awake & the mail leaves in the morning; I don't think I will have time to write any more so I will close. We are both well and Jim unites with me in love to you all. Your loving daughter   *Junie*

FORT STEVENS, OGN.,
June 30th, 1867.

Darling Eddie   Your nice little letter dated May 19th has arrived. I was very glad to get it and also to see how nicely you can spell . . . . How are your vegetables growing? Brother Jim has planted almost everything and all are up except onions and they won't grow in this sand. Have you got your dog yet? I wonder if he is as pretty as our "Guy". We have got a lot of chickens and yesterday five more little downy lumps broke through the shells. We have warm weather during the day but have to build a fire morning and evening. The sunset light don't fade from our sky till ten o'clock at night. Baby likes to be out of doors and won't sleep at all in the house except at night. So I take a little basketwagon with a pillow in it out in the yard after breakfast when she is washed and dressed and put her in it and she stays three or four hours asleep, then when she wakes I ride her about. We almost live on the porch and in the yard. I sit out there and sew.   Sister *Junie*

FORT STEVENS, OGN.,
June 30th, 1867.

My dear Nannie I *have* got some whole sheets of paper but have only time to fill this piece. Baby seriously objects to my writing letters. She is a cunning little rogue and I think is growing pretty since I have heard that *she looks like me* except having her father's eyes. She takes a great deal of notice and will look up in your face with such a sweet laugh. She exercises her lungs occasionally and a pretty strong little pair of *bellows* they must be. We are almost eaten up with swarms of flies and while I am busy brushing them away from her face she will watch them with the greatest interest twisting her little head almost around. She is a beautifully formed child with faultless hands and feet, for the latter have not grown at all and now look very tiny . . . . She was born the first day of May, I thought Jim told that in his letter. I can sympathize with your "boil." I have had *two* tremendous fellows and have lots of little ones coming, besides being devoured every night by gnats . . . . I have to be careful of my diet for my baby but I eat Graham bread altogether and dried *peaches* (*not* apples) stewed with brown sugar, and they keep us both pretty regular.

Jim has gone to Portland on business and baby & I are forlorn. Capt. & Mrs. Babbitt came down and made us a little visit last week. Mrs. B's servant girl sent baby two dear little bibs with lace around them that she made herself. Mrs. B. is going to make her a short dress to be the first one she wears when tucked. I think your little maize colored sack the prettiest she has and they fit her so nicely. Jim took us all rowing in our barge last Friday. Give a kiss to Mama & Papa & yourself from *June & Baby*

IN GOOD COMPANY

Fort Vancouver to Camp Harney

JULY-OCTOBER 1867

FORT VANCOUVER, W.T.,
July 14th 1867.

Dear Nannie   The date of my last letter received from home was May 20th, so you may imagine that I am anxiously awaiting another. The mail steamers which did ply between Portland and San Francisco every week, now only come every fifteen days so all our letters will be much further apart. You may be surprised at the heading of this letter but this is now my home (pro tempore). Jim has been ordered to report to Genl [George] Crook in the Boise district and he does not know where he will be stationed.[1] Neither can he find out until he arrives out there; consequently he has to leave baby and me here until he can ascertain what his future movements will be. You can address all letters to me, care of Capt. L.S. Babbitt, Fort Vancouver, W.T., and I will forward to Jim those intended for him, as he will write to me from every point he reaches.

We have been so busy during the past two or three weeks, packing up and selling off all we could dispose of that I have had no time to write before. The journey is so long that we cannot take much with us and will have to depend on getting things from Boise. Our little home at Fort Stevens was looking lovely and I regret leaving very much just as the summer begins. I am real sorry also on account of

Jim's garden. He has taken such pride in making it what it is and all his vegetables were doing finely to repay his trouble. We left there last Monday & reached here on Wednesday evening all well. Baby continues to grow fatter and to *outgrow* her clothes already. She is a bright, funny little puss and is growing quite pretty. I must have her vaccinated soon as we have to knock about so much; I dread to do it, too, for fear it will make her sick.

Dear Jim is obliged to leave us during this week; I will be as comfortably and pleasantly situated as I can be away from him. He first thought I better go home to you but I dreaded the journey so much without him; as I am seasick all the time I would be compelled to leave baby to her nurse more than I would wish to; for I always wash, dress and undress her myself. Besides I may be able to join him in a month or two; then we would be more likely to go home together. I made baby a cloak out of my little black and white plaid to travel in but I am going to make a white merino one and Mrs. Babbitt is going to embroider it with white silk. Won't that be pretty? The little toad is laying on the bed beside me sound asleep and looks like a fat picture. She is a restless wide-awake child during the day but very good at night. We are going to have her christened tomorrow in the chapel here. I see in *Harper's Weekly* of June 15th a map with "Camp C.F. Smith" marked on it.[2] It is the first that I have seen . . . . Jim sends love to all.   *Your loving sister Julie*

FORT VANCOUVER, W.T.,
July 31st, 1867.

Darling Mama   I can sympathize now with you as I never could before, in your anxiety for your children. I know how heavy the trial you are passing through in darling's illness. I am anxiously awaiting a letter from the Steamer which is expected in today, but I cannot receive it for a week as our mail still goes to Astoria and is redirected here. I am very comfortably fixed here, have sitting room, chamber, storeroom & two kitchens on the first floor and servants' rooms above. I am living next door to my friend Mrs. Babbitt, and I have an excellent woman with me. Mrs. Kelly went to San Francisco to live and I now have a Mrs. Bellion. She is the wife of one of the soldiers but is a perfect lady. She is a midwife by profession and never lived out as a servant before. She is consequently a splendid nurse for Baby and helps me with my sewing as the cooking for us two does not take much time. She comes for twenty dollars in gold a month and I put out my washing. (The average amount for wages is 35.00 gold per month.) This dear, delightful Vancouver is lovely as ever and if I only had you all living next door, and my husband home with me I should be so happy. I had a letter from him yesterday; he had been travelling in a stage five days but had not reached his destination, however they had passed beyond the point at which they feared Indians.

Friday, August 2nd. Last night I received another letter from Jim; he had just arrived at Fort Boise where he awaits further orders. He was well & told me to send his warmest love to you all when I wrote. Baby is well & fat. She was christened just before her papa left, and is called "Julie Melville"; your suggestion of May Stevens I think very pretty but Jim wouldn't hear of any name but Julie . . . .

I've been down to the convent to have the "sisters" make her a little white, corded sunbonnet.[3] A cap is no use in this sunny, country region. I am braiding a white marseilles cloak for her. She has nearly outgrown her little sacques. Col. [Marcus A.] Reno's wife is knitting her some large ones. Ain't she a fortunate little toad? She spoils all my dresses so I have got another calico wrapper. Do you think it pretty? It is a yard wide. It is trimmed with black & looks quite stylish. I have spread so much during the past year that none of my dress waists will fit me. I've had to gore all my skirts to get new waists out of the pieces. I'm several inches broader around my shoulders and am real fat. Tell Annie I'm copying her little crochet sacques to send to Beck. She expects her baby in September . . . . I must send this off quickly for the steamer soon sails. Tell Annie the band on the parade [ground] is playing "May Breezes"; it takes me back home. I am so anxious for my letter by this steamer to know how dear little Eddie is getting. How is Baby? I don't feed my baby at all; she never has anything but milk. I think that is the reason she is so splendidly fat . . . . Kisses & love for all from your affectionate daughter   *Julie*

FORT VANCOUVER, W.T.,
August 11th, 1867.

Dear Nannie I received Papa's kind letter of June 29 by the last Steamer but it had to go down to Fort Stevens and be remailed before I got it. I thank him so much for keeping me informed of dear Eddie's progress. It makes my heart ache to be so far from him and you all in these trials, but it is only a little more needed discipline, Nannie. Your brother has been away more than three weeks but has not yet reached the termination of his journey nor will he do so until the fifteenth of this month. He has had a disagreeable fatiguing trip, and poor fellow, feels dreadfully not being able to take us with him. He writes to me from every stopping place begging for all the letters that I can write. I have often laughed at people for writing to each other every day but I don't wonder at it now.

I have a very pleasant little home, but it looks like an old maid's mansion. Everything set up primly with no one to disturb it; no pipes & tobacco on the mantels, no gun & fishing rod in the corner, no slippers and boots in the middle of the floor, no shotgun wads & fish hooks in everything that will hold them. Oh! I assure you I miss them.

I have just heard from him [Jim]; he says he will try to come for baby and me by Oct. 1st. He said he thought maybe I better go home, but I thought not & he was too faint-hearted to urge it. I hate to leave him behind & still cling to the hope of all coming together. He has written to Genl Tompkins to see if he can get him ordered East; but this is a secret.[4] . . . Give the enclosed picture to Papa and Mama. I would send you one but they cost 4.00 *a half dozen;* that was all I could afford and one must go to her papa, one to Mrs. Gilliss, one to me and I had promised one to Mrs. Babbitt & Mrs. Weeks who have been like kind sisters to me. Maybe I will give you mine when I join Jim, then I can share his. Baby has just been vaccinated, and has gone to sleep. Her picture is not half as pretty as she is, she has squinted her eyes just like I do, and I never saw her do it before. The Steamer has just come in but will leave before I can get my letters so I will have to send this without knowing whether there are any for me or not. Tell Mama & Papa I don't look old and cynical as this picture does. I'm in excellent health & fancy look quite *handsome* as Baby is so pretty & everybody says she is the image of her mama . . . .

Jim's address is Fort Boise, I[daho] T[erritory] & the letters are forwarded. Kiss Papa, Mama & little sister for baby and   *Junie*

Baby has a bunch of grapes mark on the back of her head.

FORT VANCOUVER, W.T.,
August 20th, 1867.

Darling Mama   I have just received Annie's letter of July 8th and another Steamer arrived today but I do not know what it has brought for me. I am glad that little brother is improving. Poor little fellow; what a hard time he has had. My baby has been a little sick from her vaccination, but the sore is healing now and she is well again. How I wish you could all see her; I know you would love her, she is a very winning little thing and makes friends with everybody. She is fat & dimpled all over. Tell Annie her recommendation to always have a nurse could not very well be carried out in this country for they won't live with you for love or money unless they feel inclined. There are so few girls out here that the ambition of all is to marry, and they can marry so well that they won't stoop to a soldier; consequently the garrison possesses no attractions for them. Indeed the commonest Irish girls marry merchants & men far above them, and very disagreeable it proves sometimes. I know of several *Army officers* whose wives formerly were *washwomen*; a Surgeon proposed to Mrs. Weeks' nurse, and another Surgeon actually married the *cook* out of Mrs. Ten Broeck's kitchen. They of course become entitled to all the rights and rank of officers' wives, but you never can make ladies of them & it is disagreeable to meet them on equality.[5]

I hear constantly from Jim; he is still travelling and has worked around in a circle till he is not very far from his starting point. This is some consolation to me for he expects to come into The Dalles about October 1st. It's a dull life for baby & me, for I have no inclination to go out anywhere without my husband.

They have just created a new division called the Department of the Lakes of which Genl Crook is commanding officer and Jim will be at his headquarters wherever they may be established.[6] I don't care much about it however; I am dreadfully homesick. I think I would bring baby home, if I were not so much afraid of the voyage. I have just had a letter from Mrs. Gilliss from which I am sorry to learn that Fannie does not improve at all, on the contrary she is almost constantly confined to her bed. Poor Becky expects to meet her trial next month; she is very nervous & low-spirited about it, but she will have her mother with her which I did not . . . .

Life out here is merely a monotonous round of existence, one day is merged into another without any perceptible transition as far as marked by events. I have made a great many pleasant acquaintances & some warm friends, & I think travelling expands the mind & enlarges one's ideas—more than that it is so disagreeable to be away from home & husband at the same time.   *Junie* . . . .

FORT VANCOUVER, W.T.,
Friday, September 13th, 1867.

Dear Nannie   The Steamer which arrived on Wednesday morning brought me a letter from you of Aug. 7, and my husband himself. You may imagine my surprise when I heard he was in San Francisco. As soon as he saw Genl Crook at Camp Warner he was sent to San F. on business for the Genl.[7] He was there a week or two and then came up here. He expects to leave again next week for Camp Harney on Rattlesnake Creek, the new Post that he is to establish.[8] When it is practicable he will return for me and Mrs. Crook who is here waiting to join her husband.[9] It will be a very pleasant post I imagine, it is for three or four companies and will be as large as Fort Vancouver, the houses to be like those. One thousand rolls of wallpaper have been sent there. There will be fourteen or fifteen officers with their families, and I should like the idea of going there very much, if I had not set my heart on coming home this Fall.

Jim brought Baby from San Francisco, a box containing knife, fork, spoon and napkin ring, of the most beautiful pattern. The handles have a large medallion head on them. Mrs. Kip sent her a pair of gold sleeve loops, made like a band bracelet, that is they have hinges and both sides are solid . . . . She is very fretful all night from her teeth. She has two *jaw teeth* almost through and none in front yet. Isn't that strange? . . .

I have just finished remaking my blue silk. It is tightly gored with a new waist and tight sleeves. Mrs. Babbitt says it looks very stylish but it is my first experience of the new fashioned shapes and I felt as if I had crawled through the small side of a knothole. Jim likes it however, so that is all I care for. Baby spoils all my clothes by throwing up milk on them. Jim has been sick but is better now. I am so delighted to see his dear old face again, that is, as much of it as shows above that horrid beard . . . . It is Friday and my "Mary Ann" has just swept my rooms so I am going to dust & trim my lamps and "putter" around generally as they say in Oregon. With a great deal of love from us both to you all I am your attached   *Sister Junie* . . . .

FORT VANCOUVER, W.T.,
September 25th, 1867.

Darling Mama   Yesterday morning I received your letter of Aug. 27, and today arrived one of Aug. 15, so you see we have irregular mails at this end of the line, too. Jim left this morning at six o'clock to visit Camp Harney, our future home. He expects to return at the end of three weeks, and take me up there if it is a pleasant place. If not and he is compelled to remain there all winter, I will begin to think of coming home. It requires great courage to make the voyage without Jim and with my baby as I am seasick all the time, and I am such a miserable cry-baby without my husband. We both thank you all so much for baby's pretty things. The Red Riding Hood has not arrived yet, but the darling little ring and the cap came safely. I am going to make up the latter at once. I am very sorry that you are spending money for us that you need yourselves Mama, dear. Please don't do it. We know and appreciate your love for us without such substantial evidence & "will gladly take the will for the deed." . . .

I am so glad to hear that the health of Eddie and Baby is improving. Ask Nan what she means by only weighing so little. I weigh 116 and am ashamed that I am not heavier. I am making myself a short gored dress and short coat of black & white waterproof, as a travelling suit. I don't need anything else as these military potentates keep us always on the go. Capt. & Mrs. Babbitt started today on a trip to the English city of Victoria [Canada], the only place on this coast worth seeing except the Yosemite Valley. The stores there are said to be splendid, as foreign goods of finest textures are sent there. Jim sent for a black lace shawl for me. Ain't that nice? Of course I don't want it for winter, but it is a good opportunity to have Mrs. B. select it, as she has excellent taste. They will be absent about ten days so I am doubly lonely. I have a real nice nurse though, who is some company. She says she would like to go East with me if I go, but her husband won't let her. She is going to Camp Harney with me if I go up there. She is only nineteen but has lost a baby of her own, and is perfectly devoted to ours. Baby will put out her hands to go to her. I am surprised to see how deeply attached Jim is to Baby, but she is so cunning he can't help it. He don't like children generally and our Eddie has heretofore seemed to be the only one he cared for . . . . He says he hopes someday to have a pleasant home somewhere where you can all come and see us. We are so fond of garrison life; it has all the advantages of a country home without its loneliness.   *Junie*

FORT VANCOUVER, W.T.
September 29th, 1867.

My dear Mama and Papa   The steamer came in tonight and I expect some letters tomorrow morning. October 3rd. I received today the package containing baby's Red Riding Hood; I think it is the handsomest one that I ever saw. I won't let her wear it till she gets on her short clothes. I can't begin to thank you in words for all your kindness, but I think you will know what is in my heart . . . .

I am very tired, I have been over in Portland all day doing some shopping for the winter campaign at Camp Harney. I have canton flannel for nightgowns for baby, flannel for high neck & long sleeve shirts (I've made one for her and put it on her), little white merino stockings and a pair of kid boots which the man said were the smallest made, but her toes just come halfway down the sole, for she has remarkably small feet and hands, Nannie's prognostications to the contrary notwithstanding. I got her a crib, but I could not find a high one like you used to have for us.

I had a letter from Jim when he had been two days out on his journey. He reports the road in excellent condition. I expect he reached Camp Harney today; after he has remained there a week I shall begin to look for his return. You can't imagine how very lonely I am without him, although I am surrounded by kind friends. My nurse is going up there with me, which is an unexpected piece of good fortune . . . .

Oct. 4th. Well, I will make another attempt at this letter tonight for the mail leaves in the morning. Baby is fretful today, I think her gums ache, she bites so hard. I have had calls all day and have been trying to work a row of button holes down the front of my walking dress, two of which I succeeded in doing; baby is so hearty I have to stop and nurse her about every ten minutes. She is sitting in the nurse's lap by me, laughing in my face. She is a darling little thing. Tomorrow is your birthday Mama; I tried to get something pretty for baby to send you but did not succeed. The assortment of Portland goods is poor in the first place, and secondly we only get 69 & 70 cts for our greenbacks and it makes things cost a small fortune to send to San Francisco. So please don't think we don't remember you, and accept as a poor substitute our warmest love and best intentions . . . .

Baby is biting on a rubber ring which Capt. Haskell brought in to her.[10] She puts everything in her mouth. The clerk at the Sutler's sent her a rattle. Her gums hurt her so much that she is crying hard so I will stop and take her. With love.   *Julie* . . . .

FORT VANCOUVER, W.T.,
October 13th, 1867.

My dear Nannie   Yesterday's steamer was a happy arrival for me as it brought yours and Papa's letters of Sept. 10th, and also two from Mrs. Gilliss and from Beck, one from Mrs. Kip. The day previous I received one from my husband and one from Jack, so I have a most delicious pile in front of my desk now. I am certain that some of those I write home are lost, for I distinctly remember writing a full account of Baby's christening, godparents etc.

At the time appointed for her baptism a sudden gust arose, and as we could not go down to the Chapel, the Chaplain preferred having the ceremony at the house instead of postponing it, as he had received orders to go to Montana, and Jim was to leave me in a day or two. I demurred as we were visiting Mrs. Babbitt and she being a Roman Catholic I thought it might be disagreeable to her. But she insisted and arranged her parlor table with a silver urn of water and a stand of flowers. Furthermore Capt. Babbitt requested that he might be godfather as his wife's church prevented her from assuming a sponsorship as she wished to do. Mrs. [Susannah] McCarthy the Chaplain's wife, a dear old lady, was godmother.[11] Baby behaved beautifully and was named "Julia Melville". Tell Mama . . . our arrangement was that if a boy I should name him, if a girl, that privilege belonged to Jim. He wished her called Julia and I added Melville for *his father*. You know it was his middle name, and was to have been Jim's also but the Minister who baptized him omitted it.

There! you have full particulars, except that Capt. Babbitt who has just returned from Victoria brought Baby an exquisite short dress . . . . We have no church today and will have none in future, one Chaplain is retired & relieved from duty here and we are not to have another.

I expect Jim tomorrow; then I will know definitely what we are to do this winter. I fully expect that we will spend it at Camp Harney. Tell Mama & Papa please not to send anything out to me for there is only half a chance out of ten that we will ever get it. Jim has lost everything that I sent him from here. *All* my letters are piling up somewhere, a compass, a letter scale, 100 post stamps & baby's picture all sent at different times, never reached their destination; a box of pickled oysters and smoking tobacco which I sent him was stolen at the Dalles before it had been put on the train for Camp Harney . . . .

Baby can sit alone. She has no teeth through yet but I think will have soon; she is evidently suffering with them, is peevish & fretful at night and has high fevers till daylight. She is real goodnatured though, for the fleas nearly devour her, and she laughs all day. I caught three on her this morning and her poor little soft skin is peppered with bites. So am I. Love to Mama, Papa, Eddie and Kitten. Your affectionate sister   *Julie*

FORT VANCOUVER, W.T.,
Wednesday, October 16th, 1867.

My dear Papa   By the last steamer I received your welcome letter of Sept. 9th, and also some papers. I deferred writing by return mail in order to tell you what were to be our movements, as I was expecting my husband. He arrived on Monday and you may be sure I was glad.

We are busy now packing up, and expect to leave here for Camp Harney on Saturday morning. Genl Crook's wife will accompany us, and what is of great importance to me, my nurse is going too. Lieut. Pollock with his wife and baby are there already and Capt. Kelly's wife & three or four daughters expect to go.[12] I have no doubt we will have a pleasant post in course of time for there will be so many persons. Of course at first it will seem somewhat rough but that will initiate us into the mysteries of frontier life. I feel that Genl Halleck would not order his officers about at such an ill natured rate if he had to pack up and move with each one of them. However, I try to think it's all for the best as indeed it must be. Last May when my recovery was rapidly facilitated by the news that we were to go East so surely that we only awaited the actual receipt of the orders I felt dashed suddenly to the earth from a seventh Heaven when Capt. Porter was sent in place of Jim.[13] But he went to New Orleans and just think what we have escaped in not spending this summer there! Indeed I feel, as much as I long to be home, that it would be rash to apply to go. The very application would lessen Jim's claim to an eligible post and he might be sent down South or out on the Plains. Oh dear, I have to keep my courage up by singing "There's a good time coming boys, hurrah!" The enclosed notice is from a Dalles paper; the "promotion" means going higher up in the country, I suppose, for there is none in the fact of being on Genl Crook's Staff . . . .

My little Tot suffers with swollen and heated gums but the little pearls are long making their way through the surface. She is a perfect kitten in her fondness for scratching. No matter how short I keep her finger nails she manages to draw red parallels on everybody's face and hands and has a special weakness for getting hold of one's nose. She buries her fat little hands in her papa's whiskers and pulls with a good will and a pretty strong grip . . . . Jim sends love.   *Your affectionate daughter Julie . . . .*

UMATILLA HOUSE, DALLES, OREGON,
October 20th, 1867.

My dear Mama   Yesterday morning we sailed from Fort Vancouver, a goodly company consisting of Mrs. Genl Crook, Lieut. Charles Bird & wife, Miss Browneau (her sister), Capt. Gilliss & wife and last but not least Miss Baby Gilliss and nurse. We reached here safely after a pleasant day's travel and ate so much supper, that we astonished the natives. I went out with Jim & bought a large lamp and a pair of worsted leggings for Baby and it was real funny to hear all the Jew shopmen greet Mrs. Gilliss. Mrs. Crook says, "why the whole town knows you." We expect to pile ourselves in an ambulance and leave here about 1 or 2 o'clock today (Sunday) and ride 15 miles to our first stopping place where we remain 'till tomorrow morning. The weather is lovely but we expect to encounter a breeze from Spitzenbergen when we reach the Blue Mountains and have prepared accordingly.[14] Baby has high neck & long sleeved flannel shirts with a worsted sacque over, long leggings and her long clothes with a double flannel wrapper, to put over her canton flannel nightgowns. A big blanket shawl to envelop her, a white worsted hood & shetland wool veil. I have put on high neck & long sleeve merino shirts, & canton flannel drawers, a canton flannel skirt over my flannel one; then I have a pair of flannel drawers and long woolen stockings to put on over my shoes, legs up to my knees. My travelling suit is a short dress & coat of black & white waterproof, and a black silk bonnet, with a worsted hood for early morning & evening. Mrs. Crook has the same costume pretty much and you will think we are preparing for a trip to the North Pole. Col. Weeks & family have gone to Sitka. Lieut. Bird, wife & sister leave us here & go to Boise. I am very sorry, I like them so much. The

Sutler at Vancouver made me a *Christmas* present when I left. It is a round tray, with a decanter in the middle & half dozen wine glasses around it, *all* Bohemian glass. It is beautiful. Mrs. Crook brought Baby from Victoria a *bib* made of fine nansouk with thin wadding between, quilted in small diamonds with a tiny spray embroidered in each; under the chin is a beautiful bunch of worked flowers, the whole thing is edged with work; you can't think how pretty it is. Jim has bought everything in the line of groceries that we can use for a year & sent to Camp Harney so we will not be in danger of starvation. Capt. [Abraham] Bassford & his wife have gone there. We will have plenty of company . . . .

Please be very careful in directing your letters to us, the mail communication is irregular and many letters I've no doubt will be lost, so please don't send anything else to me unless it might be a pamphlet or newspaper, that could take the chances, for they will be very welcome (next to letters) if we ever get them. Well I must stop & get together my small baggage, "big box, band box, bag, basket, baby & bundle." With ever present, loving thoughts of you all at home I am your own daughter   *Julie* . . . .

Capt. James Gilliss, A.Q.M. U.S.A., Fort Harney, via Canyon City, Oregon.

CAMP WATSON, OREGON,
Wednesday, October 23rd, 1867.

Dear Mama & Papa   On Sunday morning we left the Dalles in an ambulance with four mules and travelled without accident or incident for fifteen miles to a Mr. Gillum's house where we remained all night.[15] Mrs. Crook, Jim, nurse, baby and myself all had to sleep in one room with three beds. These houses are public houses for the entertainment of man & beast but their accommodations are ludicrous. Next morning we started about seven o'clock and travelled forty-five miles. The country through which we pass is grand at first from the fact of being different from anything seen before, but after journeying a day or two it becomes very tiresome from its monotony. The entire stretch of Oregon from the northwest to the southeast corners is exactly the same, a continuous expanse of bare, brown hills and snow capped mountains. We travel up & down mountains all the time & in the short space of an hour we will almost melt in the valley and freeze on the hilltop. One grade called Deschutes Hill is four miles long and so steep that we all got out [of] the wagon and walked down the worst part.

From the top of this hill the view was beautiful. We were on a very small plain on the top, and at our feet lay chasms dark and deep; hundreds of miles away as far as eye could see, one after another rose the "everlasting hills," which close around us "bare, barren, bold," showing their rocky structure and total freedom from verdure, not even a blade of grass pierces their baked, rocky sides; those farther off clothed with the soft blue which distance lends them, melting off into indistinctness, till at the point where earth and heaven meet, a single snowy spire, pure and glittering, our glorious Mt. Hood still stood sentinel over our winding way. Before and on the right of us the white tops of Mts. Jefferson, Adams, St. Helens, Rainier and the Three Sisters, rose and completed the circlet of gems of which Hood is the clasp. At the base of the hill flowed the Deschutes river, narrow and deep, its dark green striped with the white foam from its numerous rapids and making it look like a band of malachite. Down the hillsides our surefooted mules carried us, into ravines where we held our breath to look; up again the steeps when it seemed almost impossible to avoid sliding backward into the abyss behind.

More than a hundred miles have we travelled over, each mile so like the last it is hard to realize that we are not going in a circle and continually reviewing the same scenes. We have had some ridiculous experiences in our nightly stopping places that have furnished merriment and kept us from feeling fatigue. Baby stands the trip very well, her tender little skin chapped dreadfully by the rough mountain air. I like the sea breeze far better. Our faces and hands are so chapped in spite of veils, gloves and mufflers that the blood oozes through the cracks. I like it here at Camp Watson very well and should be pleased if it were our destination.[16] But I suppose Camp Harney will be equally pleasant when we arrive there. The long journey is tedious, though Jim has made it as comfortable as possible. We have a large spring wagon with six seats, plenty of blankets and robes and as the roads are in excellent condition, we would not be wearied at all if it were not a six or seven-day journey. We remain here today to rest, tomorrow we expect to proceed on our way. I will write whenever I have an opportunity, but my paper has become so soiled in the valise that I am ashamed of it.

Today is overcast and the first cloudy day since we left Dalles. Jim has gone out to hunt a deer; he shot a badger on the road here. My greatest objection to this trip is that though every mile in reality draws us nearer home, yet every step of it must be retraced before we ever get to you. Well, I must not give homesick thoughts a chance to get the upper hand so I will stop writing. With love and kisses to you both and my dear little sisters and brother I remain your dusty and travel-stained but ever loving daughter   *Julie*

CAMP HARNEY, OREGON,
October 28th, 1867.

My dear Parents   The morning after I wrote my last letter we left Camp Watson. After two days' travel we reached Soda Spring, here we camped for the night.[17] It is a very pretty spot, shut in by hills; on the side of one our tent was pitched. There is a detachment of soldiers camped there and they are building a nice log house, as it is intended to be a permanent stopping place, being one day's travel from this Post. Yesterday morning we left there & reached this point about 3 1/2 o'clock. In the little valley at Soda Spring Camp there is a mineral spring which I think beautiful as it is the only one I ever saw. It is a mound formed entirely by the alkaline deposit of the water, in the centre of which bubbles the water cold and clear. The gas bubbles continually. I don't like the taste of it. Our journey hither has been always up & down mountains but the last day seemed more mountainous than ever. We passed through snowstorms on the summits and found sunshine in the valleys.

This post is destined to be a very large and very busy one, but will always be disagreeable from the fact that it is situated on a flat with alkaline dust about a foot deep. I never saw such a dirty place. We will not remain here. Genl Crook says Camp Warner is far pleasanter, and also has the advantage of having houses already built; here we live in tents, while houses are building. We expect to leave for Camp Warner in about three days. That will be headquarters and consequently the Genl & wife, Capt. Pollock, wife & baby, Dr. Dickson and a company of Infantry will all go with us.[18] There are five ladies at Warner now and when we all arrive there it will be quite a community. Our address will be *Camp Warner, Oregon, via Susanville, California.*

Baby has stood the trip very well and has been very good especially as it breaks up all her regular habits and sleeps. She is the dirtiest little towhead in the country. She cries when I won't let her suck her toes. I will be glad when we are settled once more, it is miserable to be always upsidedown. I am sitting on a trunk writing on my knee but we have two tents together with plank floors, iron bedstead, four chairs & rocking chair so I can't complain much. I have the most aristocratic home at the post & the only one with a floor. I have a nice stone fireplace & chimney too. We have had fine weather, very pleasant through the day but cold at night; blankets are plenty however. I will not be able to write again till we reach Camp Warner. Letters will be very irregular so you must not feel worried when you don't get any, for in many cases you will get a whole budget at a time . . . . I have an opportunity to send this so I will close. With love and a kiss to each of you in which Jim joins I am as ever your loving daughter   *Julie*

THE INDIAN FRONTIER
Camp Warner
NOVEMBER 1867–SEPTEMBER 1868

CAMP WARNER, OREGON,[1]
November 4th, 1867.

My dear Parents   We arrived here last night after a long journey. I like it very much and think it is destined to become the prettiest post on this coast. I hope we will remain here all winter for although it may be very romantic camping all over the country, I much prefer remaining stationary. I wish we had been here all the time that we have passed on this coast. We have had a fatiguing trip but it was not entirely without its pleasures. We had quite a large party consisting of Genl. Crook & wife, Lieut. Pollock, wife & baby, Lieut. Dodge, Colonel Johnston[2] & his clerk Mr. Halliday, Dr. Dickson, Mr. Day, Jim, baby & nurse and a whole company of the 23rd Infantry, with a train of pack mules, with their Mexican drivers, and a train of baggage wagons.[3] We made such an imposing display in crossing the country, that not a single Indian showed his face.

We had tents pitched every night, and a stove in the large one devoted to the ladies, the others had campfires before every one. It was a very picturesque sight when we pitched camp every night. Two soldiers did all our cooking. We all live in plank shanties here now, but a great many very nice houses are in process of erection and will soon be completed. I am delighted that we left miserable Camp

Harney and came here now that the travel is over. There are a great many officers with wives here. I have not seen all yet and do not know the exact number.

Baby looks so cunning she is quite a pet already. She is growing very pretty, so pretty in fact that it astonishes me to think she is my child, but she don't look like me you may know. Jim received a letter from Genl Tompkins last night; he says if [Secretary of War Edwin M.] Stanton had remained in he could have had Jim ordered East this fall, but he now has no friend at court and is afraid he cannot do it. The mail leaves here once a week and is going out at daylight tomorrow so I scratch a few lines to send you to tell of our safe arrival . . . . Your own daughter   *Julie*

Direct Camp Warner, Oregon, Via Susanville, Cal.

CAMP WARNER, OGN., VIA SUSANVILLE, CAL.,
November 9th, 1867.

My dear Parents   The Express leaves very soon and I must send some message to you although I have nothing to write about, except to say that I am well. I can't say the same, however, of Jim and Baby. They have both been very sick with what the Dr. calls "Mountain fever" caused by the climate, the rarified mountain air. Jim is nearly well, but Baby is still quite sick, I think because she is teething also. I have to give the poor little thing quinine & iron three times a day in liquid form. Jim can take his in pills. She is very fretful and wants me to hold her all the time . . . . I suppose the sudden change from seaside to the mountains affected us more than if we had been living in an intermediate atmosphere. It made me feel real seasick for a few days but it passed off. I think this is a very pretty place, somewhat windy but I expect it is healthy.

We are living in slab huts. Ours has a glass window, the only one here, but I have only a dirt floor while some of the others have planking. We put our planks in a tent, which we opened from the log room so we have two rooms. We brought with us a wooden bed and a crib, and as our dirt floor is a slope we have put blocks on the legs which stand down hill. Our walls are unhewn logs with the cracks between filled with mud, the roof is a sort of thatch of young saplings with sod covering. In the tent we have a pine table made of a packing box; a long box stood on end with two shelves in it forms our sideboard; three wooden chairs; a grey blanket on the floor for a rug; a good stove, and you have before you our combined parlor and dining room.

I expect Jim will apply to come East in the Spring; as long as his application to Genl Tompkins was unsuccessful, I think the next one will be directly to the War Department.

I have not put Baby in short clothes yet; her Papa thinks I better wait till she gets well, for fear she might take cold from it. This is quite a large garrison; there are eight ladies, several babies, and more are coming. I want to write a letter also to Mrs. Gilliss as I have not written for some time, I am afraid she will feel hurt, so I will stop before baby wakes. I am so hungry for home letters . . . . Jim has gone to the sawmill.   *Julie*

CAMP WARNER, OREGON, VIA SUSANVILLE, CAL.,
November 15th, 1867.

My dear Parents   The Express which came in day before yesterday brought us several bundles of papers and also the little package containing Baby's necklace and armlets. They are beautiful and I can't begin to thank you all. I am so glad they reached us safely, I was afraid they would be lost. I put them on her the day they arrived and they looked very pretty. Poor little baby, she has been quite ill since I last wrote. She has had Remittent fever and the Dr. one night said there was very little hope for her, but next morning when he brought another physician to consult with him she was so much better that she was pronounced out of danger. She is well now, but is still fed on quinine, beef tea and sherry wine. She got thin in two days, and fattened up again in two days more. I put her short clothes on yesterday as the weather is mild and pleasant and you can't think how comical she looks. She is delighted as it gives her an opportunity to play with her toes, which she sticks in her mouth. She is growing so lovely and has so many sweet little ways. She made a grasp for her pretty presents and put them right in her mouth. I am much obliged to you all . . . .

Jim is pretty well again but I think badness is breaking out the tips of his fingers, he is troubled with gatherings.[4] He is kept pretty busy building this Post; we generally retire at tattoo about 8 1/2 o'clock and then Miss Baby insists upon waking at four in the morning and having us play with her, so without my morning nap I am pretty sleepy all day. I used to be pretty good at sleeping, didn't I? Well I'm better at eating now than anything else. I feed Baby once a day on Farina cooked with water till about the consistency of cream; she loves it.[5] She is the noisiest, wildest little killdeer at times; then she will put on an old thoughtful expression and you can't even make her smile for a moment; then she will shout out and jump, grab your nose or hair and pull till you cry "quits." I did so long to have you see her in her lovely babyhood . . . . I don't think I ever liked children much, but now it seems to me there is nothing in the world so lovely as a baby . . . .

I am so glad that we had to come over here to Warner. If we had remained at Harney it would have been perfectly impossible to get away from there till late next Spring; here we are only a week's travel from San Francisco so if such a thing as being ordered East should happen, we could go, and that too without the sea voyage from Portland. Though to tell the truth, I would rather be at Fort Stevens than anyplace on this coast, Fort Vancouver not excepted. I was perfectly happy there in spite of the isolation and at first the incessant rain. Baby has waked and wants her bath and to be dressed so I will stop. Jim joins me in love to one and all.   *Junie*

CAMP WARNER VIA SUSANVILLE, CAL.,
November 24th, 1867.

Dear Nannie   I've nothing much to say but as the mail is going out it must not go without a trifle from me. More especially as this mail will reach you about Christmas, which we had fondly hoped to spend at home among you all. Jim and I both feel quite badly at the disappointment of a plan which we have long had in view. Knowing that this next New Year day was the twenty-fifth anniversary of Mama's & Papa's wedding and consequently their "silver wedding day," we had long intended to give them each a handsome piece of silver, but this last move of ours and our bare existence here has taken every cent that we could scrape together (except the price of *my* passage home which we will not touch under any circumstances) and even a month's pay in advance. The merest necessaries of life cost almost fabulous prices, and although we all live in log cabins of only two rooms and have to support a style of life somewhat inferior to a washwoman or woodsawyer, there is no one at the Post (not even the Genl) who can do more than make two ends meet. This *we always* do, for we have determined to do it, but it prevents our having any cash in hand, and the most provoking part is that we could live more than comfortably on our pay, if we were at home. Well! Well! I won't grumble any more but I do feel so disappointed for I had set my heart on just what things I thought Mama & Papa would like best. You need not say anything about this to them. Only tell them we feel sorry that we could not send them some little memorial for the day. I was going to have a pretty picture of baby taken & framed to send you, but in this Hottentot land I might as well wish for a piece of the moon, and possibly with more success, for we *do* see her.

I have not had a letter since we arrived here and I guess that's the reason I'm in a bad humor, for we are not altogether miserable. In fact there are a great many pleasant people here, but everybody is half or whole sick. Jim claims to be well, but looks thin & cadaverous and has sickness almost constantly. About three-fourths of the garrison have been sick with Remittent and Intermittent fevers, and I'm going to ask Dr. Powell to give Jim a certificate to send him to the seaside.[6] We have never had such good health as we did at Fort Stevens. Dr. Powell has applied for change of station for himself; he says we are so high in the mountains here, he will never get well. Baby has recovered and is as fat as butter again but she is very pale and has blue rings around her eyes; she seems to suffer with pain in her gums and that may occasion it. I wish you could see her; she is real pretty and begins to talk . . . . She almost jumps into our arms if either of [us] hold our hands out to her. She is very fond of her father and will laugh and caper when he takes her. She is quite strong and tries on all occasions to stand on her feet; we have to consequently watch her to prevent it.

November 28th. I had to stop writing yesterday, Baby pulled my paper so much . . . . I want you when you can find time to get some wool and make Mama a breakfast shawl. I have found mine so useful . . . . I dreamed last night we had just reached home among you all when the reveille bugle woke me to the realities of Camp Warner. I don't know whether the enclosed will be sufficient for the wool but think it will . . . . Jim joins me in love to you all and a Christmas kiss to each one. Your own sister   *Julie*

CAMP WARNER, OGN.,
December 15th, 1867.

My Dear Nannie   Your letter of November 9th arrived today and although it made me feel very badly to know how you are all worried at our not coming home I had to laugh at your ideas in regard to our position. You must think that we have a circle of Indian warriors around us all pointing guns & scalping knives at us. We have not seen even one. There are Indians almost anywhere in this Pacific country I know, but the *entire number* in this upper country is estimated at five hundred at farthest and they will never show their faces near a large garrison. We have such a large post here that if the Indians only would come they could be wiped out of existence and save all future trouble to Oregon.

This is a very pretty place, lots of officers with wives and children, and although the quarters are built of logs so are those at Vancouver, and just like them. I am sorry you all expected us, I think *you* forgot your usual philosophy, "Blessed are they who expect nothing, for they will not be disappointed." We want to come home as much as you want us, and Jim talks a great deal about applying, but we cannot determine whether it is wise to do so. If he does there are 9 1/2 chances out of 10, that he will either be sent out on the Plains where the Indians are a thousand [times] worse than they are here, or down south into the very jaws of Yellow fever and Cholera. And as to coming home without him I could not think of [it] for an instant, because the voyage has its perils and disagreeabilities at all times and they are greatly enhanced when travelling alone; I am seasick nearly all the time and Baby would necessarily be left too much to nurse. Too many of my friends have lost their babies on that watery journey to make me run any unnecessary risk with mine. I am living on and hoping from day to day. We talk all the time about coming home in the Spring, but it is best not to expect us till you have some basis of expectation.

I would love dearly to see our babies together. They are so different. Mine has eyes like sapphires and as bright as stars, pale golden hair with just enough curl in it to prevent it from being straight, firm white flesh, fat and dimpled, and merry as a cricket. Gentle and loving I think, for already she will smooth her little soft hand over your face and kiss with her baby mouth wide open. On the journey here she had a brilliant color, which she never had before or since, and everyone said she was so pretty, I always think of her and little sister as two kittens, one white with a blue ribbon on its neck, the other jetty black and glossy as satin with a red ribbon on its neck. Oh! I nearly forgot to tell you I have a little nephew. Beck's son was born on Oct. 2nd and she thinks him the most wonderful child ever seen.[7] I think mine is, and Mama thinks hers is so I guess this is the golden age of babies . . . .

You needn't be so fierce about Army officers let me tell you; there are some tiptop men in the service, and I think Army life very fascinating [but] it has its drawbacks as well as every other branch of life . . . . Your loving sister   *Junie*

CAMP WARNER, OGN., VIA SUSANVILLE, CAL.,
December 29th, 1867.

My Darling little Brother   I promised that the next letter should be to you, and so it must, even though I have nothing interesting to tell you. We have not yet got over Christmas frolics and I think of you all at home very much and hope you are having a nice time. We have enjoyed it very much, although we are too far away from a town to buy anything for presents, yet we had some fun from that fact for we would go [to] the sutler's store and buy anything he happened to have. One lady got a dark calico dress, another got some cans of oysters; I got two bottles of perfume, a tin box of arrowroot, a pretty collar, a dozen eggs, and a couple of apples. Eggs & apples are almost worth their weight in gold out here, so they were valuable presents. I made brother Jim a hemstitched handkerchief and a turkish tobacco bag. Baby got some pretty things from Mr. Day. He came up from Virginia City two days before Christmas and brought her a nice rubber rattle, and a large painted doll, rubber all, which cries whenever you touch it.

We were all invited to a Christmas party down at Fort Bidwell in California, sixty miles from here. Some of the officers and their wives went, but the roads are so bad and the snow so deep, that we who had babies could not venture. All of us left here behind, numbered sixteen, sat down together at a large dinner party at Lieut. [John R.] Eschenburg's; after dinner we had a dance to the music of a fiddle and a flute. Yesterday brother Jim took me sleigh-riding in a little wooden sleigh he had just made drawn by a pair of grey horses. Oh! I have another dog, a perfect beauty . . . . He is a greyhound with large soft eyes and full arching throat just like a fawn. His name is "Don". Baby loves to play with him and he is very gentle with her, but he is lazy, he wants to lay down at my feet or beside the stove all the time.

We are going to invite everybody to see us on New Year's day. I have made a big fruitcake and a bowl of eggnog. Give Sister Annie the enclosed little collar. Tell her I did not make it. It was given to me but is too small to meet around my neck. She will have to wash it I guess . . . . I wish it were possible to send you all something nice, but it is not; you will have to take the will for the deed till we get home. Baby is well, and the cunningest little fat ball you ever saw. She has one tooth which I found on Christmas Eve. There are four other babies here besides her, but they call her the "brag baby of the garrison," because she is so good natured and wants to laugh and play with everybody, I think; but they say because she is so pretty. Oh! I forgot to say Mrs. Crook gave her a little pair of gaiter boots, but they are twice as long as her foot, so I have to put them away . . . . Kiss Mama, Papa, Annie and Baby with a "Merry Christmas & a Happy New Year."   Lovingly *Sister Junie*

CAMP WARNER, OREGON, VIA SUSANVILLE, CAL.,
January 23rd, 1868.

My dear Parents   We are snowed in; have not
been able to send out a mail carrier for more than a month, consequently we have had no mail matter come in. But we are in hopes of
sending out an express in a day or two now, as it is thawing rapidly.
I am afraid you will be so worried at our long silence not knowing, as
we do, its cause. We are very comfortable and happy in spite of the
snow wall between us and the outer world. We are very well, Baby
is fat as a little pig; and although the mercury has stood at 14 degrees below zero, we have not felt the cold at all. These solid log
houses with thatch roofs are the warmest buildings imaginable. Jim
takes me out sleigh riding nearly every day and he has a nice collar
of bells which adds much to the enjoyment. Our principal amuse-
ments are giving dinner parties and making ice cream in the evening. Baby's nurse (also cook) says "this ought to be called Camp
Grubb, for nobody thinks of anything but eating." I guess mountain
air is a good tonic, but I will never love it as I do the seashore.

Apropos of mountains, I have a project in my head which would
delight me to have carried out. Mrs. Crook has been dilating on the
beauties of her home 'till I am crazy for you all to go there next
summer, if you could manage it. It is a place called "Oaklands,"...
only about a half day's ride from Washington. It is a glade, twenty
miles long, about twenty-four hundred feet above the sea. It is a favorite mountain resort; there are several large hotels and a number
of furnished cottages all owned by Mrs. Crook's father, and kept under his superintendence during the summer. She says the expense of
living there is very little. I wish you could rent one of the cottages
and take your meals at a hotel for a month or two during the summer; I know it would be such a benefit to all of you big people as well
as little Kitten and Eddie boy. I will ask Mrs. C. the name of her father's agent there, and maybe Papa could manage to run up there
some day and find out all about it. I would do it myself if I were at
home; it would just be a pleasant little ride.

Baby is growing fast, and is getting so interesting; she has two teeth through, and two more just appearing. We have lots of babies here in camp. It looks beautiful here today, the snow is two or three feet deep; indeed we have not seen the ground since the first of Dec. It is piled on the roofs and overhangs the eaves of our picturesque little cabins like softest down; the dark pine and fir trees are cased in ice every separate needle.

Jan'y 27th. Well! the mail closes tonight so I will scribble a little more. Mrs. Crook says her father is his own agent and you can find out anything about Oakland by writing to "John Dailey, Esq., Oakland, Alleghany Co., Md."[8] . . . Today is lovely, and Jim has had Baby and me out sleigh-riding. Some time ago it was so cold that vinegar froze in the castors and broke two bottles all to pieces. My girl is sick abed today and the Orderly is cooking dinner, so I must go look after him. Baby sits on the bed surrounded by pillows about half the day; she protests but it don't do much good. Your own loving daughter,   *Julie*

CAMP WARNER, OREGON, VIA SUSANVILLE, CAL.,
February 2nd, 1868.

My dearest Papa   Your letter of November 22nd has just arrived, being the first that I have received since the first part of Dec. Please don't send any more "Overland," it's a slim chance if we even get them. If you can find a map with Susanville on it you will see that Steamer letters will come right straight up to us. We are only about thirty miles from the boundary of California and *I think* about midway between the East and West corner of Oregon. I feel inclined to cry at your letter but I can't help laughing for all that. Of course so far away you can have no idea of the way we are situated but rest assured that your solicitation for us makes you imagine things infinitely worse than they are. For instance you think me reticent on the Indian question and consequently conjure up visions of terrible things when really the only reason I have said nothing on the subject is because I never thought of it. Indians seldom enter our heads except when expeditions are being fitted out.

Our Post is too large and settlements are becoming far too numerous through this country for the Indian peace of mind and they have either all left our neighborhood or hide in the ground, for several scouting parties have been out and failed to find any.

Feb. 5th. An Express is just going out so I must scribble in a hurry. We are having such lovely weather that I hope the strength of the Winter is broken. Indeed it has been very pleasant notwithstanding the snow. Jim says find Warner Lake on the map and our post lies about ten or twelve miles due west of it. We have a very large garrison, four full companies of men, between fifteen & twenty officers of whom several are married and four have children; then there are several gentlemen clerks, the sutler who is ex-rebel General Cosby,[9] with his wife & two children, his two clerks one of whom is the brother of my old school-mate Fannie Duncan, besides a long train of Mexicans who take care of the pack train and any number of other people in different capacities, so we constitute quite a village and at present have the addition of fifteen Indian scouts— the chief speaks as good English as I can.[10] We have a billiard room with a handsome Phelan table, horses, saddles, sleighs, bells, snow-shoes etc., and I only wish you were all out here just to see how nice we are. But I can't help crying over your letter, just to think of poor Mama sick, Eddie in poor health, Nannie bowed down with cares she should never feel while she has an older sister, and we with our hearts overflowing with love and anxiety to help you, compelled to remain in this banishment with our hands tied as it were . . . .

I wish you could see my baby. She is growing quite a beauty. She has magnificent eyes, dark, bright, blue with long black lashes that sweep her cheeks. Her hair is perfect golden with quite an inclination to curl, skin velvet, clear red & white and as fat as a little pig. She has cut a third tooth & tries so hard to talk. She takes up the skirt of her dress in both little fat hands & holds up before her face till I say "where's baby," then she will drop it with a shout and repeat it again. She has learned so many cunning little ways and I am thankful she has such perfect health, as indeed we all have. I do believe *now* that living in a city causes much sickness. When our ship comes in we are going to have a cottage on Staten Island, or else only *three miles out* of some city. Baby is waking and I must stop. Jim joins in a great deal of love with your own daughter   *Julie*

CAMP WARNER, OGN.,
February 12th, 1868.

Dearest Mama   Your letter of *Oct. 27th* has just arrived in this last mail and as I had previously received one from Papa written in Nov. announcing your sickness you may imagine that I am anxiously awaiting one of later date. I greatly fear that your exertions in fixing up our home so nicely has augmented your disease. Oh dear, how I wish I could help you. But indeed Mama you must not think I am not homesick because I don't come without Jim. I really cannot muster courage to do so though he is very kind about it. He says of course he would miss baby and me sadly, nevertheless if I really would go he would cheerfully make all arrangements for me to do so. But I see he does not *wish* it as long as we are comfortably fixed; he says, though, if he were in a dangerous place or liable to be sent out scouting, I should not stay out here. The annoyances and inconveniences of a sea voyage without a husband cannot be imagined without having been seen, and another thing, it is a very hard trip on babies and so many of my friends out here lost their children on the voyage that I shrink from taking our little one away from her father into danger. His whole life is wrapped up in her. Another thing; he has not relinquished all hope of coming himself this Spring. Indeed he wrote Col. Eddy saying if he were not ordered East shortly he should send in his application to Genl. Grant.[11] He intended doing so last Fall but was overruled by Genl. Steele & Col. Hodges & Col. Eddy; they thought it probable that he would receive orders during the Winter and that he would be entitled to demand a better post at the East if he did not ask to be relieved from present duty. He is still young and I do not like to urge anything that will interfere with his future prospects or advancement much as I long to come home, and in truth I believe he is equally homesick, and is so kind and indulgent to me that I dislike to take advantage of it . . . . Jim sends love to each one and so you may be sure does your own   *Junie*

CAMP WARNER, OREGON,
March 28th, 1868.

My dear Parents   .... The last letter received was from Mama date Jan'y 16th. The snow is so deep on the Sierra Nevada Mountains that the stages can't run, in fact pack-mules can't push through it, & the only mails that come through are brought on the backs of *men* who walk on snowshoes. Tomorrow we will send a mail by way of Harney & Columbia river, which you will receive long before the previous ones. Genl. [Lovell H.] Rousseau is establishing a military express via Boise & Camp Harney to this Post which will run right through three times a month. Tomorrow is the first outgoing mail on this new line and I don't know yet what the address for this route will be. I will repeat what I have said in former letters, that Jim has *sent his application to Washington* "to be stationed east of the Mississippi river." With all due allowance for delays and deliberation he hopes to hear from it in July or August at furthest. Though I am prepared for disappointment I have plenty of hope. We are enjoying magnificent weather, the snow has nearly disappeared and the trees are full of birds.

The Indians are giving great trouble killing settlers, stealing stock, etc. They do not venture near our post in daylight, but at night they often shoot arrows into our corral and have already killed sixteen mules. Whenever the troops go after them they all hide in the stronghold of Steins [Steens] Mountain. Genl. Crook with three or four companies from here & Harney have been out for several weeks on a scout [but] he returned rather unsuccessful. They killed thirteen Indians, nearly all they could find.[12] He is going out again. This persecution of the Indians goes against the grain with me. I think it is a wretched unholy warfare; the poor creatures are hunted down like wild beasts and shot down in cold blood. The same ball went through a mother and her baby at her breast. One poor little creature just the size of my baby was shot because he would some day grow up. Ugh! it makes me sick. And all for the few grains of gold that tempt the cupidity and avarice of grasping men. The land is wretched. The fact is acknowledged that this country will never be good for anything but its mineral resources, and therefore this race of human beings which God has created and given their place on earth must be crushed to the bitter end. I do not believe such an enterprize will ever be blessed and I think the Indian depredations are a just retribution on their persecutors. Well, I will change the subject, for this is one on which I feel strongly and I may say too much.

Baby has just had another dress present; I send a scrap. She is too little to wear such colors so I will not make them up now, and when we get home she can divide with Elise because she has too many. She has *six* unmade dresses besides that twelve yards of plaid nansouk. She has seven dresses made, so she is not in want . . . . Jim sends his love . . . . your own loving daughter   *Julie S. Gilliss*

CAMP WARNER, OGN.,
April 5th, 1868.

My dear little Brother   I have not had a letter from you since last Fall and I have watched for one in every mail . . . . Your little picture came safely and I was so glad to get it. I showed it to Baby and told her it was Uncle Eddie; she looked very wise and opened her mouth and tried to grab it. She thought he was something nice to eat. She is a funny little thing. She can't crawl a bit; when she tries she slips backwards and bumps her nose on the floor, so she won't try much; she thinks it's a great deal nicer to walk. She climbs up to a chair and walks all around it. Indeed I can't keep her off her feet except when she is asleep. She is very well but a little fretful now because her sixth tooth is coming through. She loves to be outdoors and screams at the top of her voice whenever there is a window or door opened. That shows she has a naughty temper . . . .

I hope you have such beautiful weather as we have; it is warm & lovely yet we are surrounded by snow. The sun is as bright & the sky as blue as I ever saw it.   *Sister Junie*

CAMP WARNER, OGN.,
April 15th, 1868.

Dear Nannie   We fortunately had a mail today or my patience would have oozed out the ends of my fingers. It brought your letter of Feb. 9th and Papa's of Feb. 20th; nothing later. Papa's was to Jim so I won't answer that . . . . I am sorry pew rents ascended just now, the vestry should learn "retrenchment," since that's the order of the day and carried to such an extent in the Army that dimensions are given of the pieces of paper to be used in writing. An officer's path don't lie all the way through roses, especially in Oregon where there is so much sagebrush.

We are having some more snow; it began on Easter Sunday and seems loth to stop. Baby had an Easter egg, about an inch long, dyed coffee, with her name & the date scratched on it and presented to her by one of the doctors. Lieut. Pollock gave her the cutest little pair of kid ankle ties. She is fretful tonight with her teeth but she is right fat with cheeks like brickbats, for that is just the color. She keeps me jumping about till all the flesh is shaken off my bones. She climbs up by a string if she can't find anything else to get hold of, and she won't keep still a half second; she puts everything in her mouth; feathers, sticks, shaving, bits of mud all go to the general receptacle. I don't dare take my eyes off her if there is anything within reach for fear she'll choke herself. She is very fond of Mary Ann but she has to be in the kitchen a great deal as she does the cooking. Tell Papa we received two packages of papers today which are only *four months* old . . . . Love from us both to Papa, Mama and the little ones, Your loving sister,   *Julie*

CAMP WARNER, OGN.,
April 26th, 1868.

My dear Parents   We have not had any mail since my last letters, but are sending out an Express tomorrow so I will write a few lines even though I have no letters to answer & very little to say. We are all well. Baby is suffering with a tooth that comes so slowly and hard that the Dr. wants to lance the gum. I have not sufficient courage to let him do it 'till he insists upon it. She is well otherwise.

Genl Crook has been ordered down to Portland in temporary command there 'till a successor to Genl Rousseau (who is ordered to Wash.) shall be appointed. He leaves tomorrow morning and leaves Mrs. Crook here 'till he finds out how long he will probably be absent.[13] We are having beautiful weather and still run along in the same groove of life, monotonous but quietly happy . . . .

Jim is ordered over to Harney to inspect property and I am grumbling at his being away for the next six weeks. So much for being important; if he wasn't chief quartermaster of the District he would be left here in peace and quiet . . . .

We are hoping to get a mail in about a week, and then I hope to have some letters to answer so you must excuse the stupidity of this one. I hope you are all well and by this time feel brightened at the prospect of our return. Though I am so anxious to come I feel really nervous at the idea of taking Baby through the Tropics while she is having so much trouble with her teeth. Everybody tells me it would be so much better if we remained here on the mountains till Fall. *Junie*

CAMP WARNER, OGN.,
May 6th, 1868.

Dear Nannie . . . . We have had no mail since April 1st owing to the deep snow on the Sierras. That is nearly over now and a mail will come in here about the 15th, & be regular after that. On July 1st a post office will be established at Bidwell nearly 60 miles from here. Jim has gone to San Francisco, with Genl Crook. They were ordered down to consult on business connected with the Department and will probably return in five or six weeks. Mrs. Crook is staying with me and we get along pretty well, but we are both the most perfect babies away from our husbands. We are going out to ride horseback with Mr. Day in an hour or two. Baby looks lovely today. I can't keep her in the house without a cry, so she has been out with Mary Ann nearly all day. Her cheeks are like roses and I can hear her little shouts of laughter all the way from the parade ground . . . .

This warm sunny weather makes me so sleepy that I am yawning at every other word. I feel homesick and as time rolls on I feel nervously expectant for the answer to our application. I say over and over again that I am prepared for disappointment but if such it proves I know it will be severe. You don't know what an intense feeling of suspense it is. I feel worried too about you all . . . . Give my love to Mama, Papa and the Babies. Little Junie kisses her hand to you all. When I ask her how big she is, she holds both hands as high above her head as she can. Your own sister   *Junie*

CAMP WARNER, OGN.,
May 15th, 1868.

My dear Parents   The Express came in last night but there was so much mail matter that they could not bring all at once so the remainder will not arrive 'till the 18th and our outgoing mail leaves on the 17th. Of course my letters were all in the bags that were left, not a single one came, but three bundles of newspapers up to Feb. 17th were the earnest of good things to come. I have heard once from my husband since he left, and will get another letter on the 18th. They are in San Francisco now, and I hope they will have a great deal of pleasure combined with their business. Lieut. [Thomas M.] Fisher has also gone away on business and his dear little wife with Mrs. Crook & myself form an exclusive little coterie. We three ride horseback almost every day and console each other generally. Mrs. Crook gave quite a brilliant little party on her birthday. All the officers were in full uniform, and the house was brilliantly lighted. Wooden frames filled with candles depended from the ceilings and the same luminaries stuck in tin reflectors fastened all around the walls. Whale lamps on tables and both ends of the mantles added to the brightness.

Camp Warner is vastly improved since Winter has finally been persuaded to leave us. I wish I could paint for you the scene that now stretches before me. Our camp is situated in a little valley or basin green as an emerald, flecked with golden sunshine and laced with a silver network of little streams, bordered by an amphitheatre of hills. Before us, they rise tier above tier, at first soft green, then melting into the rich purplish haze the distance lends them while here and there, a tawny streak of sunshine touches them like watch fires kindled by the gods on Olympus. Behind us they lift their snow-capped peaks to kiss the clouds while down their sides slope the sombre shadows of the pine and hemlock. Down among the rushes that fringe the streamlet's bank shines many a sleek sided and white horned brindle; and the whirr, whirr of the steam engine in the sawmill seems like a fierce anachronism in these sylvan shades, at which the tinkling cowbell sounds a mild defiance. Far in the north rises a cloud as yet "no bigger than a man's hand" but black and portentous, and the thick thunder growls a reply to the wind muttering its low melody in the pine tops. Anon, a blast bolder than its fellows, leaves its eyrie in the mountain top and swirls through our valley out to the Lake beyond, and the flowers and the grass bend before him and raise their heads to gaze wonderingly at his retreating footsteps .... With a great deal of love I am your affectionate   *daughter Julie* ....

CAMP WARNER, OGN.,
May 18th, 1868.

Dear Mama & Papa   Your letters of March 19th just arrived last night. Oh! do go in the country if you can. You may find some little discomforts attending the move, compared with our dear home, but those very little annoyances will be beneficial to you both because it will be something entirely different to what you have ever experienced. It is change you want; even if for the worse it is better than stagnation .... I hope sincerely that this letter will find you in the country somewhere. Our own house at home is so fully furnished that you could take lots of little comforts from there without interfering at all with renting it—the piano, some curtains & things that would make your new habitation seem home .... Both of you make yourselves miserable because you are so exclusive and shut yourselves up from the world. Now I think this is a pretty good world on the whole, and the more you rub against people and rub off the coating of conventialism the more real gems you find beneath . . . .

It makes me laugh to have you say you are too old to make new friends. I expect to be that when I am Methuselah, not before. We are truly and genuinely happy and yet the enclosed is a faithful likeness of our abode. But we have never passed a day without someone coming in & generally five or six every evening. Genl & child, matron & maid come & go in and out our houses when they like. Often some gentleman will come in and frankly say he is hungry. Our little closet is always handy where we keep bread & butter & dried applesauce (and we rarely have anything else to offer). It is eaten as heartily as if it were some delicacy. While the snow lasted we often made ice cream by freezing milk. We have some of the dearest friends who we can't help loving because we know them just as they are without any artificial "society" veil drawn between . . . . [The balance of this letter seems to be lost.]

CAMP WARNER, OGN.,
June 6th, 1868.

My dear little Brother . . . . I am so glad you went down in the country and liked it. We have just as bad weather here. On the last three days of May it snowed all the time, on the second of June it snowed about 2 feet, and ever since it has hailed, rained, snowed, thundered, lightninged, "blew and friz" all the time. This morning the sun came out so I am in hopes we will have some good weather. We had to give up our horseback rides while it was so stormy so we amused ourselves, and took exercise learning to play billiards. Tell Mama I am so much obliged for Baby's cloak, but it has not arrived yet and I am afraid that, too, is added to the list of lost articles. I made coat and cape out of Baby's marseilles long cape and braided it with white, but she is very fast outgrowing it. She has six teeth, she walks all around a chair and can walk all over the room if you take one of her hands. She tries very hard to talk but can only say the same four words, she don't learn any new ones. She is very imitative though, and does everything she sees anybody else do. She even tries to copy the expression of face, by screwing up her mouth and eyes and working her face as it seems to her (I suppose) that others do. She is considered very pretty. I know her eyes and complex-ion are beautiful but I am so disappointed in her hair. It promised to curl, but now it is about five inches long and while it is *wet* will curl up all over her head but just as soon as it gets dry it is as straight as candles. She is very plump and fat and very healthy, and I am very proud of her in spite of the "no curls".

I had one big piece of work this week to repair damages, for our roof burnt off, and made a great mess. It was thatch of young sap-lings covered with sod which in turn was covered with deep snow. The cooking stove inside had dried the young trees and they caught fire around the stove pipe burning all across, melting the snow and mud on top which came down in streams and ruined everything. I had the only umbrella in camp fastened over the baby's crib to pro-tect it from drips all the time, so that did not suffer so much as other things. Our floor is of dirt packed hard so my gunny sack rugs were washed out and can be used again . . . .

Tell Papa his Chinook bundle arrived safely with both letters in-side, much to my surprize, for when it reached here there was no wrapper on it and the different documents were all loose in the mail bag, and it was only his signature to the letter that proved our claim to it.

I look for Brother Jim's return about the 10th. I often get letters from him. (A whole brood of little chickens have just hopped in the open door) . . . . I am very much obliged to you for your description of Mr. Lincoln's monument. I had never heard of it before. It must improve Judiciary Square very much. Today is Saturday and I have got all my washing to put away and mend, and the mail is going out tomorrow morning so I won't write to Papa & Mama till next mail. Kiss every one for me.   *Junie*

CAMP WARNER, OGN.,
June 20th, 1868.

My dear Parents   The mail has not come in yet but we send one out tomorrow nevertheless. Jim came home a week ago, very well but very tired of being in the saddle. He brought me a beautiful little alarm clock and half a dozen silver tablespoons from San Francisco . . . .

The Chief Quartermaster, Col. Eddy from Vancouver, has been ordered East, and as Jim is next in rank I was in hopes we would go down there, but that means Genl Halleck has decided that Vancouver is so much of a fancy post that officers are not needed there as they are up here, consequently no one is to go. Col. Eddy is a thorough gentleman and has a good deal of influence and he says as soon as he finds out where he will be stationed East (if it is a desirable post) he is going to have Jim ordered with him. I expect he has reached New York by this time.

We are having very warm weather although five days ago we had a snowstorm. The mosquitoes are terrible and I fancy are the same size as the Arkansas mosquitoes which roost on branches of trees. Baby keeps very well and gets fatter every day, although she lives almost exclusively on bread and milk and beef tea. She drinks a teacup full of the latter every day for her dinner. I gave her a very soft boiled egg yesterday which she liked exceedingly. She is the funniest, merriest little dumpling you ever saw. Her father thinks there was never anything like her. I have not weaned her yet for I want to see her safely through this summer first, and consequently I am rather thin, but I am very well and riding horseback keeps me so. Mrs. Crook and I take our Orderlies and ride, because Jim & Genl. C. both have to ride so much on business that they rarely want to ride for pleasure, though I will say they go whenever we seem to really wish it. We sometimes combine business with pleasure and have one of the boys carry a bag and spade to dig onions, which grow everywhere. The hills are covered with exquisite flowers, the straw-colored violet, the blue iris, the tiger lily, and many other gems of our hot houses at home are rusticating all around us.

I am making two or three of Baby's calico dresses. It is impossible to keep her in white any longer. She crawls everywhere and has worn the front widths out of half a dozen white ones already. She wears white aprons with the colored ones so they don't look so very bad. Her father brought her a pair of kid slippers with bows and buckles on them & she is as proud as a peacock of them. He brought her a painted picture book, an ivory rattle with bells, and several little traps of like nature which she is very fond of. Her principal pet is a hideous India rubber doll which she kisses and hugs and puts to sleep in the rocking chair, standing up to it and rocking it. She has learned another word; when she wants to go out she shakes her hand and says day day. Wonderful is not she? Well I believe you would all be as silly about her as we are if we had her home. Jim sends love to you all in which he is heartily joined by your loving daughter   *Julie*

> **CAMP WARNER,**
> July 1st, 1868.

> *Dear Papa & Little Brother*   Your joint letter of May 13th arrived today . . . . We have not had any reply to our application yet but I hope in every mail to get one. I suppose the political world in Wash. is too much agitated to be very prompt in business that is so important to such atoms as we are. Papa dear, I thank you so much for painting that picture of Astoria and yet you just casually mention it in the little end of your letter as if it was of no importance. I will try and make a rough sketch from memory that may give you some idea of the present town . . . . I have not had a letter from Mrs. Gilliss for over two months. I'm afraid Fannie is worse, as her letters have been very regular heretofore . . . . Your affectionate daughter   *Julie*

> **CAMP WARNER,**
> July 19th, 1868.

> *Dear Mama, Papa*   Three mails have come in with no letters for me though each brought a package of papers. We have a regular mail every Monday now. I have never yet received the packages that were sent me and I have given them up as lost. Baby has been quite sick and is still ailing. Her eye teeth seem to be nearly through and pain her excessively. She still keeps fat and to all appearances, well . . . . Our camp has been very gay with visitors lately, Capt. Kelly, wife, three daughters, Lt. Ropes & wife & Lt. McCleve have been here for three or four days on their way to Camp McGeary [McGarry].[14]

They have just left and yesterday arrived ten officers from San F[rancisco], on Court Martial service. Many of our friends are among them. Added to that we have 30 or 40 Indians who in their gay dresses and paint furnish the picturesque to our landscape.

I suppose you have heard of the treaty made with the Snake Indians and they are coming in thick and fast now to be placed on a reservation.[15] There are nearly three hundred of them at Harney. Some of them are very fine looking men and very imposing in all their panoply of war, but there are several very old fellows who are perfectly frightful, from the fact that their ancient skin is as white as parchment & the red & black paint on it makes them look as hideous as one can imagine. The day the Indians came in to ratify the treaty or make terms, I don't know which, they began coming by daylight, first in twos and threes, then in larger groups, 'till the Camp was swarming with them. The troops were all on a keen watch, with small arms concealed on their persons, but pretended to be carelessly strolling around unarmed. Genl Crook stood at the head of the parade, Mrs. Crook and I stood close behind him, *apparently* as unsuspicious as if we were receiving at a ball. In reality everyone was alert, and the officers behind us were keenly watchful. *Nobody* trusts a live Indian. As they massed in front of us, on their ponies, with their guns slung across, they certainly were an ugly looking party. The General with his quiet dignity told them he would have nothing to say to them until they all dismounted, and laid down their arms. A turbulent spirit immediately broke forth. Scowls, shakes of the head, furious gestures and whirling around of the ponies looked for a moment pretty serious. I never before or since saw such ferocious looking beings. One single brave seemed to oppose the others, he rode around among the hundred screaming, gesticulating imps and with some strong influence brought them down to a sullen, muttering crowd.

In a very low voice General Crook said to us, "do not look frightened, be as calm and indifferent as you possibly can, and stand still right where you are." It *seemed* as if we stood there for hours, while those ugly braves refused to retreat unless they could retain guns and ponies. Our General stood as immovable as stone, refusing to speak unless they agreed to this first demand. Slowly, with fierce looks and ominous grunts, one after another dismounted and laid his gun at his feet. One furious chief wheeled suddenly, rode hard and fast away and was seen no more. I do not believe any man living but General Crook could have brought those Indians to even the semblance of yielding, and for one do not believe they will keep any treaty when they get ready to break it.

We had a war dance for our benefit which apart from its bloody symbolification is the most absurd thing I ever saw. They are very much interested in everything they see, especially our baby. All day they are coming to our doors and windows to see "pale papoose" and want me to "make sing" which means *cry*. She was the first child they saw when they came in camp, and one & all seem to think most of her though they have seen all the other babies since. I have been laughed at unmercifully because I was afraid they would steal her as they admired her so much.

Dr. Dixon, one of our surgeons, is going to Washington in a few days; he is an old Philadelphian and I will give him a letter to you, so he will call & tell you all about us. He is perfectly infatuated with our baby so you may expect a glowing account of her.

We have moved down in a big house and put our carpets down on the floors, and as there are only about three other carpets in camp we are considered very stylish . . . .

We have the most singular weather here I ever experienced. From sunrise till about five o'clock P.M. one suffers with the heat; from that time we have to build fires every day and not a single night yet have we been able to sleep under less than three blankets. On the tenth of July there was a quarter inch of ice on the creek and all the potatoes that were planted were killed by the frost. Consequently there are none in camp and we can't get any till the new ones are ripe in Surprise Valley . . . .

Mrs. Crook sent to San Francisco for a croquet set. When it arrived the bill was thirty-seven dollars, thirty of which was for freightage; so we all joined in a club and have now a fine court.

We have given up learning billiards because the table has been moved to the Sutler Store. We have a particularly nice store, but a very limited supply of goods. My green riding dress has worn to perfect rags. I have just made one of stone colored flannel (which was the only material I could get) and trimmed it with black braid &

jet buttons and it really looks quite stylish. I am trying to wait patiently for an answer to Jim's application, but I feel forlorn as each mail comes in without it.   *Junie*

CAMP WARNER,
[undated].

Dear Parents   I will not write by this steamer in the mail for Dr. Dixon will bring this. The little bundle is scarcely worthy of acceptance but with the two or three days' notice, it is impossible to get anything nice to send you. The dress & buttons (for Nannie) is not my taste, but was selected for me in San Francisco. The trimming was given to me but I have no use for it and I thought if you trimmed the dress with folds of cherry silk it would do for a heading. I would send the silk if I could get it. I have nothing to send but some things I have in house, but the doll has been in my trunk for a year waiting transportation to Elise. The worthless needle case, Mama, you can only value for the love that made it, and I am ashamed to send Papa's cigar case empty, but I don't believe there are cigars enough in camp to fill it. Everybody smokes pipes. The spotted linen I hope is enough to make Elise a slip. Jim sends the photographs of Fort Stevens. The three larger ones join together as the marks indicate . . . . Dr. Dixon will call and [I] hope you will like him, for he has watched and tended our Birdie so kindly during our stay here that we feel indebted to him. Her teeth make her sufficiently sick to cause us to be thankful that we are in this cool country, for the least warm weather shows us what great trouble we would probably have with her if we were in a warmer climate. And yet she keeps fat through all . . . .

CAMP WARNER,
August 2nd.

Dear Mama   I have not had a letter from you for ever so long. I am afraid that a great many home letters are lost for I received one from Papa dated May 7th and the *next* one that came was June 17th and I am sure some were written between those two dates. Everyone says that overland is now the quickest and surest mail route. Letters written may reach San Francisco in seventeen days. I shall write that way in future. This end of the [transcontinental] railroad is progressing rapidly and is now entirely finished across the summit of the mountains . . . . One can go through from Reno to San F. now in a day. I have just received Annie's letter of June 22nd. I cannot understand why a letter of mine was mailed from Red Bluffs; that is far beyond Susanville and on another road. Our nearest post office is at Camp Bidwell about sixty miles from here, but the address for our letters is still Susanville as that is where they sort the mails.

Jim has a nice buggy which he got in San F. and we can take nice rides now as all the Indians around here are in the different camps. Genl Crook has gone down below after the Pitt river Indians and expects to subjugate them this summer which will put an end to Indian warfare in Oregon, and to these outposts also I expect.[16]

Tell Annie I feel ashamed to acknowledge that Baby can't talk yet; and the worst of it is, she is too lazy to try. She says half a dozen little words and seems too contented with them to learn new ones. She calls papa as plain as I can but I have been more than two months trying to make her say "mama" and she won't try to say anything that even sounds like it. She walks into all the mischief she can find, but never without holding to something. And I know she can walk alone for if she only holds the end of a string she is satisfied. One large double tooth is through and she is perfectly well again, though the corresponding one I think will soon make her sick again as the gum is swollen and inflamed. There are two babies here, both two years old, who cannot talk as much as my baby so I think the mountain air unfavorable for talking, though baby *will be* a perfect chatterbox for she prattles all day long, but we cannot determine whether she speaks Chinese or an Indian dialect . . . .

We are having beautiful weather and make the most of it by being outdoors playing croquet or riding most of the time. We are expecting another company of cavalry here today under Capt. Hall with two Lieuts. so we shall have some additional officers.[17] We have already fifteen, and Jim ranks above everybody in camp except General Crook, so Mrs. Crook & I have things pretty much as we want them. Col. [Edward R.] Platt, one of the court martial officers, told me that he thought Jim would be removed from here to some post where there were older officers, that it was an anomaly for him to serve at a post when he ranked the commander of the post as he does here, and yet he can't take the command because he is on the Staff. Capt. Hall will take command when he gets here & he ranks Jim by six weeks so that may settle the matter, though it has gone to the W[ar] Dept. for a determination. No news yet from the application. Love from us both to Papa & children. Jim will write soon. Lovingly your daughter,   *Julie*

CAMP WARNER,
August 8th, 1868.

Dear Nannie   No home letters last mail but as it arrives every Thursday now I do not look for one *every* time. I received one from Mrs. Gilliss stating that she had sent Baby a dress for her birthday but it has never arrived. Indeed I am perfectly disgusted at the regularity with which the mail is pilfered. About half my letters and *every* package that is sent to me are missing; I think Susanville P.O. ought to be overhauled. I have heard that as it is the last distributing post office most anybody can go in there and overhaul the mails, and books, papers etc. are carried off by any who take a fancy to them. I cannot vouch for the truth of this but I think it probable as the loss of things is so systematically kept up. Mrs. Crook & several officers have subscribed for a half-dozen periodicals for a year and have never *received a single copy* of any of them. Our only subscription was for the *Agriculturist*, one of the nicest monthlies I know, but the year expired last December and we stopped it for we knew we would never get it up here.

Capt. Hall has arrived with his company. His men have organized a dramatic corps and have several hundred dollars worth of scenery and a scene painter in the company. They are now raising a subscription to build a small theatre. They have a splendid string band, and we will have a regimental brass-band this Fall. Capt. H. and his Lieut. both have buggies and horses, so a great deal of riding now interferes with the votaries of Croquet. Jim's buggy being made with leather c. springs we can ride over these rough roads much easier than the others and our horses being half Spanish and somewhat unreliable we have a nice little pair of mules now, so Baby and I can ride all over these hills in safety without fearing they will kick the buggy to pieces. We rode about ten miles yesterday and Baby is perfectly delighted, especially if she can get hold of the lines.

I played five games of billiards on Friday. Of course I did not win as I played with Lt. Pollock who is the champion of the camp, but he told me he thought if I practiced I would make a good player. Jim plays a good game and I am anxious to learn to play with him. He played with Mrs. Raymond in Vancouver and spoke so highly of her ability that I feel ambitious to learn before we go down there as they have a billiard room in their house.[18] Baby is quite well and growing more interesting every day, but developing a good deal of mischief, and I'm afraid a little temper, as she screams lustily when she wants anything I won't let her have. She is a remarkably affectionate disposition always hugging and kissing her father or me, but I am afraid he will spoil her . . . .

I am very anxiously watching the mails but as yet we have heard nothing from our application. It is very provoking, for if we do not leave by the end of November we will be snowed in here 'till Spring again. I wish Genl Meigs would try it awhile and see how he likes it.[19] Your brother says very little for he never grumbles at *anything* but I can see he is anxious and disappointed.   *Junie* . . . .

CAMP WARNER, OGN.,
August 17, 1868.

Dear Papa   No letters again this mail; I am perfectly sick of the incomplete postal arrangements on this coast. I was told a few days since that a gentleman who has recently arrived out here by the overland route found in stables and stage stations on the road (wherever it was at all rough) bags of mail tossed aside, some having been thrown off during the snows of last winter, and there they will probably remain 'till all time I suppose, for no one would dare to open them as they would be liable for robbing the mail. When you receive this we want you to mail *two* letters to us at the same time directing one the old Susanville address, and the other via Reno, Nevada, *both* overland. We think the Reno address will bring it through in half the time, for by that route letters reach San F. from New York in seventeen days and I think the trip has been made in fifteen.

Many of the officers & ladies are preparing for an excursion tomorrow down to Goose Lake,[20] but the distance is so great they will be away three or four days and the roads only passable for saddle animals so I am not going as I cannot take Baby. I never leave her more than an hour at a time for fear she might get hurt so I am going to take her tonight to a theatrical entertainment. With a mother's partiality I think she is growing very beautiful; I wish you could see her now as she sits on the floor before me. Her little dimpled limb showing from her white dress, her hair a perfect sunshine color in curls all over her head and tied back out of her eyes by a blue ribbon, equaled by the bright eyes beneath in intensity of blue. Her cheeks are always crimson and two little rows of pearly teeth show now between the rosy lips of as pretty a mouth as you ever saw. And yet you can have no idea of what she looks like for she has the brightest expression; everybody says her face is perfectly sparkling. During the last two days she has made several efforts to walk alone, and can now walk entirely across the room, but she seems a little timid about it, and I think it is rather strange for she is a very fearless child; I have seen nothing that she seems afraid of but thunder. She cries and clings to me, hiding her eyes, in a storm. She is now in excellent health although it is very warm and she has three double teeth almost through . . . .

I saw in a Sacramento paper the announcement of a death in Washington of apoplexy of Emanuel Leutze. Can it possibly be Mr. Leutze? I thought he was in Europe . . . . Your loving daughter   *Julie*

CAMP WARNER, OGN.,
August 23, 1868.

Dear Papa   Your letter of July 17th arrived two days ago, containing darling little sister's pictures. They are beautiful and she must be a lovely little thing. I now have good pictures of all but you and Nannie and I would like so much to have them. I want a head of yours to match that one I have of Mama so I can have them framed alike. I feel real provoked at the unmerited neglect with which our application has been treated, it certainly deserves an answer pro or con. Genl Crook has been ordered to Portland in command of Department of Columbia;[21] they will leave in three days; Lt. [Azor H.] Nickerson goes with them as Adjt. Genl. of the Department and that takes our three best friends away, we care nothing for those who are left. We all came here together and I don't like to see them go back and leave us behind. Genl. Crook was very anxious to order us down to Vancouver but Genl. Halleck would not let him, because Vancouver is a fancy post and he can't spare qrmstrs to put them there when there is nothing to do. Unfortunately, for some things, Jim is considered one of the best quartermasters and they always keep him where there's plenty of hard work. I'm afraid our chance of coming home depends on the [Army] reduction bill, when we may be retired on half-pay and that is not a pleasant contingency. We don't worry at all about it, for it is so much easier to go through a difficulty when you are unexpectedly brought face to face with it, than it is to calmly conjure up all the shadows that possibly can fall on you. I have never yet found a reality as bad as the anticipation made it appear through its distorted lens . . . .

I must plead your excuse for brevity for the weather is intensely warm, though as the snows generally begin here in September I suppose it will not last long. Ask Mama how to dress a baby in winter. The ladies here have high neck & long sleeve woolen dresses for them which are abominably ugly; yet the little white ones with white aprons that Birdie wears now will not be warm enough. I enclose a scrap of a dress Mrs. Crook gave Baby, but it does not seem to me to be suitable to make up, while she is young. She walks alone now and has learned to say Mama and to call "Bob," a little Indian boy.

Genl. C has returned from his scout in California, the Indians have all capitulated and the scouts are disbanded; Indian warfare is over in Oregon, till some overt act of some of the wretched whites shall make the Indians again dig up the tomahawk. The Goose Lake valley is being filled with settlers and the reservation near us has a thousand Indians. I certainly fear the future.

Just wait 'till we are retired and have to farm for a living . . . . Jim has a mania for going into wholesale business for agricultural implements, which I don't approve at all. Do not say anything of this in your letters. He says he would *never resign* from the Army, and his desire for that business would only be if he lost his position. Dr. Steele told me *never* to let him take up business or any such confining occupation, that he was not strong enough to stand it and he would only have health as long as he was always busy in the open air or being knocked about, that his present position was the best calculated to ensure his life and health. I must confess this thought is ever present with me and strong now as his uncle Thomas has just died with some brain disease, exactly as his father did, and both from close application, the one to study, the other to his ledger.[22] [His sister] Fannie is still in a critical condition, cannot admit a ray of light or an audible word in her room; has to be lifted from one side of the bed to the other, and *has no disease* or local disarrangement except *headache.* We both send a great deal of love to you all. Your loving daughter   *Junie*

CAMP WARNER, OGN.,
Sunday, September 6th.

My dearest Mama   Your letter of July 30th arrived a week ago last Thursday and on Friday morning Baby seemed poorly so I sent for the Dr. In three hours she became alarmingly ill with cholera infantum and by one o'clock we all thought it was her last hour on earth. She laid on my lap cold and rigid as stone; her eyes wide open, fixed on vacancy, her flesh grey like granite, with black circles around her mouth and eyes. There seemed nothing we could do but watch and wait. Poor Jim was crushed, his very life seems centered on our baby. In about an hour a faint flush crept over her and she turned to me and looked up in my face. From that instant she seemed to mend. The next morning she was considered out of danger, but we have watched and nursed her through a trying convalescence ever since. She is better today than she has been yet, owing (I think) to the fact that I rubbed three jaw teeth through yesterday with my thimble. She still has some traces of the disease but this is abating.

Mama, I feel so sorry for you and Papa, you must feel the loss of your friend so much, particularly Papa, to whom he was almost a brother.[23] His own family of course must feel it deeply, scattered all over the world .... Jim is as well as usual but he has never had the health out here that he had at home; he is thin as a rail and has neither appetite nor energy. I've enough for both. With much love to all I am your own daughter   *Julie*

HOMEWARD BOUND

Transfer Orders at Last

SEPTEMBER 1868–FEBRUARY 1869

FORT BIDWELL, CAL.,
September 13th, 1868.

My dear Papa   I received your beautiful letter in regard to the loss of our old friend some time ago but have been prevented from writing by the continued illness of our darling. She *seems* worse, but in fact has never been better. Her disease is inflamatory diarrhea or dysentery, and has such a firm hold upon her, it seems almost impossible to dislodge it. Our Dr. said he had done all that was in his power to do with the very limited stock of medicines he had and that as a last hope we must bring her down here for change of air, and attendance. The Dr. here formerly practiced especially on women and children and therefore knows more than surgeons generally do on the subject. We reached here night before last and will probably remain a month or six weeks or until Baby is considered out of danger, which she cannot be till the disease is mastered. It keeps me very closely occupied with her so I have to scratch a few lines as occasion offers.

This post is sixty miles from Warner and we drove the distance in our buggy between six a.m. and nine p.m.[1] As the road was very bad some places, only a bed of lava like stones, not a scrap of earth visible, it was a hard journey on the poor baby who laid on a pillow on my lap, and was unconscious most of the time.

Sept. 20th .... Today Baby is much better and while she is sleeping I will scribble a few lines to say so. The doctor says we must not take her back to Warner until Winter, so we are staying with Lt. Fitzgerald & wife.[2] The latter is only eighteen years of age so I feel quite matronly. In fact, only one lady here is older than I; Mrs. Chapin is only nineteen and Mrs. Fisher just twenty.[3] Dr. Dodd's wife is about thirty so that saves me from being the old lady of the post. The garrison is nothing like Warner, not half so pretty, but the view around is far superior. At Warner we can only see the edges of the basin in which we are; here the post lies at the base of Bidwell mountains which bound the northern view but on east and south as far as eye can reach is a beautiful stretch of country waving with grain, dotted with houses & filled with beautiful lakes, two of which are only two or three miles distant. Bidwell is at an altitude of only 4500 feet so is considered much more healthy than Warner whose altitude is over 7000 feet.[4] ... Our sister Fannie is fast nearing "the country from whose bourne no traveller returns," and a few words written at intervals with great pain, sent to her brother last week, will probably be the last that she will ever pen.[5] Oh! I have wished so earnestly that we might be permitted to see her once more, but it seems otherwise ordained.

Sept. 23rd. Baby is a great deal better today & in excellent spirits; so I have spent a few hours preserving. Do you remember those beautiful mountain cherries we once got at Harper's Ferry? I have seen none since until now. The mountains here are covered with them.[6] ...

Excuse this scribble, I have the neuralgia in my head and eyes and the latter pains me so I can scarcely see. With much love from us both I am as ever your affectionate daughter   *Julie*

CAMP BIDWELL, CAL.,
September 27th, 1868.

My dear Parents   The last mail brought me a letter from each of you and one from Nannie. Papa's enclosed a very pretty notice of Mr. Leutze which Jim and I both think he wrote. Indeed I have often wondered Papa, why you did not write, for your letters show that it would be no task for you. I will send it back when

I have a *safe* opportunity. The Susanville P.O. is only an aggrava-
tion of the spirit. I have a very good picture of Mr. Leutze in my album which I am uncertain whether I own or not, if you have no
good one I will send it home to you. Dr. Dixon was delayed a month
in San Francisco owing to the loss of his trunk; he sailed August
28th. Mama, I am very sorry that Nannie and Elise should have
throat affections too; mine has troubled me a great deal, but the Drs.
say there is no actual disease there but a great weakness and non-
performance of duty by the different members of the throat and every M.D. gives me the same tonic to use. A solution of Chloride of
Potash as a gargle . . . twice a day. I wish Annie could use it. You
can get the chrystals and re-cover them with water as fast as it is
used. I have the same bottle ever since I have been out here, they
never use up.

We have been so fortunate as to get a single officer in half of our
house. Our quarters are double houses and so few are finished that
two families have to live together. I have been in a perfect terror
about it, for I have already seen the trouble that has arisen in some
houses here from it, only adding another to the many proofs that
one roof was *never* large enough to cover two families. I wish we
could have our home to ourselves but as that is impossible it is much
better to have a bachelor than ladies in the other half.

Baby is improving nicely and is almost herself again. She is very
fretful owing to an eczema rash with which she is covered. The Photographer has arrived and expects his chemicals in a week. I will have
Baby's picture taken, though I don't know anything of the artist's
ability. I do not imagine it will be a very fine picture, but during this
illness I have wished many times that we even had a poor one of her.
We are having *very* warm weather and my fingers stick to this paper
at every line. Jim is up at Warner but I expect him down next week.
He can't stay here but a few days at a time. I sincerely wish he could
for his health is very poor. He has lost twenty lbs. since we have
been at Warner. With much love to you both and all the children, I
remain your own loving daughter   *Julie*

CAMP BIDWELL, CAL.,
October 5th, 1868.

Darling Mama I wish I had something more sub-stancial to send today than our love and best wishes. But I have no chance of getting anything and still less of safely sending. I am very sorry that you have been so sick and sincerely hope this will find you well again. I have had a slight attack of pleurisy and your sickness seems very much like it only much worse. Baby is getting along nicely; in fact is perfectly well again except a little trouble with her teeth; two have cut through this week and some more will be through soon. She is gaining flesh too, although she lost so much it will take some time to regain her old weight. She almost lives on beef-tea; in fact that has formed an important article of her diet for six or eight months past. With bread broken in it she eats it every day . . . .

I received a letter from Papa on Sept. 30 which was mailed Sept. 8th, the shortest trip any of my letters have made. He speaks of Col. Eddy; I thought I wrote that his orders (Col. E's) were changed by telegraph the day before he was to sail and he is on duty again in Portland. Jim is so thin and overworked that our Doctor says he will give him a certificate of ill health and recommend a change of station, if he wants it. Genl. Crook promised to have us ordered to Vancouver if he could possibly manage it. Genl. Halleck is the crooked stick out here to counterbalance Genl. Meigs at home. Jim has been down here for a few days; he returned to Warner this morning. It is not considered safe for Baby to go back until about November 1st, so I will stay here 'till that time unless the weather becomes inclement. I will have Birdie's picture taken next week. Today is Sunday. How I wish I could go to church again. I still hope almost against hope that we will get home this fall or winter. There are such constant changes at Warner, that we seem the only ones who have not some intimation of a change. More than half of the officers & families who came there when we did have gone away. Yesterday a whole company left for Vancouver; the Headquarters of 23rd Infty. have also been removed to V . . . . Your own loving daughter *Julie*

CAMP BIDWELL, CALIFORNIA,
October 14th, 1868.

Dear Papa   Your letter (via Reno) of Sept. 17th reached me Oct. 7, that of Sept. 16 (via steamer) has not come yet. You say Mama is a little more comfortable. Oh! I hope tonight's mail will bring news of more decided improvement. It seems harder than ever to bear our separation when some one of you is sick and suffering at home. Baby keeps so constantly occupied that I do not have much time to think, and poor Jim reproaches himself so much for being the cause of our separation that I try not to let him see how sorry I feel. He has tried in every possible way to be ordered home.

Baby is getting her teeth very hard and is scarcely ever out of my arms. I tried all one morning to get her picture taken but she moved all the time and every attempt made her face as indistinct as a ball of smoke; I am going to take her again this morning but as she is such a hard subject, and the photographer knows so little about his business I despair of success.

I am expecting Jim down this afternoon. His mother has gone down to New York to 53 West 48th St.[7] Fannie had to be moved on a bed; the water cure attempt was helpless and hopeless, she is gradually sinking .... I have a cold and my teeth and head are both acheing bad enough to be an excuse for this miserable scratch. I will leave it open till the mail comes in, as the outgoing mail does not close till an hour after.

Last night being tired, Mrs. F[itzgerald] and I concluded to go to bed early, as we were alone, her husband being away. She was to take some ale on retiring, by the doctor's advice, and not being able to draw the cork, she opened the door between our rooms, and asked me to help her. She held the bottle, I taking the corkscrew end; just as we started to pull, the floor seemed to rise up and we both sat down. Before we could regain our feet we were rolled across the room, curtains and pictures swung out, small articles fell off of the mantlepiece and I had my first very disagreeable experience in earthquakes. We had twelve slight shocks that night and by morning I felt quite willing to go back to Warner.

Oh! I'm so glad that dear Mama is better. Your letter of Sept. 24

via Reno, just came in. I'm sorry that Nannie did not see Dr. Dixon . . . . Baby seems better tonight. Jim couldn't come down; he is a member of a court martial at Warner. I'm obliged to send this to Mail right away . . . . Your own loving   *Junie*

CAMP BIDWELL, CALIFORNIA,
October 20th, 1868.

My dear Sister Nan   Your two letters of September 24 & 30 arrived this evening. I am very sorry that Mama does not improve more decidedly . . . . I should think it was a complicated disease, for some symptoms seem to be those of bronchitis and others of pleurisy and pneumonia. Don't let Mama sit up and sew or exert herself at all till she is better. Papa says you have been a dear, faithful little nurse and he don't at all know what would have been done without you.

Does Eddie begin to think about going to Annapolis? I hope he can go; I think the Naval and Army schools send more brave, noble men into the world than any other institutions in the country. Of course I except the ministry; I think that is the highest calling but so few seek to adorn it by their own consistency, and so many shine only by the dignity of the office. I should be very proud to see my little Eddie enrolled among the embryo heros of the Naval School, and to know that his would be the frame to fill the vacancy which for the first time the name of Stellwagen has made. Tell him his little niece is very fond of brass buttons, but the anchor will please her just as well and she will think Uncle Eddy something wonderful. I send another picture in this letter for fear the last did not reach you. She has all her teeth now except one incisor and four canine teeth, and can bite like a pair of nippers, though she is too goodnatured to do so except in fun . . . . I knew Dr. Dixon would be in a hurry to get to Annapolis for he is engaged to a lady there, a niece of the naval Capt. [James] Gilliss' wife.[8]

I expect to go back to Warner in a week as Baby is perfectly well now and I have been away from my dear old husband so long. I have had a very pleasant time here but will be glad to get home again . . . . your loving sister   *Junie*

CAMP WARNER, OREGON,
November 8th, 1868.

My dear Mama   We are back and settled in our new log house which is very comfortable, but is literally "two rooms and a kitchen"... we have a garret over it, not yet finished, but where our one servant, a discharged soldier, makes himself halfway comfortable. This man is a Swiss, a born cook, devoted to Baby and very faithful. He has taught Baby to say Yah! and Nein! which with Papa and "tacker" (cracker) compose her vocabulary . . . .

No letters today, no news yet from the application . . . . One of the officers on the board which met here says Jim will probably be relieved from here, because he ranks every officer at this post but can have no say in anything because he is a Staff officer as he is serving as Quartermaster and not as an Artilleryman. He says the matter has gone to the War Department for determination. General Crook has been out after the Pitt River Indians. When they are finally subjugated, if those Snakes keep quiet, I suppose these outposts will be abandoned . . . .

I bathe [Baby] in a tub of water every night before putting her to bed and it is pleasant to see how happy she is, but she gives the strongest evidence of her temper in the screams when I take her out. I have to whip her a little bit occasionally. I send some scraps to show what she is going to wear this Winter; the weather is so cold and the laundress tears up things so frightfully that I can't let her wear her white dresses. The plaid I bought at the Sutler's store; the other was a present Lt. Fitzgerald (who is an Irishman you can tell by his taste) brought to her from Chico. Ugly as it is I am going to make it; it will do for the backwoods.

Our Sutler has a very nice stock of goods. Jim bought me a beautiful balmoral from him; it is a Boulevard skirt, light grey with three bands of black velvet with white fern leaves on it, round the bottom.[9] He also bought me a calico because it was so pretty . . . . We have beautiful clear weather, but quite cold with a heavy white frost each night . . . . your own loving daughter   *Julie*

CAMP BIDWELL, CAL.,
Monday, December 7th, 1868.

Dearest Mama & Papa   I scarcely know whether I am head or feet uppermost. With Artemus Ward I could exclaim Hip! Hip! Hurrah! E pluribus unum! Erin go bragh! etc. The important orders have arrived. "Report immediately at Washington City." Orders arrived on Thursday night, we sold out, packed up & started *Sunday* morning. Wasn't that quick work?

Reached here last night, leave tomorrow morning for San Francisco. Will probably sail about January 1st. I will not bring my nurse further than New York. I am so tired and my head spins so badly, from excitement and hurry of getting out of these mountains before we are blocked in with snow, that I won't write any more. All well. Lt. Fitzgerald, wife & *new baby* will leave here & sail with us. Lovingly your daughter   *Junie*

Don't write to us after you receive this.

CAMP BIDWELL, CAL.,
Tuesday, December 8th, 1868.

Captain H[all] has ordered Jim back to Warner; says his orders were irregular as they came directly to him from the War Department, whereas they should have been sent through Captain H. as he is Commanding Officer. I could cry. Baby and I must go, Jim says, or we will be snowed in and then he could not get us away all winter. Oh dear, I wish there was not so much red tape. Why did not the War Office know better than Capt H, I wonder. I have my saddle horse, and a road wagon with robes and blankets, so will go on; as Lt. F[itzgerald] wants to take his sick wife to San Francisco we will go together using the same guard of Cavalry. My faithful old Swiss man has appeared here, having tramped the sixty miles, with his worldly goods slung over his shoulder. He says he will go all the way with us to wait on me and Baby until we go aboard our Steamer; that it was too lonely at Warner without us. Faithful old Rush!

CAMP BIDWELL, CAL.,
Wednesday, December 9th, 1868.

Jim has gone back and I am furious at the necessity. Captain M[unson], the Commanding Officer of Bidwell,[10] is going to drive us in our buggy the first two days, as we have put a mattress in our wagon for poor little Mrs. F[itzgerald]; she is too ill to sit up. Faithful old Rush will ride my horse, and take the reins of the buggy when the Captain goes back. Then I will take Baby into the wagon, and put the luggage into the buggy. We can go to Reno and take the cars, for the railroad is now finished to that point, but Jim thinks I better push on to San Francisco and wait for him, as it is very uncertain when Captain H. will let him go. I am really comforted in having Rush along with us.

OCCIDENTAL HOTEL, SAN FRANCISCO, CAL.,
December 24, 1868.

We left Fort Bidwell at daylight on the morning of Dec. 10th and reached Bears, the first stage station that night.[11] Such a station! A log house consisting of two huge rooms, one with four large wooden bedsteads in it, the other with a large openstone chimney place full of cooking, a long table made by placing boards on several barrels, with wooden benches on each side; both rooms with dirt floors. Our supper was good, and plenty of it, but the night's rest was questionable. The stage came in just after we arrived, and its passengers added to our party so filled the place that some of the men went out and sat all night in the stage. All the women were piled in the four beds; in the other room the floor was covered with rough mattresses and the rest of the men dropped on them with hats and boots just as they were. At three in the morning the stage people started, so we a little later, had a good breakfast and thankfully started away from such surroundings.

Some days our journey was charming, especially when we went down into the Chico Valley and found summer with peaches and oranges on the trees, while our start in the morning had been from the regions of perpetual snow. Some of our nightly camps were made in pretty farmhouses where we met pleasant people; one night we camped out under the stars, our baggage wagon failing to catch up with us. Sometimes we saw stealthy Indian forms lurking near, but our Cavalry escort kept them at a distance. Sometimes Rush took baby on the horse, and relieved my tired arms for hours; sometimes I got on my saddle, putting man and Baby in the wagon, while I was refreshed by a good gallop; but all the time a sore spot in my heart testified to the needlessness of my having to take this journey without my husband.

In due time we reached Sacramento, took the beautiful steamboat, on the hottest day I had felt for months, and finally reached San Francisco, coming right to our old quarters among old friends at this hotel. It seems so much nearer home, but oh! so far from Jim. Rush is here still, at some foreign boarding-house, comes every day to perch Baby on his shoulder and take her out for fresh air. Our kind friends . . . have been here insisting upon taking us to their home at the Presidio where we will go this afternoon, our trunks having been already taken this morning; so I will send this letter before I start, and hope to hear soon that Jim is on the road to me. We had expected to sail on January first but I suppose that is now out of the question.

PRESIDIO OF SAN FRANCISCO
February 20th, 1869.

I have had a most lovely visit here, and can never repay the kindness of these Army friends. I am expecting Jim tomorrow and as we will then sail on the first steamer, this will be my last letter. Jim's letter says that . . . the paymaster came up to Warner to pay the troops and was greatly surprised to find Jim still there. On learning the facts of the case he induced Captain H[all] to let him go. He said there was much comment at headquarters on account of Captain H's action in the matter, and he thought it would be wise for the gentleman in question to waive his rights and let Jim obey the War Department order. So Jim is on his way, on horseback, no baggage and he has had hard work getting through. However we are nearly gone.[12] Au revoir.

NOTES

INTRODUCTION (pp. xi-xx)

1. Family information comes from the family history compiled by Charles J. Gilliss, eldest son of Julia and James, and provided to the Oregon Historical Society by W. Weir Gilliss, Jr., a grandson. See LEAVING HOME, note 13 and ON NORTHWEST SOIL, note 3.

2. See Charles J. Gilliss family history, copy at Oregon Historical Society. On the Naval Observatory and the senior Capt. James M. Gilliss, see also *Dictionary of American Biography* and *Navy Register*, 1863 and 1865.

3. See *Oregon Historical Quarterly*, 84 (Fall 1983): 243, for honeymooners aboard a clipper ship around the Horn in 1852.

4. For an informative overview, see Susan Armitage, "Women and Men in Western History: A Stereoptical Vision," in *Western Historical Quarterly*, 16 (October 1985).

5. In the latter painting, Mr. Stellwagen was a model for one figure. See TRANSITIONS, note 11 and THE INDIAN FRONTIER, note 23.

6. Priscilla Knuth, *"Picturesque" Frontier: The Army's Fort Dalles*, 2d ed. (Portland, Oregon, 1987), 69, 72.

7. Sandra L. Myres, "Romance and Reality on the American Frontier: Views of Army Wives," *Western Historical Quarterly* 13 (October 1982): 409.

8. Abe Laufe, ed., *An Army Doctor's Wife on the Frontier: Letters from Alaska and the Far West, 1874-1878*, (1962; reprint, Lincoln, Nebraska, 1986).

LEAVING HOME (pp. 3-16)

1. Thomas H. Gilliss, younger brother of Jim's father. See THE INDIAN FRONTIER, note 22.

2. *Henry Chauncey*, a wooden sidewheel steamship of 2,656 tons, was built at New York by William H. Webb for the Pacific Mail Steamship Co. and named for a PMSS director. She left New York on her first voyage to Aspinwall on November 1, 1865. See Erik Heyl, *Early American Steamers* (Buffalo, N.Y., 1953), 205.

3. Bedloe's Island, later the site of the Statue of Liberty, was renamed Liberty Island in 1956.

4. William Ingraham Kip was first bishop of the Protestant Episcopal Church in California in 1853. He continued there, becoming rector of Grace Church in San Francisco in 1862. His son was William Ingraham, Jr. *Dictionary of American Biography* (hereafter DAB) and *San Francisco Directory, 1877*.

5. J.D. Whitney became first California state geologist in 1860. The first volume of his geological survey of the state was published in 1865. H.H. Bancroft, *History of California* (San Francisco, 1890), 7:636.

6. Described as the "fastest steamer of her time," *Golden City* was another wooden sidewheeler (3,374 tons) built by William H. Webb and owned by PMSS Co. Heyl, *Early American Steamers*, describes her as the "ultimate" of

her kind (p. 185). She made her first voyage to San Francisco in 1863 and was placed on the Panama run.

7. The mouth of the Chagres River was about eight miles west of Colon. The village there had been the main Atlantic port of the Isthmus before the Panama railroad (1855), when Colon (Aspinwall) became the main port.

8. Tehuantepec: gulf, isthmus, town on the southern Mexican Pacific Coast.

9. In the early 1860s European powers (Great Britain, Spain, and France) intervened in Mexico's troubled history. French pressure brought the offer of Mexico's crown to Maximilian of Austria, and he arrived in 1864, supported by foreign troops. There were new foreign loans as well. After the end of the Civil War in the United States, that nation found the "foreign" monarchy troublesome to the Monroe Doctrine. By 1866 Napoleon III began to withdraw troops and in 1867 Maximilian was killed.

10. Probably Julia was familiar with macadamized roads and streets, or she may be thinking of concrete or Portland cement sidewalks, or even stones as "pavements."

11. Col. René E. DeRussy, Chief Engineer, Department of the Pacific, was in his seventies. An Academy man, he entered service in 1812, was made a brigadier general March 13, 1865, for "long and faithful service," and died November 23, 1865. See Francis B. Heitman, *Historical Register and Dictionary of the U.S. Army . . .* , 1789-1903 (Washington, D.C., 1903), 1:369; Marshall Hanft, *The Cape Forts: Guardians of the Columbia* (Portland, 1973), 5.

12. Gen. Henry W. Halleck was in charge of the Military Division of the Pacific, with headquarters at San Francisco. That included the Departments of California and the Columbia. *War of the Rebellion: A Compilation of the Official Records of the Union and Confederate Armies* (hereafter WOR) (Washington, D.C.: GPO, 1897), Series 1, Vol. 50, Part 2, p. 1268. Probably Capt. P.B. Johnson, who was relieved as acting quartermaster of Volunteers, as reported by the Salem *Oregon Statesman*, November 6, 1865, p. 4, col. 1 (quoting Vancouver, Washington, *Register*).

13. Julia Stellwagen and James M. Gilliss were married in the Church of the Epiphany in Washington, D.C., October 12, 1865. See family history copy at the Oregon Historical Society, hereafter OHS, by Charles J. Gilliss (1872-1955), son of James and Julia, taken from family Bible of Capt. James Melville Gilliss.

14. Perhaps Charles Le Brun, a French painter, 1619-90, or the nineteenth-century artist Eugenie Le Brun or her aunt, Elisabeth Louise Vigee-Lebrun. See Alfred Frankenstein, "The Royal Visitors," *Oregon Historical Quarterly* (hereafter OHQ) 64 (March 1963): 6, 19.

15. Henry Inman, American artist, 1801-46.

16. Cholera morbus = acute gastro-enteritis, and not the usually fatal Asiatic cholera (so-called).

17. Col. Edwin B. Babbitt of the Quartermaster's Department; Col. Charles S. Lovell, at Fort Vancouver, Washington Territory. Most army officers may be identified either through Heitman, *Historical Register . . .* , op. cit., or the

yearly *Army Register*. (For example, see *Official Army Register for 1866*, published by order of the Secretary of War . . . , Adjutant General's Office, Washington, August 1, 1866.) These sources have been used for identification of army figures unless others are mentioned.

18. *Sierra Nevada*, a wooden sidewheeler of 1,395 tons built by William Collyer, New York. Launched in 1851 as *Texas*, she was renamed, and was owned by the Oregon & California Steamship Co., 1861-69. See Heyl, *Early American Steamers*, 391.

ON NORTHWEST SOIL (pp. 17-24)

1. S.N. Arrigoni, a Milanese Italian who married an Irish wife in Dublin, operated several hotels in Portland after arriving in 1858, including one located near s.w. Front and Stark named "Arrigoni." In the later 1860s he moved to Astoria and operated a hotel there. According to "Survey of First Half-Century of Oregon Hotels," by Alfred Powers and Mary-Jane Finke, OHQ 43 (September 1942), Mrs. Arrigoni was an excellent cook and the Arrigoni hotels were known for fine food.

2. Captain Gilliss relieved Lt. Henry Catley at Fort Dalles. (See Julia's letter of May 13, 1866.) Catley had enlisted in the new Ninth Infantry as a private in 1855, and did assorted military duty in the regular Army and in the Oregon Volunteers during the Civil War years. See Priscilla Knuth, ed., "Cavalry in the Indian Country, 1864" OHQ 65 (March 1964): 11 fn 17.

3. Steamboat Captain Ephraim W. Baughman, an Oregon pioneer of 1850 who in 1851 was fireman aboard *Lot Whitcomb*, the steamboat built at Oregon City, went on to a notable career on the Columbia and Willamette rivers and elsewhere. In 1864 he and Lizzie Thomas were married at the Episcopal church in Oregon City by Rev. Thomas Fielding Scott, according to the Portland *Weekly Oregonian*, July 2, 1864, p. 3, col. 3. Lizzie (or Elizabeth) was the daughter of John Thomas, of English birth, and his wife Jane, born in Massachusetts. The family lived in Oregon City in 1860, according to the U.S. Census for Clackamas County, Oregon. Probably "Uncle William" Thomas and his wife, "Aunt Jane" Tucker, an older sister of Julia's mother, Eliza Tucker Stellwagen (see A NEW HOME, note 9), lived in or near Washington, D.C. The Pioneer Card File at the Oregon Historical Society indicates that John Towson Thomas, born in Devonshire in 1808, settled in Massachusetts, then the District of Columbia, then Missouri, where Elizabeth was born. John married Jane Gage Goodhue in 1847, and they crossed the Plains to Oregon in 1850. His occupation is given as "draughtsman, boatbuilder," and he built the "first boat on Missouri River, 1834, the *Far West*. In 1851 he built the *Hoosier*, first steamboat above Willamette Falls. His grandfather, John Thomas, invented and built the first sectional dry dock in America." See also Julia's letter of July 22, 1866.

4. Geologists (1989) date Mt. Hood's last eruption at about two hundred years ago and class the mountain as active. Newspapers reported vapor or "smoke" from time to time in the last half of the nineteenth century, often with questioning

comments. See *Oregon Statesman*, August 30, 1859, p. 2, col. 3; September 6, 1859, p. 2, col. 6; letter, October 4, 1859, p. 2, col. 4; February 2, 1864, p. 3, col. 2; October 16, 1865, p. 2, col. 2; and for comment on smoke emitted on January 11, 1866, see the January 22, 1866, issue, p. 3, col. 1. Harvey W. Scott's *History of the Oregon Country* (Cambridge, Mass., 1924), 5:121, refers to a possible smoke report in the Portland *Oregonian*, March 29, 1886, and mentions S.A. Clarke's comment that he had seen smoke from Mt. Hood's crater several times.

5. The Indians Julia saw must have been lower Columbia River Chinook, who practiced head-flattening. A good many commentators made the same error. The Indians of the interior confusingly named "Flatheads" were Salish, and did not flatten their heads. In regard to the "Cascades Massacre" in March 1856, Howard M. Corning, in *Dictionary of Oregon History* (Portland, 1956), 47, states that three people were killed and others wounded, but most of the forty or so settlers around the Cascades took refuge in the Bradford & Co. log storehouse. Others escaped downriver to Fort Vancouver. Lt. Phil Sheridan and forty dragoons went upriver to effect the rescue, and shortly u.s. Army troops who had gone to Fort Dalles previously, arrived back to join the attack. A military garrison of nine men was also besieged in the small blockhouse. Two additional blockhouses were built later. The "tenantless shells" were more likely due to economic reasons, and followed the abandonment of the larger military activity and building at the Cascades that took place during the army movements and Indian disturbances of 1856-60.

6. The *Idaho*, built in 1860 on the middle Columbia River, was "absorbed" by the Oregon Steam Navigation Co. In 1881 she was piloted over the Cascades by Capt. James Troup, and was sent to Puget Sound in 1882, according to E.W. Wright, ed., *Lewis & Dryden's Marine History of the Pacific Northwest* (Portland, 1895), 92.

7. Born in Dublin, John McNulty was a seafaring man who arrived in Portland in 1852, where he began a steamboat career. He moved to The Dalles and "for over a quarter of a century ran the Oregon Steam Navigation Company and Oregon Railway & Navigation Company boats between there and the Cascades." *Lewis & Dryden's Marine History*, 93.

8. A "Mexican saddle" had a large, wooden horn. Julia must not have been riding sidesaddle.

A NEW HOME (pp. 25-45)

1. The Commanding Officer's quarters at Fort Dalles burned on December 23, 1865. Though The Dalles City Fire Company tried to put the fire out, it "could be of little use, there being no reservoir on this Post. The few buckets of water immediately available extinguished all apparent fire, but breaking out afresh, all efforts to overcome it were fruitless." (Col. John J. Coppinger to Capt. W.I. Sanborn, December 24, 1865, Record Group [hereafter RG] 92 Consolidated Correspondence File, Fort Dalles, National Archives [hereafter NA].) Dr. D. Walker, surgeon, who was there at the time, later wrote that "there was no wa-

ter nearer than Mill Creek and the barrels that had been filled for domestic use." Two howitzers on the front porch, he recalled, were rolled over into a snow drift. "The soldiers, finding that any attempt to stop the fire was useless, proceeded to save the contents. The stove and dishes in the kitchen, the side-boards, wardrobes, tables, windows and doors and even their casings were re-moved." Lulu D. Crandall, "Covered Wagon Stories," undated clipping from a newspaper from The Dalles in Crandall scrapbooks at Wasco County Library, The Dalles (courtesy Mrs. Gladys Seufert). Faulty fireplaces were blamed, as they were when one of the officers quarters burned on October 24, 1864. See Knuth, "Picturesque" Frontier: The Army's Fort Dalles, 2d ed. (Portland, 1987), 69, 107.

2. Capt. (brevet colonel, as Julia subsequently refers to him) John J. Coppinger, 14th Infantry, from Ireland, was not an Academy man. He fought in the Civil War and against hostile Indians, 1866-68, and went on to become brigadier general in 1895 and major general of volunteers in 1898, retiring that year. The colonel's wife was a daughter of James G. Blaine, according to the Crandall clip-ping cited (A NEW HOME, note 1).

3. Alden H. Steele was the surgeon. He and his family—and the Gillisses for one night—occupied what is now the only surviving building at Fort Dalles, the Surgeon's Quarters (on the National Register of Historic Sites). Later, Steele was Acting Assistant Surgeon at Fort Stevens when the Gillisses were there. Often, post doctors were civilians under contract with the Army. Dr. Steele's wife, whom he married in Oregon, August 8, 1854, was Hannah H. Blackler. (See Oregon Statesman, August 22, 1854, p. 3, col. 3; Weekly Oregonian, Au-gust 19, 1854, p. 2, col. 5.) In the U.S. Census for Oregon, 1860, under Oregon City precinct, Clackamas County, Steele is listed as a physician and surgeon, age thirty-seven, born in New York; his wife, Hannah A., age thirty-four, was born in Massachusetts, and there were then two children, both born in Oregon (Fannie, four, and Frances, two), as well as Mrs. Steele's sister, Lydia H. Black-ler, age twenty-three, born in Massachusetts.

4. A small field piece—that is, a small cannon on wheels.

5. James and Julia Gilliss moved into the quartermaster's house. Officers quarters at the post were exceptional—and controversial—built from Andrew Jackson Downing's popular house patterns. (See Knuth, "Picturesque" Frontier, 30-31.) Capt. Thomas Jordan was the quartermaster in charge of the building ex-pansion at Fort Dalles, 1856-58, during the time of the Indian wars of the later 1850s (usually called the Yakima War) and the fort's greatest importance. He did not anticipate how soon the post would be eclipsed by surges into the inte-rior of the country following gold discoveries in eastern Oregon and Idaho, any more than General Halleck, after the Civil War, could understand Fort Dalles' importance in the late 1850s. Jordan was sharply criticized by the QM Depart-ment for what it felt was his grandiose execution (carried out with the help of German immigrant Louis Scholl as "supervising architect"). The last of several court-martial trials based largely on Jordan's method of financing on the distant frontier without army funds in hand might have succeeded—or been completed

one way or another—except the progress of events in the region and then on the national scene brought the beginning of the Civil War during the time of his last trial (in Washington). A Southerner, he resigned and became a Confederate officer.

6. Probably E.G. Cowne, one of the proprietors of The Dalles *Mountaineer*, who died January 18, 1866, of pneumonia. See Portland *Weekly Oregonian*, February 10, 1866, p. 1, col. 3; George S. Turnbull, *History of Oregon Newspapers* (Portland, 1939), 283-84. Julia sometimes wrote her letters over several days.

7. *Klatawa*, to go, get out, in Chinook jargon. See Edward H. Thomas, *Chinook: . . . a History and Dictionary* (Portland, 1935), 82.

8. Thomas Condon is famous as the discoverer of the John Day Valley fossil beds, and for long work with fossils. See Robert D. Clark, "From Genesis to Darwin: The Metamorphosis of Thomas Condon," in Thomas Vaughan, ed., *The Western Shore: Oregon Country Essays Honoring the American Revolution* (Portland, 1975), 199ff. When Julia wrote, Condon, as she says, was pastor of The Dalles Congregational church, built in the fall of 1862. (See her comment in her April 26, 1866 letter.) For more on Condon see Clark's *The Odyssey of Thomas Condon: Irish Immigrant, Frontier Missionary, Oregon Geologist* (Portland, 1989).

9. Jane Tucker Thomas was Julia's mother's sister. Jane's father, James Tucker, was born in Devonshire, England, in 1784, and died in Washington, D.C., August 7, 1865. His wife was Jenifer Castle Booth, only child of Sir William and Lady Alice Booth of Jenifer Castle. The Tuckers, then with two children, came to the United States in 1819 with some of the Thomas family in a sailing vessel belonging to the latter. Tucker worked at the Navy Yard in Washington until his death. Julia's "Aunt Jane" of the letters, born in Washington in 1820, has been mentioned as the wife of William Thomas (see ON NORTHWEST SOIL, note 3) whose brother John lived at Oregon City. Julia's father, Charles Kraft Stellwagen, found work with the Navy Department through James Tucker. Tucker family information was obtained from W. Weir Gilliss, Jr., and is attributed to Mrs. W.F. Chamberlain of Kirkwood, Mo., and family Bibles.

10. "Jim's clerk" was the Mr. Day Julia mentions from time to time. He went with the Gillisses to southeastern Oregon and worked for Captain Gilliss apparently as long as the latter was in Oregon. L.H. Day is identified as "Clerk, writing in the office of the Q.M." and employed beginning March 1, 1866, at Fort Dalles for $150 a month, in a Camp Harney "Persons and Articles Hired" list of September 1867 and in the Camp Warner list of November 1867. There is a special entry noting Day's work in January 1869 with the Camp Warner lists. NA, RG 92, Reports of Persons and Articles Hired for selected camps, microfilm copies at OHS (courtesy R.K. Clark). "Mr. Porter," whom Julia mentions immediately after, was probably the J.W. Porter listed as clerk at Fort Dalles from September to December by Lt. H. Catley, in the December 1866 "List of Persons and Articles Hired" for that post.

11. Jim's sisters: Fannie, born in 1843, and Rebecca, born in 1838. Julia often refers to the latter as Beck or Beckie.

12. Similar to pinochle but with sixty-four cards.
13. Major General Steele assumed command of the Department of the Columbia at Fort Vancouver on February 24, 1866, according to his annual report dated October 1866. See H.R. Ex. Doc. No. 1, 39 Cong., 2 Sess. (Washington, D.C., 1866), p. 37.

TRANSITIONS (pp. 46-81)

1. Julia's comparative "Drachenfels" (a high cliff on the Rhine in Germany, with castle ruins) may be "Grant's Rock," located east of West Scenic Drive at about Eighth Street in The Dalles, according to Jim Beers of that city. He could not recall any rocks on the west side of Mill Creek that resembled castle ruins.
2. Capt. John C. Ainsworth of the Oregon Steam Navigation Co. and Mrs. Fannie Babbitt Barker, daughter of Col. E.B. Babbitt, were married in San Francisco, as announced in the *Weekly Oregonian*, February 6, 1864, p. 3, col. 4. See also Julia's letter of July 22, 1866.
3. Of three Captains McKibbin in the 1866 *Army Register* (all born in Pennsylvania), two are listed in the 14th Infantry (a battalion of the 14th Infantry was stationed in the Department of Columbia when Steele assumed command, he notes in his 1866 report, op. cit. (A NEW HOME, note 13). These two were Lt. (bvt. Capt.) Chambers McKibbin, and Capt. (bvt. Col.) David B. McKibbin.
4. Calico, as now, an inexpensive cotton cloth with figured pattern; delaine, woolen, or woolen and cotton cloth used for dresses; linsey woolsey, coarse cloth of cotton and wool or linen and wool.
5. Agent for the OSN Co. at The Dalles, Dodge was also elected to the Oregon legislature from Wasco County in 1866, which Julia mentions in her June 10, 1866, letter. See 1865 *General Directory . . . east of the Cascade Mountains . . .* , comp. by George Owens (San Francisco, 1865); David C. Duniway, comp., *Members of the Legislature of Oregon, 1843-1967* (Ore. State Archives, *Bul. No. 2 Rev.*, Salem, 1968).
6. A form of gelatin made from air bladders of fish (sturgeon, cod, etc.).
7. Gustavus V. Fox was Assistant Secretary of the Navy during the Civil War, and resigned in May 1866. See also Julia's letter of June 10, 1866.
8. T.B. Kelly, "Druggist, resident on the Bluffs," The Dalles, is listed in the 1865 *General Directory . . . east of the Cascade Mountains* (see TRANSITIONS, note 5).
9. Thomas F. Tobey, regimental adjutant, born in Rhode Island.
10. The branch U.S. mint was built about 1868, but before it was completed the gold rush into Idaho and eastern Oregon had fallen off, and the mint was never in operation. The stone building is still standing.
11. The painter Emanuel Leutze (1816-68) was born in Germany, but his family moved to the United States and settled in Fredericksburg, Virginia, then Philadelphia, where he studied. Like Bierstadt, he also studied and painted in Germany and Europe (1841-59). He returned to the United States in 1859, and spent his time in New York and Washington. Like Bierstadt, too, he traveled to the West to see for himself. He died July 18, 1868, in Washington (see Julia's

letter of August 17, 1868, and THE INDIAN FRONTIER, note 23).

12. Probably Mrs. John E. Andrews. Mr. Andrews was identified as the father of Frederick who died at the Cascades, according to the *Oregon Statesman*, January 25, 1864, p. 2. col. 7. The Gillisses stayed with the Andrews family on their way upriver (see Julia's December 24, 1865, letter, in December 27 entry).

13. Edward Myers, born in Germany, major and bvt. lt. col. during the Civil War, of the 1st Cavalry (1866) and 7th Cavalry (1867).

14. Bvt. Lt. Col. Richard F. O'Beirne, 14th Infantry, and Capt. George H. Weeks, depot and post QM at Ft. Vancouver. Weeks was married to another daughter of Col. Edwin B. Babbitt. See Julia's letter of July 22, 1866.

15. Delicate net lace.

16. It is not clear which "Oregon artist" Julia means. Perhaps encouraged by Bierstadt's 1863 visit and subsequent publicity, the popularity and awareness of Mt. Hood paintings was increasing regionally. More people could "enjoy" the mountain in the region, too, when they were not dealing with the difficulties of mountain passes and slopes at the end of a long journey over the Oregon Trail. There were other travelers of some renown who painted the mountain as well, such as California artist William Keith. His 1868 painting of the mountain's west side favorably impressed Oregonians (see Portland *Evening Bulletin*, July 8, 1868). For a discussion of Bierstadt's Oregon visit in 1863 and Mt. Hood paintings, see J.D. Cleaver's unpublished manuscript, "Oregon Country Illustrated," in OHS museum and library.

17. Bvt. Lt. Col. Eugene M. Baker, 1st Cavalry, was sent to Camp Watson on the Canyon City Road. See Col. Chas. S. Lovell to Capt. W.I. Sanborn, May 29, 1866, NA RG 393, U.S. Army Commands, Fort Vancouver, Letters Sent, 1857-67, microfilm copy at OHS.

18. Capt. Charles Lafollett, Co. A, 1st Oregon Volunteer Infantry, and his company in 1865 built Camp Polk, in present Deschutes County about three miles from Sisters. The camp, located on a route across the Cascades, was abandoned in 1866, and captain and company were mustered out in June. See under Camp Polk in L.A. and L.L. McArthur, *Oregon Geographic Names* (5th ed., OHS 1982) hereafter OGN; also *Report of the Adjutant General of the State of Oregon, 1865-6* (Salem, 1866), 217.

19. Probably the artist William Birch McMurtrie. He worked for the U.S. Coast Survey in Washington, D.C., and accompanied William P. McArthur on the first survey of the Pacific Coast in 1850. In the 1860s he worked in Philadelphia and Washington as well as on field trips to the eastern and southern coasts. He died in Washington in 1872. Julia mentions McMurtrie several times. Some of his Pacific Northwest views are reproduced with Robert D. Monroe's "William Birch McMurtrie: A Painter Partially Restored," in OHQ 60 (September 1959): 352-74.

20. Alvin P. Hovey, born in Indiana, judge and then governor of the state, became a brigadier general of volunteers during the Civil War, and late in 1865 was appointed minister to Peru, where he remained for five years. (DAB).

21. Julia reflects the attitudes and prejudices prevailing in her society at the time.

22. Reuben F. Bernard is better known in the Pacific Northwest for his action during the Bannock War. See George F. Brimlow, *The Bannock Indian War of 1878* (Caldwell, Idaho, 1938), 87-88. Responding to Maj. Gen. Frederick Steele's request for cavalry to deal with the Indians in the eastern Oregon, Idaho, and Nevada gold mining area, General Halleck sent four companies of cavalry, two by sea to Fort Vancouver in April. The other two companies of the 1st Cavalry came from California by land (Capt. David Perry's and Capt. James C. Hunt's), and were stationed at Camp C.F. Smith and Camp Lyon. See Steele's annual report, 1866 (A NEW HOME, note 13).

23. Capt. Lawrence S. Babbitt, of the Ordnance Department, in charge of the Vancouver Arsenal, was born in Massachusetts. He was the son of Col. Edwin B. Babbitt, Chief QM of the Department of the Columbia. The latter retired July 29, 1866. For more on the Babbitts, see Julia's July 22, 1866 letter.

24. Opened in 1863, the Portage Railroad at Celilo was incorporated by the Oregon Steam Navigation Company under the name The Dalles Railroad Co. It was used until the Ore. Railway & Navigation Co. built its line on the Columbia's south bank in 1882. Later it was rebuilt by the state and finally replaced by a canal in 1915. See Howard McKinley Corning, ed., *Dictionary of Oregon History* (Portland, 1956).

25. With Steele on his inspection tour of the Department were George E. Glenn, of the Paymaster's Department, and Richard P. Strong, AAAG and ADC, Headquarters, Department of Columbia. On June 5 Steele and Strong, with a ten-man escort, left for Camp Watson and continued from there with Bvt. Major Myers and Co. I, 1st Cavalry, to Camp Currey and the Harney Valley, then to Camp Lyon and Fort Boise in early July, where Steele met General Halleck. See Steele's 1866 annual report, op. cit. (A NEW HOME, note 13) and NA, RG 393, U.S. Army Commands, Fort Vancouver, Letters Sent, op. cit. (TRANSITIONS, note 17).

26. On April 18, Bvt. Lt. Col. J.J. Coppinger and Co. A of the 14th Infantry marched from The Dalles to Fort Boise, "scouting the country." In June he and A Company went to the assistance of some citizens attacked by Indians in the Owyhee mining district. In July his company and other troops moved to the Three Forks of the Owyhee, and in September he was ordered to establish a winter camp fifteen miles east of the Three Forks. See Steele's annual report, 1866, op. cit. (A NEW HOME, note 13), pp. 38-40.

27. The Stellwagen home in Washington, D.C., was at 1105 H St., NW.

28. That is, "Sikhs Siwash nika ticky mika chako tomollo, iskum tenas salmon"— Friend Indian I want you to come tomorrow, to get a small salmon. Thomas, *Chinook* . . . (A NEW HOME, note 7).

29. Chenowith Creek, Wasco County, enters the Columbia River just west of The Dalles (southeast of Crates Point). Named for Justin Chenowith, who settled a donation claim west of The Dalles. McArthur, OGN.

30. Fort Walla Walla public stores not useful at other posts were directed to be sold at public auction. General Halleck also directed that the fort was to be closed and left in charge of a non-com or agent. See Halleck to Steele, Portland, July

23, 1866 (NA, RG 393, Army Commands, Dept. of Columbia, Letters Rec'd, Box 7, P59). Captain Gilliss and "lady" arrived at Fort Walla Walla on July 6 according to William M. Hilleary, Co. F, 1st Oregon Volunteer Infantry. Hilleary, an educated young man for his times, was involved in paper work for the small group of Oregon Volunteers still at the post. On July 7 he wrote: "The Quarter master and Commissary Stores are being turned over to Capt. James Gilliss by Lieut. [John F.] Noble. The Capt. will act as 'Inspector' before he receives any thing that is not fit for issue. He has authority to Inspect and Condemn Government Property. There is a quantity of Commissary Property that will be condemned, because it is rendered worthless by being worn out or broken. Some deficiencies exist in the Whiskey and Sugars. I presume that who ever drank the whiskey had to have it well sweetened." See Herbert B. Nelson and Preston E Onstad, eds., *A Webfoot Volunteer: The Diary of William M. Hilleary, 1864-1866* (Corvallis, Oregon, 1965), 211.

CONNECTIONS (pp. 82-96)

1. Thomas Fielding Scott was Episcopal bishop of Oregon. See Thomas E. Jessett, "Thomas Fielding Scott: Bishop of Oregon." OHQ 55 (March 1954): 45-72.
2. Maj. Gen. Henry W. Halleck, Hilleary wrote, was "a very plain man. I would have taken him for some old pedlar from his dress. His sunburnt face is very dark, his eyes a dull black some what glassy. His dress an old straw hat, Linen duster and Cheap John Pants. No Frills!" *A Webfoot Volunteer*, 210 fn 113.
3. Wife of Lt. John F. Noble, 1st Oregon Volunteer Cavalry. She was reported to be a niece of U.S. Vice President Hannibal Hamlin. When Hilleary arrived at Fort Walla Walla on May 27, 1866, the post was occupied by twelve men of the 1st Oregon Cavalry and Noble was CO, AQM, and ACS. Hilleary, who did not drink, had a low opinion of Noble, who drank a good deal. See *A Webfoot Volunteer*, 196, fns 113, 202. On Noble, see also Knuth, "Cavalry in the Indian Country" (ON NORTHWEST SOIL, note 2), 15fn-16fn.
4. Described as the first on the Columbia with a wheelhouse, the 155-foot sternwheeler *Cascades* was built in 1864 and purchased in 1865 by the OSN Co., which used it on the Cascades route. John H. Wolf was captain. *Lewis & Dryden's Marine History*, 123.
5. Lt. Gen. Winfield Scott, born in 1786, served in the U.S. Army from 1808. By 1841 he was the senior major-general, and "from 1815 until 1861 he was the most continuously prominent public man of the country." *Officers of the Army and Navy (Regular) Who Served in the Civil War*, ed. by Wm. H. Powell and Edward Shippen (Philadelphia, 1892), 369. Scott retired in 1861 and died at West Point, N.Y., May 29, 1866.
6. General Halleck commented on disposing of Fort Dalles in December 1865 (*Sen. Ex. Doc. No. 70*, pp. 303, 50 Cong., 1 Sess.), and ordered the breakup in 1866 (see Knuth, *"Picturesque" Frontier*, 107 note 157). However, when it was decided to enlist Indian scouts (done by Lt. William Borrowe at The Dalles and the Warm Springs Indian Reservation), Fort Dalles was occupied again from December 1866 until July 15, 1867, when it was finally abandoned. (See NA,

Reservation File: Fort Dalles, Oregon, 1848-80, RG 94, Adj. Gen's Ofc., report on Fort Dalles Military Reservation by AAG R.C. Drum dated May 25, 1880.) Gen. George Crook employed these Indian scouts, under William C. McKay and John Darragh, as well as another group under Archy McIntosh, in his 1867-68 campaign in southeastern Oregon and adjacent areas, when James and Julia were at Camp Warner. See Keith and Donna Clark, eds., "William McKay's Journal, 1866-67: Indian Scouts," Parts 1 and 2, in OHQ 79 (Summer and Fall 1978).

7. Gilliss was AQM at Ft. Stevens from September 1866 to June 1867, where he succeeded Lieutenant Borrowe, AAQM. In April 1867 Captain Gilliss reported that construction at Fort Stevens was nearly completed, including officers quarters, company quarters, storehouses, stables, hospital and guardhouse. See Marshall Hanft, *Fort Stevens: Oregon's Defender at the River of the West* (Oregon State Parks and Recreation Branch, 1980), 59-67.

8. The *Oneonta* was OSN Co.'s fine new sidewheel steamboat on the middle Columbia, built at the Cascades in 1863. First commander was Capt. John McNulty. See *Lewis & Dryden's Marine History*, 115.

9. Chinook jargon for no or none.

10. Henry S. Stellwagen, born October 13, 1809, died July 15, 1866, a naval officer and inventor who was with Perry at Vera Cruz. (Stellwagen family history supplied by W. Weir Gilliss, Jr.)

11. Cape May is the southern tip of New Jersey, now a National Monument, and has been described as the oldest coastal resort town in the United States.

12. McDonough Stellwagen.

13. Brig. Gen. John Pope. General Halleck, commanding the Division of the Pacific, notified General Steele, commanding the Dept. of the Columbia, by telegram on November 17, 1866, that orders would be sent transferring Steele's headquarters to Portland. NA, RG 393, Army Commands, Dept. of Columbia, Letters Rec'd, Box 7.

14. Bvt. Lt. Col. Henry C. Hodges, of the Quartermaster's Department.

15. Probably James Gilliss' younger brother, John R. Gilliss.

16. Bvt. Maj. Gen. of Volunteers Rufus Ingalls, QM Department, later Quartermaster General, had been stationed at Fort Vancouver for most of the 1850s. For Beckie's marriage see ON THE COAST, note 7.

ON THE COAST (pp. 97-128)

1. John Jacob Astor's fur trade post at the mouth of the Columbia, Astoria was renamed Fort George when the Canadian North West Company took over in 1813.

2. The sloop *Belle* (or *Bluebell*, as Julia names it in her February 10, 1867, letter) was used for mail and supplies. *Lewis & Dryden's Marine History*, 126, fn 34; Hanft, *Fort Stevens*, 45 (see CONNECTIONS, note 7).

3. That is, William Borrowe (see CONNECTIONS, note 6).

4. Capt. Leroy L. Janes, 2d Artillery, CO at Fort Stevens, October 1865-November 1867. He resigned from the Army in December 1867. Co. C, 2d Artillery,

provided the Fort Stevens garrison from October 1865-71. See Hanft, *Fort Stevens*, 273, 54, 271.

5. Ehrenbreitstein was a famous fortress, a suburb of Coblenz, Germany, rebuilt 1816-32 into one of the strongest in Europe. It survived World Wars I and II. Hanft, *Fort Stevens*, 39, states that at the end of June 1866, five 10-inch Rodman smoothbores and five 200-pounder Parrot rifles were at the fort, but not yet mounted. On the way from New York were thirteen more 10-inch Rodmans. By the end of June 1867, twenty-six guns were mounted.

6. Now Scarboro Hill, it was named for James Scarborough, Hudson's Bay Co. captain who retired to a land claim near the mouth of the Columbia River on the north bank earlier called Chinook Hill. He acted as a river pilot. See Edmond S. Meany, *Origin of Washington Geographic Names* (Seattle, 1923).

7. Jim's older sister, Rebecca Melville Gilliss (1838-85), married Maj. Carrington H. Raymond November 28, 1866, in Washington, D.C. Major Raymond was the son of Capt. Israel W. Raymond of the Panama Steamship Line. Family information from WWG, Jr., and CJG.

8. Petroleum V. Nasby was the pen name of David R. Locke, popular nineteenth-century American journalist and political humorist.

9. Fabric of silk or wool or both, with ribbed surface.

10. The Gillisses had very nice new quarters—viewed militarily in the light of the degree of permanency for a defensive river mouth (coastal) fort, compared to the temporary nature of posts in the developing interior. Gen. U.S. Grant had already authorized the "disposal of the public property at The Dalles," and the opinion of the Chief of Engineers was "that Fort Dalles will never be of value as part of the system of permanent defences of the country." (Sec. of War Edwin M. Stanton to Sec. of Interior O.H. Browning, February 5, 1867. NA, RG 92, Office of QM Gen., Consolidated Correspondence File, Box 230, Fort Dalles.) General Halleck wrote General Steele on July 23, 1866, "Fort Stevens will be a permanent post." (NA, RG 393, Dept. of Columbia, Letters Rec'd, Box 7, P59.) (See TRANSITIONS, note 30.)

    The first three sets of officers quarters at Fort Stevens were all the same plan, with gable roof. They had covered porches in front, and were a story and a half high, with an ell at the rear of one story in height. Fronts were painted and sides whitewashed. The ground floor had four rooms with 10½-foot ceilings: 14x16 parlor, 12x12½ bedroom, 12x13 dining room, and 12x12 kitchen with adjoining storerooms. A loft over the kitchen provided servants' quarters. Under each kitchen was a well, with a pipe to a kitchen pump. A covered porch protected passage to the privy in the ell. There were fireplaces in two rooms downstairs, and other rooms had stoves. Hanft, *Fort Stevens*, 64.

11. Since it is "Mr." DeRussy, probably he was a civilian employee at the post, though he may have been a relative of Col. René E. DeRussy (see LEAVING HOME, note 11). A Lt. René E. DeRussy, 2d Artillery, joined the Department of California in 1866. See Guy V. Henry, *Military Record of Civilian Appointments in the United States Army* (New York, 1869), 1:200-201.

12. Artemus Ward was the pen name for another nineteenth-century American humorist, Charles Browne. Both Ward's and Petroleum V. Nasby's writings (Julia mentions him in her January 13, 1867, letter) were popular with Lincoln.

13. As "draughtsman" in the Navy's Bureau of Ordnance, according to the *Navy Register, 1865*, Charles K. Stellwagen had a salary of fourteen hundred dollars a year; in the 1868 *Navy Register* his salary is eighteen hundred dollars.

14. "Snakes" was very loosely used to refer to Indians in central, eastern, and southeastern Oregon, as well as adjoining parts of Idaho, Nevada, and California, and even further afield. In Oregon they were mostly Northern Piute, and they made difficulties for travelers on the routes to the mines in the 1860s. During the Civil War years the Oregon Volunteer Cavalry and Infantry made efforts to deal with their raids: in 1864, in a two-pronged expedition into southeastern Oregon under Capt. George Currey and Capt. John M. Drake; in 1865-66, in Currey's plans to build winter camps in their country. Brig. Gen. George Crook succeeded to the task after the Civil War, and it was Captain Gilliss' part in Crook's campaign that took James and Julia to the second Camp Warner in 1867. For background on the Snakes see the Clarks, "William McKay's Journal" (CONNECTIONS, note 6) and Drake's journal, "Cavalry in the Indian Country" (see ON NORTHWEST SOIL, note 2). Drake's "The Oregon Cavalry," in OHQ 65 (December 1964): 398-400, summarizes events of the Snake War in the earlier 1860s.

15. Julia's sewing materials included brilliant, a cotton fabric probably with a raised flowered pattern that would appear brilliant in the right light; "nansouk" or nainsook, a soft, light-weight cotton muslin with a lustrous finish on one side, used especially for children's clothes or lingerie; jaconet, another thin cotton fabric; Cluny lace, originally from the town in France, a net with darned design; vandyke points, sharp points. See Florence M. Montgomery, *Textiles in America, 1650-1870* (New York, 1984).

16. The more usual location for finding marked chunks of beeswax was Neahkahnie Mountain, just above the Nehalem River entrance in Tillamook County. The story is that a Spanish ship carrying blocks of wax to Pacific Coast missions was wrecked there. One estimate is that twelve tons of wax had been found, mostly on the sand spit at the mouth of Nehalem River (OHQ 60:158). Isaac Flint, who arrived by sea at the Columbia's mouth early in 1850, noted (OHQ 63:51) that he had a lump of beeswax that "lay in the ocean 50 years and is as good as new. It came from China in a Chinese junk and went to bottom along with the crew who brought it."

17. Usually *Fidelater*, a propeller steamship that made a maiden voyage from Victoria to Portland in June 1866. *Lewis & Dryden's Marine History*, 127.

18. Bvt. Col. George H. Mendell, of the Corps of Engineers, was married to Ellen, daughter of John Adair, first Collector of Customs at Astoria (Salem *Oregon Statesman*, November 9, 1858, p. 2, col. 7). Rodney Glisan, *Journal of Army Life* (San Francisco, 1874), 385-86, on August 6, 1857, wrote of "brilliant" parties that Ellen Adair and Mendell attended. Another Adair daughter, Katy,

married Lt. William T. Welcker at Fort Vancouver in 1857. Lieutenant Welcker was dismissed from the Army at the beginning of the Civil War, and became a captain of Artillery in the Confederate Army.

19. Astoria's first church, built 1853-54, was Methodist (OHQ 4:135). Nearby Clatsop Plains had a church built in 1850. Probably Julia refers to the first church of her denomination: the first building of Grace Episcopal Church was erected in 1866, perhaps completed inside in 1867. Material from Sharon C. Turner, *Methodist Ministers and Churches in Astoria*, and Bruce Berney, Astoria.

20. Probably a reference to H.R. 896, "making appropriations for the legislative, executive, and judicial expenses of the Government for the year ending 30th June 1863." (See *Congressional Globe*, March 2, 1867, p. 1995, H.R. 896 signed.) Julia refers to the army pay bill and a bill providing an increase in her father's salary in her letters of April 14 and 28.

21. "Toston, Chief of the Clatsop Indians has lived for many years at Point Adams . . . . He has an excellent reputation at the mouth of the Columbia," George H. Elliott, Corps of Engineers, wrote from Fort Stevens on April 25, 1865. Toston was also one of the Indians party to a treaty ceding land to the United States made on August 5, 1851, by Anson Dart, Oregon Superintendent of Indian Affairs. See W.W. Raymond papers, Mss 555, OHS.

22. According to family information (in OHS Vertical File) from Joseph A. Minott, a grandson, Glisan was born in Maryland, January 29, 1827, of English ancestry, graduated from the medical department, University of Maryland in 1849, practiced in Baltimore, then was appointed Assistant Surgeon in the U.S. Army. He served five years on the Plains and six years in Oregon during the Indian wars, resigned from the Army in 1861 and spent a year in San Francisco. Then he came to Portland and continued to practice medicine up to the time of his death on June 3, 1890. He was a professor in the first medical institution in Oregon, the Oregon Medical College (later the Medical Department of Willamette University), President of Multnomah Medical Society 1872 and 1876, and of Oregon State Medical Society 1875-76, a member of the American Medical Association, delegate to International Medical Congress in London 1881, and to that in Washington, D.C., in 1887. He traveled, wrote numerous articles on medical subjects and several books. He married Elizabeth Raines Couch, a daughter of Capt. John H. Couch, and they had four children. See also Heitman, *Historical Register*, and Olof Larsell, *The Doctor in Oregon* (Portland, 1947).

A WELCOME ADDITION (pp. 129-37)

1. The U.S. Census for Astoria for 1870 lists an Elizabeth Brown, age sixty-six, born in Pennsylvania, whose occupation is given as "boarding house." Probably she was Mrs. John Brown (his name immediately precedes hers). U.S. Census of Northwest Oregon, typed and alphabetized by Mrs. Henry I. Hiday (Salem [1965]), 3.

2. Dr. Trunhard does not appear in the 1870 census, but Mrs. W.W. (Elmira) Raymond, age sixty-one, is listed as then keeping house for her husband in

Lexington. W.W. Raymond and his first wife, Almira, and Elmira (then Phillips) all came to Oregon with the Methodist missionary group in 1840 on the *Lausanne*. Almira divorced him in 1864. See W.W. Raymond papers, Mss 555, OHS, and Olga Freeman, ed., "Almira Raymond Letters, 1840-1880," in OHQ 85 (Fall 1984): 291-92.

3. Julia, born May 1, 1867, died June 5, 1955. (CJG family information.)

IN GOOD COMPANY (pp. 138-53)

1. Bvt. Maj. Gen. George Crook left New York in November 1866 to join his regiment (23rd Infantry), and arrived at Fort Boise, Idaho Territory, in December. He comments that he found hostile Indians all over the region. The gold discoveries and mining rushes into the Pacific Northwest interior in the 1860s multiplied opportunities for difficulties with the native inhabitants of the interior region, and their often rather narrow area of balance with the environment. When Crook arrived he commanded the new District of Owyhee in the Department of Columbia. He had earlier experience with Indians of the Pacific Northwest and California in the mid-1850s. See Martin F. Schmitt, ed., *General George Crook, His Autobiography* (Norman, 1946), 142-43; also Clark and Clark, eds., "William McKay's Journal," OHQ 79:131-32.

2. Camp C.F. Smith in later Harney County just east of the Alvord desert, was established in June 1866 to replace Camp Alvord, then at its second site on "Horse" (now Wildhorse) Creek on the east side of Steens Mountain. Alvord was one of the camps set up by the Oregon Volunteers, 1864-66, in an effort to reach and defeat the Indians during winter; during summer the Volunteers did more chasing than catching. A road from California and Nevada mines to the Idaho mines ran north through this region. Crook's effort cleared some of the difficulties, and Camp C.F. Smith was abandoned in 1869 (see THE INDIAN FRONTIER, note 1).

3. Presumably the Sisters of Providence convent in Vancouver, Washington Territory.

4. Bvt. Brig. Gen. Charles H. Tompkins, Quartermaster's Dept.

5. The wife of Maj. (bvt. Lt. Col.) Peter G.S. Ten Broeck, a Surgeon and Medical Director, Dept. of Columbia. Glisan, Julia's "favorite doctor in Portland," in his *Journal of Army Life* states that when an officer married a social inferior, "he commits an offence toward army society that is rarely forgiven . . . ." (p. 452) "Army society is essentially aristocratic." (p. 453).

6. As Crook's campaign to pacify the Indians of the interior proceeded and he gained a better idea of where they moved, the District of the Lakes was created for his command in August of 1867. It included parts of southwestern Idaho, southeastern Oregon, northeastern California, and probably a little of northwestern Nevada.

7. The first Camp Warner was established July 15, 1866, and abandoned September 1, 1867, when Crook moved the location from the east side of Hart Mountain to some miles west of it just north of what was named Crook Peak. The second site was on Dent Creek, a small tributary of Honey Creek in Lake County,

Oregon. See McArthur, OGN, under Camp Warner and Fort Harney; also
T. W. Symons, *Itineraries of Routes and Tables of Distances, in the Department of the Columbia* (Vancouver Barracks, 1881), under the list of military
posts. For more on the second Camp Warner, see Julia's November 4, 1867, letter and THE INDIAN FRONTIER, note 1.

8. Camp (later Fort) Harney, in later Harney County not far from Burns, was established August 16, 1867. Crook made a circuit of the Harney Valley, looking
for "a suitable site for a three-company post." Lt. Greenleaf A. Goodale, who
was with him, describes the search, and after Crook picked the canyon at the
mouth of Rattlesnake Creek (where Oregon Volunteers had camped in 1864),
the lieutenant and his company began to build. Goodale called it Camp Crook,
but Crook renamed it for Department commander Gen. Frederick Steele, who
renamed it for Gen. William S. Harney. The post was abandoned in 1880. See
G. A. Goodale, "Military Life in Oregon," ed. by Roy Goodale, OHS Mss 681.

9. Margaret Dailey, daughter of John Dailey, married George Crook in 1865. Her
home was a resort "about a half day's ride" from Washington, D.C., according
to Julia's letter of January 23, 1868. See Schmitt, *General George Crook*, 306.
(See THE INDIAN FRONTIER, note 8.)

10. Probably Capt. Joseph T. Haskell, 23rd Infantry, Acting Chief Commissary,
according to Goodale, "Military Life in Oregon" (IN GOOD COMPANY, note 8).

11. Rev. John D. McCarty arrived in Oregon in 1853, and was (Episcopal) chaplain
to the 4th U.S. Infantry at Fort Vancouver. (See Thomas E. Jessett, "Origins of
the Episcopal Church in the Pacific Northwest," OHQ 48 (December 1947):
303.) He brought a wife to Oregon in 1856. McCarty left the region in April
1868, retiring to Washington, D.C., where Mrs. McCarty died in 1879. (See
Jessett, "Thomas Fielding Scott: Bishop of Oregon," OHQ 55 (March 1954): 43,
70; *Daily Oregonian*, February 7, 1879, p. 2, col. 2.)

12. Lt. Otis W. Pollock, 23rd Infantry, was AAQM and ACS to a detachment en-
route from Fort Dalles to Baker City, Oregon, in 1867, and AAAG, District of
the Lakes, at Camp Warner. See Henry, *Military Record of Civilian Appointments*, 1:422 (see ON THE COAST, note 11). William Kelly, born in Ireland,
was a non-com in the U.S. Army from 1843-53. He was in the 4th Infantry in
the Pacific Northwest in 1853, became a lieutenant in the 1st Oregon Volunteer
Cavalry in 1861, a captain in 1862, and was mustered out in 1866 (he saw service at Fort Klamath). Kelly became a captain in the regular army's 8th Cavalry
in 1866 and was brevetted major in 1868. He died in December 1871 in Denver,
survived by a wife and five children in Portland. (*Daily Oregonian*, January 1,
1872, p. 3, col. 1; Henry, *Military Record*, 163.)

13. For David W. Porter's 1st Oregon Vol. Cavalry service, see the journal of Capt.
John M. Drake, OHQ 65:11-17, 19-22, 26-111 *passim*. Porter died in 1871.

14. Julia may mean Spitsbergen (now Svalbard), an island in the Arctic Ocean. So,
cold breeze.

15. Perhaps the William D. Gilliam listed with his family in 15 Mile Precinct in
Wasco County in the 1870 U.S. Census. See typed copy (at OHS) transcribed by
Mrs. Wayne E. Gurley (1965), 40.

16. Named for Lt. Stephen Watson, 1st Oregon Vol. Cavalry, who was killed in an 1864 battle with the Snake Indians (including Paulina) in Central Oregon. Camp Watson was on Fort Creek in what is now Wheeler County, about five miles west of Antone. It was established in 1864 in an effort to deal with Indian raids on that route to the eastern Oregon-Idaho mines. After the Oregon Volunteer troops were mustered out in 1866, the post was occupied by regulars for several years before it was abandoned. In the winter, troops there had suffered from scurvy. See McArthur, OGN. See also Judith Keyes Kenny, "The Founding of Camp Watson," OHQ 58 (March 1957): 5-16.

17. Soda Springs was the last stop before Camp Harney on The Dalles-Canyon City Road, about thirty miles beyond Canyon City. Goodale describes the springs in almost the same words and mentions the small log house, manned for the winter by four men of his company. "Military Life in Oregon," 14 (IN GOOD COMPANY, note 8).

18. "Acting Assistant Surgeon Dickson as medical officer" is mentioned by Lt. Col. W.R. Parnell in his "Operations Against Hostile Indians with General George Crook, 1867-'68," in *The United Service* magazine, June 1889, p. 628, though Julia spells his name Dixon in her later references (July 19, October 20, 1868). He was the John M. Dickson, Assistant Surgeon, USA, who was at Fort Stevens, June 14, 1879 to October 11, 1880. See Hanft, *Fort Stevens*, 87 (CONNECTIONS, note 7), and Camp Warner Post Return for November 1867, which indicates he was assigned as Acting Assistant Surgeon during the illness of camp Assistant Surgeon Richard A. Powell (see THE INDIAN FRONTIER, note 6). NA microfilm of Camp Warner Post Returns, courtesy Jules A. Martino, Salem.

THE INDIAN FRONTIER (pp. 154-85)

1. The Gillisses arrived at the second Camp Warner a month or two late for Crook's most trying battle of 1867, at the "Infernal Caverns" near the forks of Pit River in northern California. Crook was looking for a new location for Camp Warner as early as spring. See James B. Fry, AAG (writing for General Halleck), May 17, 1867, to CO, Department of Columbia, NA, RG 393, Dept. of Columbia, Box 8, P41. Joe Wasson, a reporter with the expedition, says Crook had selected the new Warner location by the end of July (Silver City *Owyhee Avalanche*, August 17, 1867, p. 3), and notes that it was five hundred feet lower than the first Warner on Hart Mountain. (See HOMEWARD BOUND, note 4). Parnell describes it as "about 45 miles west of the old [Camp Warner] and situated at the base of Mount Crook." (In "Operations," *The United Service*, May 1889, p. 492). Crook himself reported that the new camp was "about ten miles from the west side of [Warner] Lake, in a well sheltered place, where there is plenty of timber, grass and water, and is easy of access, with an open country between there and Camp Bidwell Cal.: via which place all supplies and communications should be sent; thereby avoiding the terrible road between Camp C.F. Smith and this place .... I respectfully recommend that the new Station be called Camp Wood, in honor of the present Governor of Oregon and

also that it is the only *Woods* in this country." (Crook to Bvt. Capt. R.P. Strong, AAAG Dept. of Columbia, Portland, August 2, 1867, NA, RG 393, Letters Rec'd, Box 7, C23.)

2. Bvt. Lt. Col. William H. Johnston, Army paymaster, and Lt. Frederick Dodge of the 23rd Infantry.

3. The whole party, baggage and all, must have used Crook's new "bridge" across the fluctuating wet area of the Warner lakes just west of Hart Mountain. In order to reach the new camp by the most direct practical route, Crook had filled in a passage at the narrowest part with rocks, etc. In his August 2, 1867, report to Strong (op. cit., RG 393, Box 7, C23) Crook noted that the "causeway across the Lake is completed so that laden teams can cross it, saving at least one hundred miles in distance." The building of "Crook's causeway" is described in *An Illustrated History of Central Oregon* . . . (Spokane, Washington, 1905), 808-15. Remains could still be seen a few years ago.

4. Swellings, abscesses.

5. Farina, a fine meal made of grains and nuts and sometimes sea moss.

6. Richard A. Powell, born in Ireland, was Surgeon, 88th New York Volunteers, 1861-64, Assistant Surgeon U.S. Army May 1867, and Post Surgeon at Camp Warner. (Henry, *Military Record of Civilian Appointments U.S. Army*, 1:106 (ON THE COAST, note 11).

7. Jim's oldest sister's first child, Ward Raymond. Family information gathered by CJG.

8. Allegany County, Maryland. Oakland is presently in Garrett County, just west of Allegany.

9. George B. Cosby, born in Kentucky, graduated from Military Academy 1848, was in the 2nd Cavalry, resigned 1861 and became a brigadier general in the Confederate army 1861-65.

10. Crook used more than one group of Indian scouts, but he mentions Donald McKay and thirteen scouts specifically in his February 24, 1868, report from Camp Warner, stating that he and Co. H, 1st Cavalry, the mounted portion of Co. D, 23rd Infantry, and McKay and the scouts had left on February 11 to "operate against the hostile Indians in the vicinity of Steens Mountain." (NA, RG 393, Dept. of Columbia, Letters Rec'd, Box 8, C18; and see Julia's March 28, 1868 letter.) Crook also says that the Boise Indian scouts had arrived so tardily that it interfered with his plans for a winter campaign. He hoped to capture enough younger hostiles in his campaign against the "Snake" (Piute) Indians that they might be trained to "make very good scouts" and he would not have to depend on the Boise Indians. Three-quarters Indian Donald McKay and his half-brother Dr. William C. McKay both served as leaders of Indian scouts for the Army. Donald went on to greater fame in the Modoc War. See Keith and Donna Clark, eds., *Daring Donald McKay* (Portland, 1971), ix-x. Both were sons of Tom McKay, who had worked for the Hudson's Bay Company in fur trade days.

11. Asher R. Eddy, in the Quartermaster's Dept.

12. In his report of activities for the year Crook states: "*March 19, 1868.*—I was in

command of the district of the lakes; all available mounted troops were ordered to rendezvous at the north end of Warner's lake, but, owing to the non-arrival of supplies, was unable to reach there as soon as expected. On the 14th I reached 'Donner and Blitzen' valley, near Steen's mountain; found a band of Indians up a large canon, killed and wounded several, how many could not, from the nature of the ground, be ascertained. Supplies being exhausted, returned to camp the 26th." In *Message and Documents*, 40 Cong., 3 Sess., *Abridgement* (Washington, D.C., 1869, ed. by Ben: Perley Poore), 382-83.

13. Brig. General (bvt. Major General) Rousseau took command of the Department of the Columbia after General Steele's death (on January 12, 1868, in California). Crook's stay in Portland, where department headquarters was located, was short, and he did not move there until fall. See Schmitt, *General George Crook*, 158-59, and Julia's letter of August 23, 1868.

14. Camp McGarry was in northwestern Nevada, south of Oregon's Alvord Valley and Camp C.F. Smith. James M. Ropes was a second lieutenant in the 8th Cavalry, William McCleave, a first lieutenant.

15. Parnell describes the winter campaign of 1867-68 and the surrender of the Piutes, and mentions that one band surrendered at Camp Warner, though most came in at Camp Harney. ("Operations . . . ," *The United Service*, June 1889, 633-34.) When Crook arrived at Harney he found We-ah-we-wa and all his tribe waiting to surrender. Capt. Azor H. Nickerson's description of the event is quoted in Schmitt, *General George Crook*, 307-309. As soon as the settlement was made, Parnell says, Crook asked Chief We-ah-we-wa for ten men to go with the Army on an expedition against the Pitt (Pit) River Indians, and obtained ten volunteers. General Halleck, in his report of September 22, 1868, states: "The Indian war which has been waged for many years in southern Oregon and Idaho, and the northern parts of California and Nevada, has been conducted with great energy and success by General Crook since he took command in that section of country. On the twenty-second of August he reported that about eight hundred hostile Indians had surrendered, and that the war was virtually closed." *Message and Documents*, 40 Cong., 2 Sess., *Abridgement*, op. cit., 367; see also Crook's report in ibid, 383.

16. That is, Crook went south into northern California to deal with the Indians involved earlier that year at the Battle of the Infernal Caverns (see THE INDIAN FRONTIER, notes 1, 15), at a site a little southwest of present Alturas. The earlier name of Goose Lake, Modoc County, in the northeast corner of California, was Pit Lake, and a branch of Pit River ran out of the southern end of the lake. See Erwin G. Gudde, *California Place Names* (3rd ed., Berkeley & Los Angeles, 1969); on the Pit River area Indians see John R. Swanton, *The Indian Tribes of North America*, Bulletin 145, Smithsonian Institution, Bureau of American Ethnology (Washington, D.C., 1952), p. 479ff, under Achomawai. The second Camp Warner was abandoned October 2, 1874, after the Modoc War. It had no formally declared military reservation. See Elmer O. Parker, NA, to P. Knuth, December 23, 1965, and NA, RG 92, Consolidated Correspondence File, Box 1206 (Camp Warner), No. 465.

17. Capt. James A. Hall (bvt. Major), 1st Cavalry.
18. Perhaps the wife of Capt. Charles W. Raymond, of the Engineer Corps.
19. Brig. Gen. Montgomery C. Meigs of the Quartermaster's Dept.
20. Goose Lake was a large, rather shallow body of water with its northern end in Lake County, Oregon, and southern part in Modoc County, California. The present town of Lakeview is on the east side of the lake area in Oregon (see HOMEWARD BOUND, note 1).
21. No doubt the treaty with the Indians contributed to Crook's official transfer to the position of commander of the Department of the Columbia, where he remained until August 8, 1870.
22. According to the family history written by Charles J. Gilliss, James' father, James Melville Gilliss, died in Washington, D.C., on February 9, 1865, of a brain hemorrhage. He had "welcomed home his son James from Libby Prison, Richmond," on February 7. Thomas Handy Gilliss, a younger brother of Jim's father, died at the age of forty-five on June 16, 1868, in New York City, where he had a banking firm. (See *New York Times*, June 17, 1868, p. 5, col. 7.) James Gilliss did continue in the Army, and was stationed at Governor's Island, New York, when he died suddenly on November 13, 1898, after a pleasant day on the Hudson.
23. Emanuel Leutze, the artist, whose death Julia mentions in her letter of August 17. In the Stellwagen genealogy sent by W. Weir Gilliss, Jr., in the comment on Charles Kraft Stellwagen, Julia's father, it is mentioned that Leutze boarded with the Stellwagens when he was painting "Washington Crossing the Delaware." In that painting "The figure of a soldier wrapped in a shawl, was posed by Mr. Stellwagen." According to Fred A. Myers' article, "Bierstadt's Small Paintings . . . ," in the October 1985 (vol. 7, no. 4) issue of the *Gilcrease Magazine of American History and Art*, Leutze is best known in the United States for two large paintings, "Washington Crossing the Delaware" and "Westward the Course of Empire Takes Its Way."

HOMEWARD BOUND (pp. 186-95)

1. Fort Bidwell, at the northern end of Surprise Valley in Modoc County, California, was named in 1865 for John Bidwell, then a congressman from the state and a general in the militia. (Gudde, *California Place Names*, 28.) Just south of the post the Southern Immigrant Route to Oregon (or Scott-Applegate Trail) crossed the Lassen Pass west into Fandango Valley before turning north into Oregon at Goose Lake. In 1872 Lt. Stephen P. Jocelyn, just ordered to Bidwell and then to Camp Warner, wrote that the latter was the larger and better built post. Two photos of the Warner buildings then are in *Mostly Alkali*, by son Stephen P. Jocelyn (Caldwell, Idaho, 1953).
2. Michael J. Fitzgerald (born in Ireland), 9th Infantry, a captain by 1873. A biographical sketch is in *Officers of the Army and Navy (Regular) Who Served in the Civil War*, ed. by Wm. H. Powell and Edward Shippen (Philadelphia, 1892), 146.
3. Wife of Capt. Robert H. Chapin, 8th Cavalry, who was in the Civil War with

New York volunteers, 1861. Henry, *Military Record of Civilian Appointments*, 1:144; wife of Lt. Thomas M. Fisher, 23rd Infantry, who saw volunteer service in the Civil War, then joined the regulars in 1867.

4. The second Camp Warner site was above fifty-two hundred feet; Crook Peak is reported as about seventy-nine hundred feet elevation.

5. In spite of Fannie's illness, she lived for another fifty-eight years, dying in 1926. Family information from WWG, Jr., and CJG.

6. Probably choke cherries, *Prunus demissa*, a dark red or purple astringent fruit, harvested in September. Donald F. Menefee, born in Fandango Valley, wrote that local people of the area make choke cherry jam or jelly. Also harvested at that time are wild plums, *Prunus subcordata*, larger and used as canned fruit or for plum butter. The fruit is bitter but delightful when sweetened. There are recently planted orchards in Modoc and Lake counties.

7. The address of Thomas H. Gilliss, who had died in June. *New York Times*, June 17, 1868, p. 5, col. 7.

8. A James H. Gillis, lieutenant commander, appears in the 1865 *Navy Register*, p. 28, as does John P. Gillis, a retired captain at the Philadelphia Navy yard, p. 16. In the 1868 *Navy Register*, p. 20, James H. Gillis, born Pennsylvania, is in command of the *Wateree*: John P. Gillis (p. 90) is a commodore on the retired and reserved list "awaiting orders." John was born in Delaware. W. Weir Gilliss, Jr., found no information on the naval Captain Gillis in the Gilliss family records he has.

9. Balmoral (named for the Scottish castle), a woolen petticoat worn under a looped up skirt.

10. Capt. Samual Munson, 9th Infantry, CO at Fort Bidwell in the *Pacific Coast Business Directory, 1867* (San Francisco, 1867), 20. Crook refers to him (Schmitt, *General George Crook*, 159).

11. Probably what is identified as "Bare's ranch," at the south end of Surprise Valley, on Silver Creek ("altitude 4,679"), about fifty-three miles from Fort Bidwell, in Table No. 56, in Symons' 1881 *Itineraries of Routes and Tables of Distances, in the Department of the Columbia* (see IN GOOD COMPANY, note 7).

12. Capt. James Gilliss, AQM, left Camp Warner "for Washington, D.C., January 12, 1869," according to the January 1869 Post Return. NA microfilm, courtesy Jules A. Martino.

SOURCES

BOOKS

Bancroft, Hubert Howe. *History of California*, 7 volumes, San Francisco, 1884-90.

Brimlow, George F. *The Bannock Indian War of 1878*, Caldwell, Idaho, 1938.

Clark, Keith and Donna, eds. *Daring Donald McKay*, Portland, Oregon, 1971.

Clark, Robert D. *The Odyssey of Thomas Condon: Irish Immigrant, Frontier Missionary, Oregon Geologist*, Portland, Oregon, 1989.

Corning, Howard McKinley, ed. *Dictionary of Oregon History*, Portland, Oregon, 1956.

Cullum, George W. *Biographical Register of the Officers and Graduates of the* U.S. Military Academy . . . 1802 . . . 1866- 67, vol. 2, 1841-67 (New York 1868).

Glisan, Rodney. *Journal of Army Life*, San Francisco, 1874.

Gudde, Erwin G. *California Place Names*, 3d ed., Berkeley and Los Angeles, 1969.

Hanft, Marshall. *The Cape Forts: Guardians of the Columbia*, Portland, Oregon, 1973.

———. *Fort Stevens: Oregon's Defender at the River of the West*, Oregon State Parks and Recreation Branch, 1980.

Henry, Guy V. *Military Record of Civilian Appointments in the United States Army*, New York, 1869.

Heyl, Erik. *Early American Steamers*, Buffalo, New York, 1953.

An Illustrated History of Central Oregon . . . , Spokane, Washington, 1905.

Jocelyn, Stephen P. *Mostly Alkali*, Caldwell, Idaho, 1953.

Knuth, Priscilla. *"Picturesque" Frontier: The Army's Fort Dalles*, 2d ed., Portland, Oregon, 1987.

Larsell, Olof. *The Doctor in Oregon*, Portland, Oregon, 1947.

McArthur, L.A. and L.L. *Oregon Geographic Names*, 5th ed., Portland, Oregon, 1982.

McCormick, S.J., comp. *Portland Directories*, 1865, 1866, 1867.

Meany, Edmond S. *Origin of Washington Geographic Names*, Seattle, 1923.

Montgomery, Florence M. *Textiles in America, 1650-1870*, New York, 1984.

Nelson, Herbert B. and Preston E Onstad, eds. *A Webfoot Volunteer: The Diary of William M. Hilleary, 1864-1866*, Corvallis, Oregon, 1965.

Owens, George, comp. *General Directory . . . east of the Cascade Mountains . . .* , San Francisco, 1865.

Pacific Coast Business Directory, 1867, San Francisco, 1867.

Powell, William H. and Edward Shippen, eds. *Officers of the Army and Navy (Regular) Who Served in the Civil War*, Philadelphia, 1892.

Schmitt, Martin F., ed. *General George Crook: His Autobiography*, Norman, Oklahoma, 1946.

Scott, Harvey W. *History of the Oregon Country*, Leslie M. Scott comp., 6 vols., Cambridge, Massachusetts, 1924.

Thomas, Edward H. *Chinook: . . . a History and Dictionary*, Portland, Oregon, 1935.

Turnbull, George S. *History of Oregon Newspapers*, Portland, Oregon, 1939.

Turner, Sharon C. *Methodist Ministers and Churches in Astoria*, Astoria, Oregon (Astoria Public Library).

U.S. Census of Northwest Oregon (1860, 1870), Mrs. Harry I. Hiday, trans. Salem, Oregon [1965].

U.S. Census, Wasco County, Oregon (1870), Mrs. Harry I. Hiday, trans., and Mrs. E. Gurley, indexer, [1965].

Vaughan, Thomas, ed. *The Western Shore: Oregon Country Essays Honoring the American Revolution*, Portland, Oregon, 1975.

Wright, E.W., ed. *Lewis & Dryden's Marine History of the Pacific Northwest*, Portland, Oregon, 1895.

NEWSPAPERS AND PERIODICALS

Congressional Globe, March 2, 1867.

Evening Bulletin (Portland, Oregon), July 8, 1868.

New York Times, June 17, 1868.

Oregonian (Portland, Oregon), August 19, 1854; February 6, 1864;

July 2, 1864; February 10, 1866; January 1, 1872; February 7, 1879; March 29, 1886.

Oregon Statesman (Salem, Oregon), August 22, 1854; November 9, 1858; August 30, 1859; January 25, 1864; November 6, 1865. (See *Oregon Statesman Index, 1850-1866*, indexed by W.P.A. Newspaper Index Project, David Duniway, ed. for reproduction. Sponsored by OHS, now being prepared for reproduction by the Marion County Historical Society, Salem, Oregon. Vols. 1ff; the letter "O" is number 14 in the series, with more to come. A useful source for people and events.)

Silver City (Idaho) *Owyhee Avalanche*, August 17, 1867.

ARTICLES

Clark, Keith and Donna, eds. "William McKay's Journal, 1866-67 Indian Scouts," Parts 1 and 2, *Oregon Historical Quarterly*, (hereafter OHQ) 79 (Summer and Fall 1978).

Frankenstein, Alfred. "The Royal Visitors," OHQ 64 (March 1963).

Freeman, Olga, ed. "Almira Raymond Letters, 1840-1880," OHQ 85 (Fall 1984).

Jessett, Thomas E. "Origins of the Episcopal Church in the Pacific Northwest," OHQ 48 (December 1947).

——. "Thomas Fielding Scott: Bishop of Oregon," OHQ 55 (March 1954).

Kenny, Judith Keyes. "The Founding of Camp Watson," OHQ 58 (March 1957).

Knuth, Priscilla, ed. "Cavalry in the Indian Country, 1864," OHQ 65 (March 1964).

Monroe, Robert D. "William Birch McMurtrie: A Painter Partially Restored," OHQ 60 (September 1959).

Myers, Fred A. "Bierstadt's Small Paintings . . . ," *Gilcrease Magazine of American History and Art*, October 1985, vol. 7, no. 4.

Parnell, Lt. Col. W.R. "Operations Against Hostile Indians with General George Crook, 1867-'68," *The United Service*, May and June 1889.

Powers, Alfred, and Mary-Jane Finke. "Survey of First Half-Century of Oregon Hotels," OHQ 43 (September 1942).

MANUSCRIPTS

Army Commands, Record Group (hereafter RG) 393, Dept. of Columbia, Letters Rec'd, 1857-67, particularly Boxes 7 and 8, National Archives (hereafter NA).

Army Commands, RG 393, Dept. of Columbia, Letters Sent, 1857-67, NA (microfilm copy at OHS).

Camp Warner Post Returns, 1867-69, copies of NA microfilm, courtesy Jules A. Martino, Salem.

Cleaver, J.D. "Oregon Country Illustrated," unpublished manuscript, Oregon Historical Society (hereafter OHS).

Consolidated Correspondence Files for selected camps, RG 92, Office of the Quartermaster General, NA.

Gilliss, Charles J. Gilliss family history, partial copy at OHS; family Bible material; correspondence with W. Weir Gilliss, Jr., and Nancy Joan Gilliss.

Goodale, G.A. "Military Life in Oregon," ed. by Roy Goodale, OHS Mss 681.

Minott, Joseph A. Glisan family information, OHS Vertical File.

Raymond, W.W. OHS Mss 555.

"Reports of Persons and Articles Hired" lists, RG 92, NA. Microfilm copies for selected camps available at OHS (courtesy R.K. Clark).

Reservation File: Fort Dalles, Oregon, 1848-80, RG 94, Adj. Gen's Ofc., report on Fort Dalles Military Reservation by AAG R.C. Drum dated May 25, 1880, NA.

GOVERNMENT DOCUMENTS (FEDERAL AND STATE)

Duniway, David C., comp. *Members of the Legislature of Oregon, 1843-1967*, Oregon State Archives, *Bul. No. 2 Rev.*, Salem, Oregon, 1968.

Halleck, Gen. Henry W. Comments of December 1865, *Sen. Ex. Doc. No. 70*, 50 Cong., 1 Sess. (Washington, D.C., 1866).

Heitman, Francis B. *Historical Register and Dictionary of the U.S. Army . . . 1789-1903*, 2 vols., Washington, D.C., 1903.

Navy Register of the United States 1865, 1868.

Official Army Registers for 1865, 1866, 1867, 1868 (January and August), 1869 (January and September), Adjutant General's Office, Washington, D.C., for those years.

Poore, Benjamin Perley, ed. *Message and Documents*, 40 Cong., 3 Sess., *Abridgement*, Washington, D.C., 1869.

Report of the Adjutant General of the State of Oregon, 1865-6, Salem, Oregon, 1866.

Steele, Maj. Gen. Frederick. Annual Report, October, 1866. See H.R. Ex. Doc. No. 1, 39 Cong., 2 Sess. (Washington, D.C., 1866).

Swanton, John R. *The Indian Tribes of North America, Bulletin 145*, Smithsonian Institution, Bureau of American Ethnology, Washington, D.C., 1952.

Symons, T.W. *Itineraries of Routes and Tables of Distances, in the Department of the Columbia*, Vancouver Barracks, 1881.

War of the Rebellion: A Compilation of the Official Records of the Union and Confederate Armies, Series 1, vol. 50, parts 1 and 2, 55 Cong., 1 Sess., H.R. Doc. No. 59, Part 1, Washington, D.C., 1897.

INDEX

COLOPHON

THERE ARE PUBLICATIONS that are cared for and nurtured, works that have a quality that marks them apart from the routine, the everyday. *So Far From Home* is one of these books, a work imbued with the special soulfulness of caring human beings. Its basic heart, of course, comes from the mind and pen of Julia Gilliss. Without her words we would not have this wonderful story about life in the West in the 1860s. We are all grateful to Julia Gilliss for taking the time to give us her remarkable view of her world.

Through her words, Julia Gilliss' spirit was caught by Charles J. Gilliss, who took the time to transcribe her letters. Without his transcriptions the subsequent loss of the original letters would have meant Julia Gilliss' story would have been lost to us all. An appreciative nod to Charles Gilliss, one of those often invisible preservers of our collective past.

Yet, the transcriptions might have languished for good, had it not been for William Weir Gilliss, Jr's bringing the transcripts to the attention of the Oregon Historical Society, and for the assiduous, painstaking and passionate work of Priscilla Knuth. Ms. Knuth's devotion to placing Julia Gilliss' letters in the reader's hands demands another "thank you" from us. Ms. Knuth has made the read easier for us all, through thousands of editorial decisions and giving context to Julia Gilliss' four years in the Oregon Country.

Finally, thanks must be accorded the late George T. Resch, whose careful and visually coordinating mind produced the design for the interior of this book. *So Far From Home* is one of two final designs evolved by Resch. To use Julia Gilliss' last words in this, your last work, *au revoir*, George.

Typesetting	In Aldus, text, and Palatino, titles, by The Typeworks Point Roberts, Washington
Printing & Binding	On 60-pound Glatfelter by Edwards Brothers Ann Arbor, Michigan
Cover	Designed by Karen Bassett Portland, Oregon
Original Cover Paper	Reproduced with permission of paper artist, Peggy Skycraft Skycraft Designs Estacada, Oregon
Illustrations & Map	Karen Beyers Portland, Oregon
Produced by	The Oregon Historical Society Press Portland, Oregon